10TH ANNIVERSARY — COLLECTOR'S EDITION

NECRONOMICON

THE ANUNNAKI GRIMOIRE

A MANUAL OF PRACTICAL BABYLONIAN MAGICK

by Joshua Free

*Originally published in four installments by the
Mardukite Chamberlains in 2009-2011
as the Complete Year 3 Research & Curriculum,
Revised & Expanded for this 2019 Edition.*

PUBLISHED BY THE **JOSHUA FREE** IMPRINT REPRESENTING

Mardukite Truth Seeker Press — **mardukite.com**

© 2009–2019, JOSHUA FREE

ISBN : 978-0-578-50594-7

Cover Graphics by Kyra Kaos

— NECRONOMICON GRIMOIRE —

Raw Power. Real Magic. Primordial. Nearly Forgotten... The path of true Babylonian magic is a spiritual dedication to the Sumerian Anunnaki, a path once seemingly inaccessible—beyond our reach and understanding. Rediscover the most ancient magical system on earth, secretly recorded on cuneiform tablets thousands of years ago in Mesopotamia...

Here is the definitive modern collection of ancient magic including Anunnaki invocations, Mesopotamian gate rituals, Babylonian exorcisms, banishing rites and protective spells.

Joshua Free, world renown esoteric expert, Director of the modern "Mardukite Research Organization," and author of the underground bestselling "Mardukite Core," including *"Necronomicon: The Anunnaki Bible"* and *"Gates of the Necronomicon,"* invites the Seeker on an incredible progressive esoteric journey to illuminate the most ancient and powerful magical tradition within the text of this final volume of the "Mardukite Core" 10th Anniversary Collector's Edition "Necronomicon Trilogy," revealed with perfect clarity—including revised and rewritten materials from *"Magan Magic—the Enuma Elish," "The Complete Book of Marduk by Nabu," "The Maqlu Ritual Book"* and as a special appendix: the original *"Enochian Magic & the Kabbalah"* discourse.

Originally published in four installments,
this special *Necronomicon Grimoire* anthology
collects some of the most practical contributions from
the modern Mardukite Research Organization
as developed underground for the past decade.

MARDUKITE
10TH ANNIVERSARY

NECRONOMICON

THE ANUNNAKI GRIMOIRE

A MANUAL OF PRACTICAL BABYLONIAN MAGICK

by Joshua Free

**MARDUKITE
CHAMBERLAINS**

— TABLET OF CONTENTS —

THE ANUNNAKI SUPERNAL TRINITY

THE BOOK OF ZAGMUK BY NABU

THE BOOK OF GATES BY NABU

PART TWO—THE MAQLU RITUAL BOOK (LIBER M)

THE MARDUKITE "M-SERIES" ARCHIVE

THE MARDUKITE "LIBER-M" ARCHIVES

APPENDIX B—THE ANUNNAKI TAROT (LIBER T – EXCERPTS)

PREFACE TO THE 10TH ANNIVERSARY EDITION

We are entering the second active decade since the public modern Mardukite inception—ten years have now passed by since materials from the *"Mardukite Core"* started circulating privately among the Mardukite Research Organization (*Mardukite Chamberlains*). Anthology volumes comprising this comprehensive "core" esoteric research library are also available as part of this 10th Anniversary Collector's Edition hardcover trilogy—including *"Necronomicon: The Anunnaki Bible"* and *"Gates of the Necronomicon: The Secret Anunnaki Tradition of Babylon."*

The complete *"Mardukite Core"* library collection is a revolutionary *"New Age"* advancement in authentic historical, spiritual and mystical research drawn from a unique unparalleled combination of archeological findings and esoteric mystical-magical traditions. A wellsprings of hidden information and cuneiform tablet translations awaits the seeker—drawn from ancient folds of forgotten lore: Sumerian, Babylonian, Akkadian, Assyrian, Chaldean, Egyptian, Yezidic, Zoroastrian and more. A holistic research-intensive path, rooted in the heart and soul of humanity in Mesopotamia, is laid out clearly for the "Truth Seeker" to see —in its pure and undefiled state.

In the midst of this, now in the 21st century, the "Mardukites" are a very real modern philosophical and meta-spiritual "New Thought" movement aligned specifically with the *Anunnaki* paradigm. In ancient Babylon, this was famously founded upon the followers of *Marduk*—recognized among the local pantheon as patron of Babylonian tradition and *"King of the Gods"* for this branch of the Mesopotamian *mythos* with special assistance by the Nabu priesthood of "Mardukite" scribes...

Yet—*maps are not the journey*—and while *many are called; few are chosen.* This path, although marked in signs and beacons, is not clearly or widely tread. This "pure undefiled" *Self-Honest* journey to the *Source* is not a path of the *masses*—and even those esoterically-inclined have many times retreated from its fundamentals and antiquated semantics, returning to more familiar veils and shadows run rampant throughout modern *"New Age"* movements. Others have attempted to "cherry-pick" the most practical applications from our earlier works—ironically, the very same coveted collection of materials now revealed in *Necronomicon: The Anunnaki Grimoire*—the final volume of this trilogy

Our present volume brings together the most "practical" materials from the "Mardukite Core" to provide the most pragmatic "grimoire"—both applicable to modern times and remaining true to the *Anunnaki Legacy* demonstrated in ancient Mardukite Babylon. Within these pages, the *Seeker* will discover instructions and rites given in two recently revised stand-alone "spellbooks"—*Complete Book of Marduk by Nabu* (containing *Mardukite Liber-W, Z* and parts of *G*) and *The Maqlu Ritual Book* (otherwise *Mardukite Liber-M*).

To properly prepare the *Seeker* and introduce this work with integrity, I have also rewritten and updated material from *Liber-E*, the classic text released publicly as *Magan Magic*—from which I begin this anthology with an "Introduction to Babylonian Magic." Finally—to complete our "Mardukite Core" 10th Anniversary Collector's Edition trilogy, *Liber-K*, also known as *Enochian Magic & Kabbalah*, is featured as an appendix.

While many other texts appear within the *Mardukite Library*, it is the original "Mardukite Core" that modern Mesopotamian movements build their foundations from—and while the *Seeker* is strongly encouraged to at least pursue the greater legacy represented by all three volumes of the newly restored "Core," there is more than sufficient information supplied for personal and practical exploration of these esoteric mysteries within this current "grimoire" But—be warned, for I am entrusting to a *Seeker* this volume apart from the supporting literature as it stands; and without impunity. Yet—for those who have already accumulated and worked through our bulky pile of research tomes—this current edition will be welcomed and celebrated for its revolutionary accessibility.

Within these pages a newcomer might glean the beauty of the system—but more adept experienced *Seekers* of the mysteries will undoubtedly discover much more with little further suggestion and even less prompting, The resurrection of this *lost book* will most certainly be as well received now as it was ten years ago—if not even more so today, as the work of the *Mardukite Research Organization* continues to reach new and wider audiences.

May the personal possession of this most treasured tome bring you infinite blessings on your path.

In Peace, Love & Unity – Always,

~ "NABU" Joshua Free
Beltane – May 2019

10TH ANNIVERSARY — COLLECTOR'S EDITION

NECRONOMICON

THE ANUNNAKI GRIMOIRE

A MANUAL OF PRACTICAL BABYLONIAN MAGICK

by Joshua Free

LOVINGLY DEDICATED TO:

MARDUK & SARPANIT
My Lord & Lady of Babylon
—who gave me life.

&

ANU + ENLIL + ENKI
The Spirit of the Supernal Trinity
—who gave us all life.

—INTRODUCTION—
BABYLONIAN MAGIC
(LIBER E)

— 1 —
THE MAGICAL TRADITION OF BABYLON

*"In the Enuma Eliš... it is Marduk who is now given
given credit for creating not only the
inter-dimensional portals,
but also the BAB.ILI Gateway of the Gods on earth
—control of which was usurped in Babylon."*

—<u>Necronomicon: The Anunnaki Bible</u>

The *Enuma Eliš* cuneiform tablets are named after its opening lines—in Babylonian-Akkadian language, meaning: "When in the heights..." This series of seven clay tablets is best known among both academic scholars *and* esoteric seekers as the "Babylonian Epic of Creation" or "Seven Tablets of Creation." They are *Babylonian* or Mardukite—venerating the Anunnaki god *Marduk*—and <u>not</u> *Sumerian* (pre-Babylonian or *Enlilite*) in origin, as they are so often misrepresented. In essence, they constitute the main "systemology" of religion and magic in Babylon.

Archaeologists discovered the *Enuma Eliš ("e-numa elish")* series in 1849 when the first copy of these cuneiform tablets were recovered from an expedition of the Royal Library of King Ashurbanipal in "Nineveh." The translated tablet series first appeared in public academically as George Smith's *"Chaldean Genesis"* in 1876, receiving critical global attention from historians, mythographers and biblical scholars—and not simply due to their antiquity, but because of how significant the work is when deciphering the secret "methodology" of Babylonian civilization: both its inner *esoteric* mystery tradition and its outward *exoteric* demonstrations of religion among the masses.

Scholars determined the *Enuma Eliš* resonated so highly with the Judeo-Christian (Hebrew) *Creation-Genesis* epic that it was most likely the ancient source behind Jewish primordial lore—yet virtually every seeker of *Mesopotamian Mysteries* will eventually run across the *Enuma Eliš* and will discover an understanding that is far deeper than any of the usual interpretations and diluted "bedtime story" renditions. The epic places emphasis on creation of humans and their ordered reality in the cosmos as demonstrated from within a specifically "Mardukite" worldview.

Critical examination of the *Enuma Eliš* reveals multiple levels or facets of potential holistic understanding. The discourse carries a "political" feature while at the same time relaying its "theological" perspective, in a most significant context for Babylonian systematization—specifically elevating the power of Babylon's patron god Marduk over the Anunnaki pantheon of Mesopotamia.

Literal interpretation of cuneiform tablets provides few clues toward the definitive differentiation between "religion" and "magic" (as we often describe such terms today) among ancient Mesopotamians of Babylon. In fact, outwardly among the general population, a distinction may not even have existed. However, more recent underground contributions of the modern "Mardukite" interpretation draw semantic lines with greater clarity than demonstrated in research of our academic predecessors. In this instance: the *esoteric* "magical" knowledge and higher learning of the priests, priestesses, scribes and magicians in contrast to the *exoteric* "religious" demonstrations and general public awareness.

Another uniquely "Mardukite" appropriation of semantics distinguishes the purely *"Babylonian"* ancient *"Mardukite"* paradigm from its earlier *"Sumerian"* or *"Enlilite"* roots. Historically we see a cultural emphasis toward "Mardukite" (Babylonian) paradigms from *Akkadians*, *Assyrians* and *Chaldeans*—overshadowing and replacing a loosely organized "Enlilite" tradition of former *Uruk Sumerian* and *Ur* dynasties that tended to focus on material politics and geographical conquest rather than spiritual and intellectual pursuits, such as we see later in Babylon with the rise of the scribe-priests and literary cults of the Anunnaki god Nabu, heir-son of Marduk and herald of the "Mardukite" tradition.

Cuneiform tablets that make any reference to Marduk and Nabu are purely "Babylonian" or a direct influence thereof. The elevation of Marduk in the Anunnaki pantheon clearly distinguishes this—using the first systematization of mass consciousness to seal the "Mardukite" tradition of Babylon as "World Order."

Earlier "Sumerian" civilization resembled a more "tribal" approach to the Anunnaki pantheon, observing a patron deity specific to the location, city infrastructure, natural resources and geographical terrain. This loose organization solidified and systematized for the first time in Babylon, host of the first official "national religion," but systematized under the "Mardukite" paradigm—which is equally reflected in practices and beliefs cementing the "magical tradition" of Babylon.

Usurpation and transfer of Mesopotamian "power" to Babylon, control of the empire by priest-magicians and dragon-kings, literary catalogues of authoritative spiritual and religious systems defining humanity and its relationship with the Anunnaki "Sky Gods"—was all shown or proved to be executed and systematized by "Divine Right" and in accordance with the established "World Order" decreed by the Anunnaki Supernal Trinity—*Anu*, *Enlil* and *Enki*—in prehistoric times...

...it was the *Enuma Eliš* that made this all possible.

The *Enuma Eliš* empowered the "Law of Marduk"—such as the Code of Hammurabi—in the community. Marduk's "Creation Epic" also contributed an intellectual and spiritual foundation to all Babylonian magical and religious ceremonies. As a preliminary "rite" of invocation, specialized priests and priestesses performed dramatic reenactments from the tablet text—such as those for personal "*gate-rituals*," the "*maqlu*" and the Mardukite Spring Equinox Aries Festival of "*Akiti*" or "*Akitu*" (the Babylonian "New Year")—all of which, including the *Enuma Eliš*, are translated in greater detail elsewhere in the current anthology.

As a cornerstone of the political, spiritual and magical development in Babylon, the *Enuma Eliš* is inseparably paramount to all related esoteric and academic ventures—including any true *understanding* (and possible "theoretical" *implementation*) of the ancient "Mardukite" Mesopotamian religious paradigms, spiritual worldviews, magical or occult sciences, and the later evolution of the same into various *kabbalahs* and "Mystery Traditions" throughout the world. The *Enuma Eliš* demonstrates transfer of Anunnaki power and Mesopotamian world-order to the "Mardukite" Babylonian paradigm, marking a significant turning point in global consciousness at its apex—again, apparent in all resulting magical and spiritual practices and traditions.

A new brand of "Mesopotamia" emerges synchronous with the *Age of Aries*—*Age of Marduk*—appropriated mathematically as c. 2100 B.C. by ancient scholars. Babylonians elevated Marduk in the pantheon to coincide with a shifting era, clearly marked by Celestial Time—what we call "astrological ages" today. On the Spring Equinox, celebrated as the Babylonian New Year, the sun rises in a position relative to one of twelve equal sized thirty-degree zones that encompass our view of the cosmos like a band, each specifically distinguishing an era named for a correlating "zodiac" constellation. But the actual observed size of each constellation is not equal—some are larger, extending past their "zone."

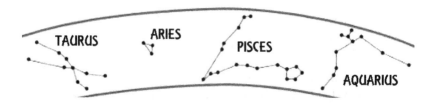

Conflict between the new "Mardukite" systemology and former *Enlilite* standards resulted from the discrepancy between the mathematical shift and the visibly apparent or observed shift in Celestial Time. In brief: the constellation of *Aries*—the *Ram of Marduk*—is dwarfed by the sprawl of *Taurus*—the *Bull of Enlil*—that marked the preceding "Sumerian" age. It seemed to "Mardukite" Babylonians that the former *Enlilite* indigenous development period would never end! *For when..?* asked Marduk.

Eventually a "Mardukite" Babylonian era did arrive—but it was always contested and often only allowed isolated points in history in which to peacefully thrive. Since the new "Mardukite" priest-scribes could not obviously wait for the "stars to properly align," an elevation of Marduk in human consciousness would have to be demonstrated another way. A new "Mardukite" (Babylonian) era brought with it a revolutionary way of socially programming human consciousness.

Learned reality perceptions of life experience were installed in Babylon consistent with the Mardukite systemology. This facet is already clearly illustrated in our previous volume *The Sumerian Legacy* (also available in the 10th Anniversary *Gates of the Necronomicon* anthology edited by Joshua Free), wherein is described origins of a unique literary tradition in Mesopotamia regarding cuneiform script refinement and its societal use by the Babylonian "scribe-priests" of Nabu, son of Marduk. Critical to a successful paradigm ushering in the *Age of Marduk*, perhaps the most profound demonstration was, in fact, forging the *Enuma Eliš* tablet cycle—for reasons that should be by now, or will become, increasingly obvious to the seeker.

In the *Enuma Eliš* text (translated in our *Necronomicon: The Anunnaki Bible*, used for *The Complete Book of Marduk by Nabu* and reprinted in this current anthology) the priest-magician is not only given the keys to the "kingdom," but keys to *all* "kingdoms"—*on earth* as it is *in heaven*. The first six of the seven tablets are "tablets of ordering" corresponding to six primary "gates" or "veiled thresholds" fragmenting our existence from the *All* to manifest an energetically-condensed material reality (as we shall continue to explore throughout this volume). Significance of this correlation should be profound enough for seasoned *seekers* of these mysteries to make useful—but for those still coming to understand this "legacy," the complete story will have to unfold as the *seeker-reader* works through the remaining material. Our purpose here is, of course, to not reiterate the several volumes of background information and source books previously released by the *"Mardukite Truth Seeker Press."*

In many modern esoteric renderings, the seventh or *"secret"* tablet of the *Enuma Eliš* is often treated somewhat separately as an extension of the earlier tablets—and this is reflected in contemporary "Mardukite" literature, such as in *Necronomicon: The Anunnaki Bible*, where these tablets are cataloged as Series-F, the *Fifty Names of Marduk*, companion to the Series-N *Enuma Eliš* (first six tablets). Some go as far as to make the *Fifty Names of Marduk* the entire basis for modern *"spellbooks."*

Following the inception of the modern "Mardukite" movement in 2008, a wide-spread revival of interest in the *Anunnaki*—and specifically the Babylonian god *Marduk*—has ensued: as planned, predicted and plotted during synchronized global ritual (intention-based) energetic movements or shifts in mass consciousness. These meditation exercises often coincide with what some call the "Beltane Gate" or "Fires of Bel" festival observed on "May's Eve" (April 30–May 1), roughly midway between the Spring Equinox (*"Akiti"/"Akitu"*) and Summer Solstice.

In contrast to the "magical" and "priestly" literary tradition of Babylon, older *"Sumerian"* (or "Enlilite") texts emphasize documenting the many "firsts" offered by *Anunnaki* gods and developed as the "Arts of Civilization" toward establishment of the first cities in Mesopotamia. As time bore on, a new brand of "Babylonian esoterica" shaped systems of early human civilization, preserved within the knowledge base of priest-magicians, priestesses and scribes. This greatly furthered a class distinction not only between *Anunnaki* and humanity, but between select humans of an "elite" *esoteric* inner circle of understanding and those of the general population. This "magical" or "sacred" class of citizen—mainly kings, priest-scribes, and priestesses—served as intermediaries between what is *"divine"* and the more mundane worldly affairs of humanity. Naturally the general population was only given (or capable of receiving) a diluted outward *exoteric* demonstration of higher mysteries of cosmic wisdom. These publicly visible "mythologies" are mostly all that has survived.

When compared to earlier pre-Babylonian "*Creation Tablets,*" one can easily determine the *Enuma Eliš* carries a much more advanced complex systematization with a wide array of intended applications. The "outer teachings" were so influential (as the first "systemology") that they went on to affect not only Babylon proper, but also greater Mesopotamia and beyond—the Assyrians, Akkadians, Hittites, Phoenicians, Chaldeans, Semitic-Jews, and yes, even in Egypt, where *Marduk* was also known as "*Amon-Ra*" and later as "*Aten*" to priests of Akhenaton's secret order. In contrast, purely "Sumerian" *Epics of Creation* are hardly "epic"—the whole cosmology often only briefly summarized in opening lines:—

> *AN carries off heaven;*
> *ENLIL carries off earth.*

After which *Enki* is given control of the first city—his home in *Eridu.* Eventually the "Arts of Civilization" are moved from *Eridu* to *Uruk* and Sumerian culture ensues, continuing to operate on this loosely defined simplistic methodology. It was rudimentary, but unchallenged, simply standing as its own as what *was* and *always had been* the case. This changed with emerging "Mardukite" paradigms and an inception of the "Ancient Mystery Tradition" permeating global spiritual and mystical factions thereafter—from *Kabbalahs* to *Hermetics*, and all throughout better recognized "arcane lore" and "esoteric sciences" imported by the Europeans in their own customs and traditions.

Marduk's spiritual and worldly supremacy is demonstrated on *Enuma Eliš* tablets as an epic describing his victorious conquest over the Great Cosmic Dragon of Chaos—TIAMAT. We can further appreciate the Babylonian opinions of Marduk when we couple to this lore of cosmic ordering the fact that Marduk also received a direct apprenticeship in the *esoteric sciences* and "Arts of Civilization" from *his father*, Enki, while residing in the ancient southern-most Mesopotamian city of *Eridu*—near the *Persian Gulf*—during much of the early "Sumerian" development period, where he is not ranked among the "Enlilite" Anunnaki pantheon and appears nowhere on pre-Babylonian tablet sources.

Prior to "*her*" identification on *Enuma Eliš* tablets as *Tiamat,* a Great Dragon of similar repute is found on older Enlilite tablets as KUR—also the *Sumerian* word for "mountain" that connects the "conquering of the dragon" with the "king of the mountain" motif—which is explored more deeply in a supplemental Mardukite *Liber-D* text released underground as the "*Draconomicon*" by Joshua Free.

This dragon-theme is so paramount—an icon that eventually comes to represent the god Marduk himself—that it later reappears in virtually all connected mythos defining "royalty," "divine right" and "dragonblood." In fact, several earlier vague Sumerian attempts to similarly show reign of power among the Anunnaki hierarchy also concerned the "dragon"— or *Kur*. In pre-Babylonian epics, a "slayer of serpents" title is attributed to just about every other figurehead among the Anunnaki *but* Marduk— and this would make sense if they are of a pre-Babylonian "Sumerian" origin. The very fact that Marduk does not make an appearance early on in the *Enuma Eliš* suggests the epic is drawn from earlier sources and/or meant to simply replace all previous Anunnaki "claims" to authority. In all instances, the "dragon-conquering" event is almost always denoting a "change in power"—a *paradigm shift*.

We can conclude that using a host of esoteric knowledge from *Eridu*— and thereby *Enki*—the priest-scribes of Nabu that developed the *Enuma Eliš* (as national propaganda enforcing a "Mardukite" church-state in Babylon) integrated a legacy of secret wisdom and practical lore from which the entire *corpus* of Babylonian magical curriculum is derived. It should also be noted that as a "legal document" the *Enuma Eliš* transfers power to Marduk after first chronicling the alignment and control of the preexisting ruling cosmic order starting with the Primordial: the Abyss, the Dragon; then shifting focus to the Anunnaki Supernal Trinity, Anu, Enlil and Enki; and finally Marduk as the hero of a "younger pantheon." [The nature of the *"primordial abyss"* and *"primeval dragon"* is further explored in Mardukite *Liber-50*, available in the 10th Anniversary *Gates of the Necronomicon* anthology by Joshua Free, or *Sumerian Legacy*.]

Beyond the points already illustrated, *Enuma Eliš* tablets additionally allude to a dualistic fragmentation of reality existence. This dichotomy is demonstrated in religio-political beliefs of "Babylonian versus proto-Sumerian," but also in terms of an interdimensional separation between the *heights* and the *depths*—the "seen" and "unseen" aspects of the All. This is of utmost importance to the magician or mystic that seeks to use and affect universal cosmic energies. We see a direct reference to this division graphically illustrated in the "dragon cycle" as two "halves" of the beast: the *dragon's head* and *dragon's tail* respectively:

> *Ti-a-mat e-Zi-ti*
> "lower" Tiamat—the "Body"
> *Ti-a-mat Shap-li-ti*
> "upper" Tiamat—the "Head"

Where many contemporary readers will be quick to recoil back to more familiar Semitic or Judeo-Christian frameworks—we can demonstrate connections there too. For example: in the *Book of Genesis*, the original waters (*"primordial abyss"*) were separated, giving rise to the "deep," rendered as "*tehom*" in Hebrew, but which is derived from the Akkadian *Tiamat*. What follows (in all accounts) describes an ordering of creation or systematization of the cosmos—the essence of materially condensed energies fragmented or separated from a "primeval source."

The ancient Babylonian magical tradition—or any magical tradition—is dependent on a practitioner's abilities to understand *true knowledge* of themselves, the cosmos, and the relationship between. Ever since the days of ancient Mesopotamia, these same magical traditions become increasingly dependent on the "local" (material realm) systematization of this knowledge in the form of "magical correspondences." Although universal cosmic energies are a constant—as much today as in *Sumer*—any systematized division and classification of these forces appeared *first* in the Babylonian Mystery School, assigned in *writing* the *first* time for secret libraries of "Mardukite" priests, priestesses, scribes and kings.

Where many resources and materials over the past century and a half primarily deal with a base recovery of source texts and an interpretation of the outer *exoteric* mythographic understanding of cultures, the unique quality of the modern "Mardukite" literary contributions rests in its clear emphasis on the inner *esoteric* knowledge—not necessarily understood by the general populations of any era or region—maintained by those of the "*priestly,*" "*mystic,*" "*royal*" and "*scribal*" classes: those with established relationships with *Anunnaki gods*—and the cosmic forces they represent back of and behind the scenes of all religious, spiritual and political activity. This is the *real subject* of ancient Babylonian "magic."

— 2 —
A TRUE "NECRONOMICON" GRIMOIRE

"Now that the fate of the Universe has been decreed.
Now that the dyke and canal have been given proper direction;
The banks of the Tigris and Euphrates have been established;
O Anunnaki—Ye Great Gods:
What else shall we do?
—What else shall we create?"

—A Broken Cuneiform Tablet Fragment

As a staple of the Babylonian religious, political and magical tradition, we have demonstrated the primary historic significance of the *Enuma Eliš* in our previous chapter. Beyond academic, archaeological and even biblical studies, the first modern "New Age" instigation of *Enuma Eliš* tablets for popular mainstream "Mesopotamian Neopaganism" occurs with the infamous *"Simon Necronomicon"* cycle, where a bastardized rendition appears within it as the *"Magan Text."* Lore from *Simon's* book does correlate loosely with some magical elements of ancient Babylon, but it does not relate a complete tradition in itself, nor does it pretend to, styled after a "magician's notebook" and not truly an account of one that is initiated into the Babylonian priesthood proper, or a specific Mystery School based thereupon—although the publication of the book has gone on to certainly incite the formation of many quasi-orders and societies.

Although *"Simon's Necronomicon"* is not the main subject of our current volume and anthology—(so not to reiterate what appears in *Mardukite Liber-R* and *Liber-555*, currently available within the 10th Anniversary *"Gates of the Necronomicon"* anthology edited by Joshua Free, or the forthcoming commemorative anniversary paperback of *"Necronomicon Revelations: Crossing to the Abyss"*)—there are correlative aspects that often seem impossible not to mention when discussing modern "New Age" revivals of the Mesopotamian paradigm in the strictest esoteric or occult sense. The fact is that most people introduced to the Mardukite paradigm already carried with them an affinity to the mythology alluded to in *"Simon's Necronomicon"* and hence the name has invariably stuck. Ancient cuneiform tablets collected for the Mardukite system never historically carried such a *title*, but that speaks only of its outer packaging.

The first six tablets of the *Enuma Eliš* epic—(cataloged as *Mardukite Tablet-N* in our *"Necronomicon: The Anunnaki Bible"* and also included later within the present anthology)—clearly provide a scriptural basis to the ancient Mardukite Babylonian paradigm and its modern revivals. We suspect its inclusion in all rites, rituals and meditations aligned to the specifically "Mardukite" interpretation of Mesopotamian spirituality and civic systemology. Additionally, there is a seventh tablet of the *Enuma Eliš*, the *"Tablet of Fifty Names"*—(given as *Mardukite Tablet-F* in our catalogue; transcribed later in this current anthology)—appearing more frequently in modern "Babylonian Magick" discourses than any other, and of course bastardized in *"Simon's Necronomicon"* as a *"Grimoire of the Fifty Names of Marduk."*

In *"Simon's Necronomicon"*—(also called the *Schlangekraft Recension* to those O.T.O. students of Kenneth Grant)—the *Magan Text* is introduced as a "lingering remainder" drawn from "sacred texts" of "cult priests" following the *"Old Faith"*—but, specifically described as a cult existing "at a time before Babylon was built..." Such statements may or may not have any true precedent on the *Enuma Eliš*, at the same time we know from the mere mention and centralization of Marduk that the text cannot possibly be "pre-Babylonian"—clearly the "Seven Tablets (Epic) of Creation" are *not* "Sumerian," but they *are* "Babylonian" verbatim.

Original campaign efforts to install a "Mardukite" paradigm in Babylon actually began prior to a centralization of Babylon as a city or nation by cult-like Nabu-tribes in dedication to Marduk. These newly forming priest-scribes re-invented and refined civic, social and psychological use of cuneiform script. A different cuneiform style previously represented a more primitive application of the earlier *eme-gir* or "mother tongue" of the "Sumerians" using fingernails to make impressions in soft clay. The greater widespread use of writing to represent human systematization resulted from invention of a reed-stylus "pen" by Nabu. The stylus now allowed for more influential writings, data collections, and history records to affect human consciousness—this is how Babylonian tradition became the first systematized standard of ancient Mesopotamia. But a pristine piece of paper folded once may just as soon be folded again—the methodology of systematization unleashed on human consciousness was ever thereafter copy-and-pasted into all developing human cultures, then shaped and formed based on unique local geography, mythologies and language. This revised literary tradition supported developmental progression of early human society using themes we most conveniently identify as "magic" and "religion."

As with the modern *"Magan Text,"* the historical *Enuma Eliš* tablets are a main *corpus* or body of instructional and supportive materials for the Babylonian ("Mardukite") priest-magicians, priestesses and scribes who aided ushering in a new metaphysical dynamic in human consciousness. In addition to "setting the stage" for a ritual performance or ceremonial observance in the literal sense, the complete *Enuma Eliš* provides both a mental "framework" ("paradigm") and energetic link specifically to the "Marduk-current stream." Likewise, the first six tablets *"empower"* a seventh that transfers power and authority of the Anunnaki pantheon to Marduk—and combined they *"empower"* a spiritual hierarchy supporting practical realizations of Babylonian religious and magical tradition.

Contrary to popular "Hollywood" conceptions of ancient religion, magic and the *"Necronomicon,"* today the Mardukite tradition is revived in a greater state of Self-Honesty and dedication to cosmic wisdom. All of the literary materials suggest a focused dedicate intellectual and spiritual pursuit as a prerequisite of true initiation—which can only be bestowed from *"above,"* by authority and permission of the *"highest."* The power is not *in* the words, it is *in* the *Self*—the true and absolute *"I-Am"* that is really undergoing an initiation to paths representing cumulatively more advanced degrees of *awareness* and *ascension*. Mispronouncing archaic words will not cause some primordial denizen to consume the operator; nor is any mere utterance of the *Enuma Eliš* sufficient to produce some "supernatural" result. The operator—*priest, priestess, magician, &tc.*—uses the tradition, system or standard as a "catalyst" to tap or activate very "natural" (but dormant) mystical connectivity with the cosmos, of which there are no "words" except those that truly and matter-of-factly resonant in consciousness exactly the nature of what they are meant to label. In short—the words and names can only carry the meanings given to them by an operator that pursued the true and underlying meanings.

The most ancient pure streams of mystical practice differ greatly from those more "Western" approaches popularly revived in modern "New Age" and metaphysical movements. Occult revivals tend to emphasize a focus only on elements that can be superimposed onto existing forms of modern magical practice or the esoteric obsession with obscure and popular "grimoires" that yield their best results in the form of self-delusion and thought-forms born from mental masturbation. Commonly, the seventh tablet of the *Enuma Eliš*—*"Fifty Names of Marduk"*—(*Mardukite Tablet-F*) is revived in exclusion to the remaining lore, isolated as a modern "spellbook" or *short-cut* variety to tapping the total power of the greater "Mardukite" Mesopotamian legacy.

Several modern occult "writers" have demonstrated that the "*Grimoire of Fifty Names*" may be successfully employed by operators for strictly ceremonial magic forms of "spellcraft"—much like the more famous derivatives of the same: such as the *Goetia* or *Keys of Solomon*, which for all intents and purposes are rooted in a "Judeo-Christian" paradigm, and are not authentic "pagan" texts. Any real universal power exercised from the *Fifty Names* is activated by the preceding six tablets, demonstrating an older and more "priestly" methodology than what is traditionally prescribed in modern occult reconstructions. As a spiritual prerequisite, the six preceding tablets directly correlate to the first *six gates* that bring the *seeker* to the footsteps of Marduk for initiation and the opportunity to observe him as "Patron of Babylon" and King of the Anunnaki gods.

Since the modern inception of Mardukite tradition, a main tenet of the paradigm is repeatedly professed—the spiritual and magical abilities are not ends in themselves, but rather results from a true and faithful "Self-Honest" relationship with Anunnaki beings and the cosmic wisdom they definitely *guard*. After the first six tablets of the *Enuma Eliš* are intoned —after the operator passes through the first six "*gates*" (or *steps* on the "ladder of lights" or "stairway to heaven") and have attuned to the *gate-current* of Marduk, then and only then, may names and powers of the "seventh tablet" or any other *gate-work* from the BAB-ILI tablet texts given later in this current Mardukite "grimoire" anthology. This critical component is necessary to operate any of true Babylonian (*Mardukite*) *gatework* ("spiritual pathworking") or star-magic proper. By the seventh tablet of the *Enuma Eliš*, the priest-magician has assumed control of the "Mardukite" Anunnaki hierarchy and is conducting ritual incantations as if from the perspective of *Nabu*, acting on behalf of his father:—

> "*The incantation of Marduk is the Incantation of Eridu;*
> *It is not I, but Marduk that speaks the incantation...*"

Invoking the "*Incantation of Marduk*"—or "*Incantation of Eridu,*" as it is also called, is among the most prominent and widely revived aspects of the ancient Babylonian (*Mardukite*) tradition. But be aware that doing so strengthens a spiritual connectivity between the practitioner and this specific ancient, raw, and powerful alignment to the *Anunnaki*. Magic of this tradition is a "*holy magic,*" originally reserved to a select group that maintained "higher" understandings of the universe and mythic symbols used to represent this knowledge. It definitively invokes powers of the Anunnaki by "birth-right," calling on the ancient "covenant" alleged to be "sworn between the gods and man."

The authentic ancient concepts defined by the ancient "Mardukite" ideal in Babylon is revived today in spirit of work produced by the *Mardukite Chamberlains* (Mardukite Research Organization)—a group of specific individuals seeking to free humanity from the spiritual and intellectual slavery that keeps us from the *Truth*, and as a result has kept many of us from a true *Self-Honest* spiritual evolution. Yes, we are "chamberlains" and stewards of an ancient mystery tradition, but we serve the cause "on commitment" and in dedication to the "*Highest*," not as some arbitrarily observed idol-worship in the name of *Marduk*—which is a commonly made mistake by outsiders and purely academic archaeologists. What's more—at its most abstract and fundamental level: modern *Mardukites* seek to prepare the "House of Marduk" and "Temple of Heaven-Earth" as one-to-one with the *Self*, the *Earth* and the *Cosmos*—All-as-One!

Unlike traditional occult revivals—usually dependent on the *Kabbalah*, medieval *grimoires*, European peasant-folk traditions and other similar sources—the specifically *Mardukite* interpretation of what some brand "Mesopotamian Neopaganism" is truly rooted in an ancient pre-Christian, pre-Judaic paradigm from the "cradle of civilization" and its writings coupled with an exquisite balance of "New Thought" vocabulary that is most resonant with the current times. Although the greater legacy holds a wide-angle view of developmental progression of global systems after Babylon, the modern *Mardukite* works forward in their understanding, beginning logically at the beginning and following the course of events as they have unfolded up until now—and possibly an insight into what is to come later. An authentic type of "magic" employed in this tradition simply defines a "path" of practical processes promoting intellectual self realization and spiritual initiation. Outward demonstrations of the art as "dramatic reenactments" or "ritual magic" are only conducted from a point of *Self-Honesty* and not *self-delusion*—which is another common flaw in many of the more widely spread modern "occult" traditions.

As described previously in modern *Mardukite* knowledge lectures: All power comes from *Self*, the true "alpha spirit" or "I-AM" within-and-as *Self*. Any system, teaching or method that displaces focus of power and connectivity to the *All-as-One* "Source" away from *Self* is a deception. If we are to classify the practice as "magic," then such a word is defined proper as: *Self*-directing the *Will* of the true *Self*. These terms should not be used to glorify the "artificial ego-self" developed in *this* world—an artificial facade personality worn by the *Self* as a temporarily sheath of true identity. To be successful, it is this mortally fabricated persona that practitioners of mystical arts must shed from their mind like snake-skin.

Modern practices of a similar nature—often dubbed "ceremonial magic" —typically adhere to a strict ritual criteria. When not arbitrarily added to a ritual for ridiculous purposes, many traditional magical, spiritual and/ or religious practices are performed in *imitation* of events first observed and recorded at the most ancient temple-shrines—such as in Babylon and Sumer, otherwise "Mesopotamia." Obviously this legacy went on to affect not only the local population, but also the later-derived practices of "Hermetic" traditions of ancient magick on a global scale—and often attributed to the "cult of Nabu" but under whatever local relative terms and names defined "Mercurian scribe-librarian gods"—whether *Nabu*, *Nisaba*, *Thoth*, *Hermes*, *Mercury*, *Apollo*, *Tir*, *Ogmha*, *Menrva*, *Seshat*, *Teshmet*, *A'As*, *Odin*, *Tiwaz*, *Tyr*, *Anahita*, *Minerva*, *Mergen* or *Merlyn*...

Modern *Mardukites* describe three aspects (or types) of magic or ritual found within the *Mardukite* work inspired by ancient Babylon:—

Firstly...the work that leads to *Self-Honest* knowledge and experience of *Self* and the *Anunnaki*—a true and faithful dedicated devotion already emphasized as a prerequisite to all of Babylonian tradition in general. One might classify this first form of "magic" as "prayer"—it is based on a transmission of intention that also establishes a necessary relationship (or communication) with the same "spiritual" forces that one is later acting as an intermediary ambassador or "priestly" catalyst. Systematic prayer-books—composed of clay tablets, of course, such as given later within this current anthology volume—were kept in private collections and bed-chambers of the most successful ancient priests, priestesses and kings in Babylonian history. Although this part of the path is primarily "introspective" and personal in nature—meant to prepare the individual for ascent up the "stairway of godly evolution"—it may also be studied, researched and developed among couples, groups, large orders and even priesthoods, just as it once was quite definitively in ancient times—and perhaps even among an unbroken underground stream since then.

Secondly...the *Anunnaki Star-Gate System*—of which Babylon is boldly named for directly. As with most *"true magic,"* this type of exploratory practice is also "introspective" and to such an extent that it consists of only the most secret *"private esoteric"* practices of the Ancient Mystery School ("priesthood," &tc.), sharing in a relationship with the *Anunnaki* that is not as evident in the more *public exoteric* demonstrations or folk-beliefs and customs within the range of common knowledge. It is of the common and uninitiated folk—and traditions prepared for their benefit —that most dry academic and archaeological interpretations are derived.

As a method of practice and tradition of personal development, the Gate motif of Babylon—also known to some as the "*ladder of lights*"—is not concerned with further accumulation of additional fragmented energies or "layers of consciousness," but rather the removal of these "artificial light filters" that inhibit *Self-Honest* experience of the "mystical" unity of *All-as-One*. Secret tablets reveal that these fragmented "levels" and "layers" representation that *Anunnaki* influenced as systematic parameters of awareness—what humans were capable of experiencing of reality. This more *cosmic* development of practice could be classified as a "Celestial" form of Ceremonial Magic. But, this is not necessarily the same, one-to-one, with the contemporary understanding of what is called "Ceremonial Magick" today. And yet, at the same time, archetypal Mesopotamian practices of "high magick" did later evolve into more familiar or popularized systems of Greco-Egyptian "Hermetic," European Druidry, and the traditional forms of Hebrew Mysticism, better known as the "*Kabbalah*," which directly evolved from the Babylonians, as did the entire "Babylonian Talmudic" and Rabbinical tradition of the Jews.

Finally...the *Cultural Magic* most closely identifiable with what anthropologists and archaeologists study—quite frankly because it is the only aspect of ancient tradition that allowed for public observation and participation. Compared to previously described "religious" and "celestial" forms, this practice is highly qualified to earn a title of "low magic" in many respects. It reflects everything we have come to expect from the cultural archetype (and stereotype) of *Babylon* proper—the national rites of public spirituality and religion that further strengthened the "system" and the popular belief in it among the population. There is no shortage of archaeological evidence to support an *outer tradition* rich in colorful cultural annual festivals; ritual gestures, idol-statues, talismanic amulets and trinkets to accomplish protective, fertility and healing effects; even the effigy personification of negativity, pestilence, demons and wicked-doers (*witches* and *warlocks*) that are destroyed with symbolic burnings as described on *Maqlu* tablets given later within the current anthology.

An elementary description of ceremonial instruction may be derived from the *Mardukite Tablet-Q* series given in *Necronomicon: The Anunnaki Bible*: "...make your invocation prayer to *Marduk* and *Sarpanit* and then invoke the Supernal Trinity—*Anu, Enlil* and *Enki*—followed by a conjuration of the fire and four beacon-lamps of the four watchtowers. Then perform the *Incantation of Eridu* and call forth a presence of your personal watcher '*sedu*' guardian-spirit." Excerpted *Mardukite* texts to support these (and other) ritual instructions are given in this anthology.

Basic modern applications may be respectively adapted from the following materials as they appear within this current *anthology* (and throughout the greater *Mardukite* literary legacy):—

- The "Incantation of Eridu." *Liber-W* and *Tablet-Y.*
- Conjuration-incantations of the Four Watchtowers: the four corners of the cosmos (and their *gate-seals*). *Tablet-X.*
- Conjuration-incantations for the fire: god-fire, beacon-lamps, cauldron, candles, &tc. *Liber-M* and *Tablet-Y.*
- Invocation-prayers to the Anunnaki "Gates of Babylon," the Supernal Trinity and Babylonian Pantheon (including representative *gate-seals*). *Liber-W*, *Tablet-B* and *Liber-50.*

In Simon's *Necronomicon Spellbook,* a practical use of the *Fifty Names of Marduk* is suggested, reminiscent of modern spellcraft far more than any ancient practices—and most importantly: skipping all of the above listed essentials to traditional ritual magic, of Babylon or otherwise. And while some indications of these methods appears in the original Simon volume, the later released frugal spellbook emphasizes only information of the seventh *Enuma Eliš* tablet (sometimes indicated "Tablet-VIb" by some scholars) concerning the *Fifty Names* of Anunnaki power usurped as "Names of Marduk" (*Tablet-F*) for *hierarchical magic* in Babylon. In the present volume—and the greater *Mardukite* literary legacy including our *Necronomicon: The Anunnaki Bible* and *Gates of the Necronomicon* edited by Joshua Free—we have sought to render a more complete and *Self-Honest* relay of this specific paradigm of ancient Mesopotamia.

Babylonian Anunnaki "incantation-prayers" and "gate invocations" are essentially synonymous, often only differentiated by intention (application) or a few statement lines. Those appearing in the Mardukite *Liber-W* (or *Tablet-W*) series—given as the *Book of Marduk by Nabu*—denote a very strong and deeply powerful devotional system adopted by priest-magicians, priestesses, scribes and kings of the Babylonian Empire. The religio-spiritual practice is indicative of a harmonic relationship with the Anunnaki "*gods.*" Petitions and prayers made before images of the gods in temples or private shrines may have yielded "spell-like" results, but as a "holy magic" that is not typically observed in contemporary "New Age" system-traditions. The powers of *above* are not "pulled down" by force and coercion, or by cryptology of some secret number and name, but are based on cosmic laws of *attraction*, *equity* and *vibration*, earned as "graces" by living the "Right Way"—a pious life dedicated to all that is positively promotes *Life* in harmony with natural law...*All-as-One.*

— 3 —
THE MAGIC OF BABYLONIAN STAR-GATES

"My spell is the spell of Enki.
My incantation is the incantation of Marduk.
Power and blood of Marduk is within me.
It is not I, but Marduk, who performs the incantation."

—*The Incantation of Eridu*

The purpose of our present volume—within the full context of the entire modern *Mardukite* literary legacy—is to provide sufficient historically accurate *esoteric* lore and *cosmic law* teachings of the Ancient Mystery School. From this we expect modern practitioners, or esoteric archaeologists at the very least, to glean a new interpretation of ancient Babylon and its spiritual, magical and otherwise national religious tradition. For some, the literary legacy we provide is a god-sent to incite an evolution of revivals and reconstructions found amidst the *"New Age"* today.

A magician, priest or priestess operating at any period in history may in fact benefit from Babylonian cuneiform "incantation" tablets so long as they are employed within the appropriate *Mardukite* paradigm. Tablets describing the *Anunnaki gods,* and the *Stargates* of Babylon they represent, are primarily given as "incantations." Unlike traditional catalogues of knowledge we might create today, Babylonian systematization is very carefully hidden within a body of tablets describing a handful of epics— but the "incantations" appear more abundantly than anything else. It is from these religious and magical tablets that we draw details about the individual figures, rendering additional insights that, for example, reading *Enuma Eliš* tablets in isolation would not provide.

Over the past century, the most frequently cited Babylonian incantation tablets mainly pertain to the *"Lifting of the Hands"* series, made popular through academic translations unleashed from the British Museum since the early 1900's. The series is named for a common ceremonial gesture used in "praise" or "adoration" of the *highest* or *sky-gods*. The standard gesture of priests and priestesses is displayed on some statue images of *Nabu* and *Teshmet* where the hands are resting in front of the body, with the right hand clasped around the left wrist.

Our premise for a modern magical revival of Babylonian tradition begins with the idea that the *Enuma Eliš* is far from primitive—that these *Seven Tablets of Creation* are a basis for a programmed material reality received by the most antiquated systematized societal civilization on the planet: in *Mesopotamia*. Surpassing even this, for practical purposes of modern esoteric experimentation, is the strong *seven-fold* structure motif observed in ancient Babylon—the same *sevenfold* theme that defines an archetypal basis for relevant correspondences: numbers, planets, colors, notes of music, &tc. We can see evidence for a *sevenfold* fragmentation of the *All* everywhere we turn in our condensed material-physical realm.

The very lore that gifted Babylon its name—*Gates of the Star-Gods*—led to a systematic understanding of the world. Both esoteric practitioners and commoners alike still operate under its spell to the present day. When we consider the division of the visual spectrum of color; the audible range of notes of music; the methodology behind the seven original sacred cities in Mesopotamia—considered energy points or even space ports by some scholars; the ordering of the "rays," "levels" or "days" of creation/manifestation; and, above all, a representative ritual or ceremonial observation of the whole thing—physically displayed by the *seven-stepped ziggurat* "high temples" of Babylonia... a spiritual, philosophical and religious standard becomes clear—one that can be easily adapted for modern-day exploration and experimentation.

As a hermetically sealed system in Babylon, the standards put forth by the *Enuma Eliš* demonstrate a clear spirto-magical and religio-political sentiment motivating the account—specifically as it relates to elevation and centralization of *Marduk* within a greater Mesopotamian Annnnaki framework. By entrusting *Marduk* with a position as *King of the Gods*, he became responsible for the "ordering" of the physical universe—the cosmos as perceived by evolving humanity—a race first bred as a superior work animal, then upgraded yet again by *Enki* for the modern design humans exist as today. But we also know that beneath this programming lies the very cosmic code of the ancestral *god-race*, and that the proper use of the *esoterica* they have left behind for us is, in turn, a "map" that may guide the "unfoldment" of dormant spiritual evolutionary potential.

First established on earth by *Enki* in *Eridu* (proto-Sumerian), and then transferred by *Inanna-Ishtar* to her city of *Uruk* (Uruk-Sumerian), the *Enuma Eliš* demonstrates further transfer of Anunnaki power and world order to Babylon during the "Age of Aries" shift—and with it, control of the *Arts of Civilization* and the keystone called the *Tablets of Destiny*.

The *"Tablets of Destiny"* are only alluded to throughout Mesopotamian lore—no specific candidate for such a relic has been unearthed, pushing the subject into the realm of legend and to the same proportions as other "mythic books" of renown. Without more literary details, the *"Tablets of Destiny"* maintain residence primarily in forums of scholarly debate. It is difficult to even determine definitively from academic records as to whether this specific tablet (or series of tablets) is indeed a physical literary cuneiform object or if it is perhaps something else altogether. In the *Enuma Eliš*, the tablet is first in possession of the great primordial dragon *Tiamat*. She tattaches it to *Kingu*, her vizier-messenger or quality of action and communication across the Abyss. After *Marduk* defeats *Kingu*, he removes the *Tablet of Destiny* and attaching it to his breast, he assumes the same empowerment of authority and power—and it is this unique talisman contributing to his victory over *Tiamat*.

Considering all collected lore of the *Tablet of Destiny*, *Tablets of Destiny* or *Tablet of Destinies*, the work—if literal—would be synonymous with the collected *cosmic wisdom* or *secret knowledge* of the "gods." Those traditions that inherited the Babylonian system (in part) later understood the same as a *Book of Life*, or among mystics as the *Akashic Records* or the *Arcane Scrolls (Tablets)*—a hidden core behind the Ancient Mystery School. If we are to take them as a metaphysical construct, then we can assume—as E.A Budge originally translates—that these are *Tablets of Fate*, though we know ancient Mesopotamian languages viewed "fate" and "destiny" as two different aspects, unlike today where semantics are often blurred. In short—as described in our discourse on *Sumerian Language*—a "destiny" is a irrevocable inevitable "destination," whereas "fate" is a pathway chosen to reach that "destination."

—Key to the Babylonian Sevenfold Anunnaki Pantheon—

Mesopotamian	*Sabian*	*Classical*
SHAMMASH	Samas	Sol, the Sun
NANNA-SIN	Nanna-Sin	Luna, the Moon
NERGAL	Nergal	Mars, Ares, Zivis
NABU	Nebo	Mercury, Woden
MARDUK	Bel	Jupiter, Thor
INANNA-ISHTAR	Beltis	Venus, Freia
NINURTA-NINIB	Kronos	Saturnus

~ *Robert Graves, "The White Goddess"*

When the *seeker* combines a traditional sevenfold-schema knowledge base with corresponding *Anunnaki* figures represented by planets and days of the week, it is easy to see how a complex system developed. Both physically (the seen, the below, the earth) and metaphysically (the unseen, the above, the cosmos), each of the seven aspects are described as a particular "quality" or "nature" of the *totality* of existence—or else the *All* fragmented into "*sever*-al" parts more easily beheld or classified than the pure mystical unity that has no names or numbers and is known only to the *Highest* cosmic order—and true "initiates" of the *Highest.*

The *All-as-One* may be fragmented by consciousness into any number of "fractions," each making perfect sense, fit within a context of total wholeness of "parts." In Babylonian tradition, this is observed as seven, and we can assign or reduce all aspects from other schemas back to this if we choose—dividing colors, lights, sounds and aspects into a two-fold (duality), three-fold (triads) and elemental four-fold paradigms in most popularly known occult traditions, yet they may also be assigned to the seven-fold division of reality described on Babylonian tablets. We can also see how the Babylonian Star-Gate system expanded or evolved into the traditional ten-fold *kabbalistic* models, demonstrating seven gates of the "younger" Anunnaki pantheon with the "Supernal Trinity" added to the system—and seven plus three equals ten.

An entire lifetime—perhaps several—may be spent decrypting a myriad of appropriated names and lore from various "mythologies" spanning all times and places. However, it becomes clear that the "visible spectrum" of archetypal energies—as we receive and experience them—is best documented and relayed in original source texts of the Ancient Mystery Tradition from Mesopotamia—and in many cases, specifically Babylon. Each key "quality" of existence—or *ray* of the spectrum—is directly associated with key figures of the Anunnaki "*pantheon,*" a systemology or model of understanding all aspects of the cosmos—it is not restricted only to Mesopotamian or Anunnaki applications. As a result, we find so many direct correlations to later emerging "mythologies" that it would detract from the current purposes of this volume to discuss further. It is enough to draw attention to this point. In the oldest tradition of Babylon, with literary origins significantly predating classical mythologies, we are given, for example, the role in a pantheon represented by the planet *Jupiter*—recognized as the position of *Enlil* in older Sumerian lore, but identified with *Marduk* for the actual systematization of Mesopotamian esoterica. This position shares particular "religious" affinity for services held on Thursday, which we name for *Thor*—the Norse "*Jupiter*" &tc.

Retained within the "ancestral spiritual tradition" of Mesopotamia, the "elder pantheon" is observed as a "Supernal Trinity" extending outside the "visible" or traditionally accessible aspects of creation. This means ancient Mesopotamian astronomers may have had some "otherworldly" knowledge of more than the "ancient seven visible planets," but their astronomy logically included only those that were "visible" to the naked eye—those carrying the greatest influence felt here on earth. We find these beyond (or "above") the *seven* and also encompassing them—and we see its influence in the traditional "*kabbalah*" ("*cabala*" or "*qabala*") as well, the system which most "Western magic" is based on, and this is explored more extensively in the "Mardukite Liber-K" *appendix* within this volume, *Enochian Magic & Kabbalah*. Suffice it to say that where the ancestral figures—or Elder Gods of Sumer—such as *Anu*, *Enlil*, and *Enki* appear frequently in older sagas, it is the offspring of these gods—the "younger pantheon" of Babylon—that represents the more visible and accessible forces of the universe. These are the forces that constitute the main substance of spiritual, mystical, magical and religious work. Above, beyond and more widely encompassing the "ten-as-one," we find three additional spheres—called "*ains*" in the Semitic Kabbalah—the ALL, the Abyss and the Dragon.

When we approach the mysteries of ancient Babylonian Tradition and read from tablets like the *Enuma Eliš*, we actually glean greater esoteric understanding of these mysteries than thought academically possible. Although the full *Enuma Eliš* text is given later in this anthology—in the grimoire portion designated *Mardukite Tablets N+F* in the *Liber-Z* portion of *The Complete Book of Marduk by Nabu*—it will benefit the seeker to preview an outline of these tablets for our current discourse.

Enuma Eliš—The Seven Babylonian Tablets of Creation

I.

a.)—ABSU (*the Abyss*) and TIAMAT (*the Cosmic Dragon*) are first forms form the One (*All*).

b.)—Generations of "gods" are born and make too much "noise."

c.)—TIAMAT entrusts her vizier KINGU the power to fight for her.

d.)—TIAMAT creates calamity and a horde of monsters as ammunition.

II.

a.)—ENKI reveals the plot against the gods to ANSAR.

b.)—A primary discourse from the first tablet is repeated.

III.

a.)—ANU, ENLIL and ENKI do not stand fit to battle against TIAMAT.

b.)—MARDUK is petitioned to champion the *Anunnaki* gods.

c.)—MARDUK asks for supreme divinity if successful; to be the *Chief God*.

IV.

a.)—The *Anunnaki* agree to MARDUK's terms and prepare him for battle.

b.)—MARDUK receives a "cloak of invisibility."

c.)—MARDUK enchants his favored weapon: a bow.

d.)—MARDUK destroys KINGU with a thunderbolt.

e.)—TIAMAT is slain; her minions are scattered and sent to "secret places."

f.)—MARDUK fashions a "*Gate*" to seal these energies separate from the material universe.

V.

a.)—MARDUK seals the cosmic systems of "Lights," "Spheres" and "Degrees" under himself.

b.)—The material-matix *below* is fragmented by the "seven," while the *heights* remain divided into "twelve."

c.)—The "*Anunnaki Star-Gate*" system is sealed throughout the Universe.

d.)—MARDUK sets up a throne for himself next to ANU.

VI.

a.)—The *Anunnaki* praise MARDUK for his feats.

b.)—The "Key to the Gate" (of the *Abyss* and the *Dragon*) is "hidden" in genetic memory of the "*Race of Marduk*," including humans upgraded by ENKI.

c.)—Babylonian systematization begins.

VII.

a.)—Having slayed TIAMAT and granted power over material creation, MARDUK takes the names and numbers of ENLIL.

b.)—MARDUK takes the "signs" and esoteric knowledge ("magic") of ENKI.

c.)—MARDUK fractures then seals all systems on Earth under his name.

Magical power, spiritual evolution and mystical arts all represent a deep understanding of the energetic relationship between all forces in the cosmos—and in truth, all aspects in the universe are connected—but it is the key correspondences from "our side" of reality that become a base knowledge contributing to many popular modes of "New Age" thought, tradition and occult practice. It is difficult for many to to understand the simplicity of the original and most ancient traditions because of how much has been obscured, added and encrypted since. Until we can shed this skin—overcoming a lifetime (or more) of personality-programming —we will always be restricted to see the complete spectrum of reality specific only to our set of "lenses."

Traditional Creation—Sevenfold Fragmentation

  I. Sunday: Sun—Light
  II. Monday: Moon—Division (of Waters)
III. Tuesday: Mars—Dryness (land, pasture)
IV. Wednesday: Mercury—Celestial Bodies
          (planets, stars, cosmic order)
  V. Thursday: Jupiter—Primordial Life
          (plants, sea-beasts, birds)
  VI. Friday: Venus—Terrestrial Life
          (land-beasts, primates/humans)
VII. Saturday: Saturn—Repose

~ Robert Graves, "The White Goddess"

  I. —Light
  II. —Particles
III. —Atoms
IV. —Molecular Matter
  V. —Plant Kingdom
  VI. —Animal Kingdom
VII. —Completion

~ Douglas Monroe, "Deepteachings of Merlyn"

The fundamental sevenfold Anunnaki "gate" system of Babylon presented within this "grimoire" clearly has many "*esoteric*" applications—of which its foremost (and original) purpose being: the "sealing" of reality, meaning the perceptions of energetic experience throughout the cosmos, or else (at its most rudimentary level), what humans consider "truth" in regards to "existence." This includes what we know (and don't know) of our origins (in the past) and the purposeful utilization of knowledge (in the present) toward an appropriately destined future. But it is this "future" aspect that always remains in debate. There is no consensus as to the "best use" of active energies in the present. The spiritual evolution of the human species—its spiritual "*hybridization*"—is entirely dependent on an intentional "return" to the *Source of All*. Just because there is no "common vision" among the masses, does not mean that the *seeker* commits error in following this path. Quite the contrary. It has always been the case that a select few—the highest minds and magicians among society—are those responsible and in power to affect and shape the general global consciousness. It is these folks, who have themselves walked the "ladder of lights" or "stairway to the stars" and returned among men.

— 4 —

CLIMBING THE STAIRWAY TO HEAVEN

*"The length of the animistic period of religion in Babylonia
is not known, but there is abundant evidence that by
the fourth millennium B.C., the Sumerians had
formulated a system of gods in which
each held a well-defined place."*

—E.A. Wallis Budge, *"Babylonian Life & History"*

Relaying the inter-dimensional model of *"Stargates"* would be much easier if we could do it in a *linear* fashion—the way we understand and learn most things in a very condensed physical material world. But such is not the case—rendering most 2-Dimensional depictions of any real *kabbalistic* system very "deceptive,"models that tend to emphasize the division of "levels" and *"fragmentation."* But the *"Veils of Existence"* are just that—*veils*. They may enshroud what we experience of existence, but they can not truly divide or separate the *All* from the *All*. They can only further fragment what they are created from with more *veils* and more perceived levels of semantic division—of which esoteric sects and occult orders have found little difficulty in doing throughout time.

Babylon is named for its paradigm—a "stairway to the stars"—an iconic representation of the seven-leveled *high temples* of Marduk and Nabu. These *ziggurat* pyramids demonstrated the "visible" spectrum of energy radiating between the "heavens above" and the "earth below"—meaning all of existence between the unknowable "heights" and "depths" of the cosmos. *Bab-Ili* texts cited throughout modern Mardukite literary work and esoteric (spiritual/mystical) experimentation are collected references from throughout greater cuneiform tablet collections. This original name for its system, nation, city and peoples—*Bab-Ili*—is the word for "gate," "doorway" or "entrance" combined with "god," "star," or "heaven."

Although the ceremonial (ritual) methodology of *"gatewalking," "gate-keeping,"* or *"starwalking"* (&tc.) is traditionally traversed from an earth oriented sequence (e.g. the *first gate*), instruction of a Babylonian "sys-temology" of esoteric magic, spirituality and religion is best aligned to the *Enuma Eliš*—from the beginning...

In the beginning...the *Ancient of Days*—before time and space had been fragmented into existence; before the heaven and earth had come into existence; before reality was separated into existence—there was simply the *All-as-One*—the *Absolute*; all existences as *One Existence*; all being as *One Beingness*...

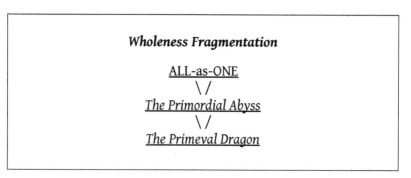

Wholeness Fragmentation

ALL-as-ONE
\ /
The Primordial Abyss
\ /
The Primeval Dragon

The full sequence of fragmentation is explored in the Year-2 materials of the Mardukite Core—contained within the *"Gates of the Necronomicon"* hardcover anthology by Joshua Free or *"The Sumerian Legacy"* volume. We can summarize some key points here as they apply to the theory and practice of magical traditions within the Anunnaki paradigm of Babylon.

Regarding the *"Wholeness Fragmentation"*—or the ALL—we direct the *seeker's* attention to an Arcane Aphorism from *"Secret Doctrines of the Cosmos"* that states: "Other than *The Law*, there is but *Infinity*, which is *Nothingness*. But in that *Infinity of Nothingness*, there is *Unmanifest*, the *Latency*, *Possibility*, *Futurity*, *Potentiality*, and the promise of *Manifest Everythingness*. It is the *Chaos* from which, under *The Law*, emerges the Cosmos. It is the *Womb of the Cosmos*." Therefore the ALL took on a beingness of its own, embedded into ALL entangled existence as a state of *"Infinite Potentiality"*—the *Primordial Abyss*.

When the *waters* were separated to give rise to the *First Form,* the *First* Cause—the *Primeval Dragon* separated as active consciousness and energy in motion. This separation from the Source is *Ego*—the perspective or consciousness of the cosmos—knowledge and motion, represented by a "creature" which rose out of the "depths" of the "infinite sea" to give *form* and *function* to a "manifest universe." It is from the start that many metaphysical schools of thought and occult lodges mistakenly confuse the terms of *Absolute Law* and *Infinite Nothingness*. *"Absolute Law* is not an infinite capacity for expression of power—it is *Power-in-Itself."*

Supernal Fragmentation

ANU—The Heights (Uranus)
\ /
ENLIL—The Airs
\ /
ENKI—The Deep (Neptune)

Celestial fragmentation—manifest reality in consciousness—appears in the Sumerian Anunnaki paradigm as the "Supernal Trinity" represented by the *Heavenly One* [ANU], the *Lord of Air-Space* [ENLIL] and the *Lord of the Deep Earth* [EA–ENKI]. These ancestral figures appear as "Elder Gods" in the Babylonian pantheon—or in more recent themes of the "*Necronomicon*" in the New Age. This progression is not progenerative—both *Enlil* and *Enki* are sons of *Anu*—but it does illustrate the hierarchical division or fragmentation of these *higher powers* concurrent with the highest three power stations or *kabbalah sephiroth.*

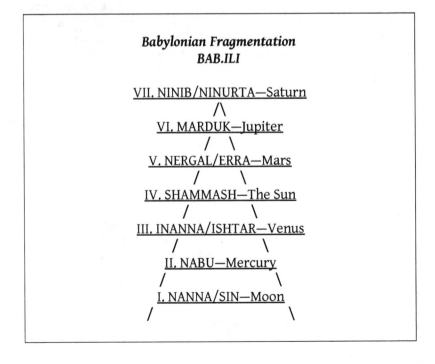

Babylonian Fragmentation
BAB.ILI

VII. NINIB/NINURTA—Saturn
/\
VI. MARDUK—Jupiter
/ \
V. NERGAL/ERRA—Mars
/ \
IV. SHAMMASH—The Sun
/ \
III. INANNA/ISHTAR—Venus
/ \
II. NABU—Mercury
/ \
I. NANNA/SIN—Moon
/ \

The BAB-ILI formation (sequence)—the *sevenfold path*—is based on a tradition specific to Mardukite Babylon, demonstrated in its correlation to the seven-fold stepped path to ascension—a bridge connecting the most concentrated mundane physical world with the heights through a successive series of veils or fragmentation. All of the "practical magic," or ritualized realizations of mystical energy used in Babylon, is reflected in this paradigm. Use of it is most clearly demonstrated in the grimoire portion of the current anthology—specifically the selections composing *"The Complete Book of Marduk by Nabu."*

It is important that magical pursuits are always balanced with the mystic arts—for it is essential that the *seeker* does not fix to strongly to the plethora of "linear" representations of fragmentation that are possible (even within this specific paradigm). The nature of the "fractured" universe outside of the *All-as-One* is actually "recursive" or "cyclical" in a material sense. This idea is always represented by the universal symbol of the *Cosmic Serpent* encircling all of creation while devouring its own tail—the *Great Universal Dragon* unfolds its form to manifest all existence and beingness. And at its most concentrated level or degree—as is expressed in the *Enuma Eliš*—the head or consciousness of the dragon is indicative of "space" and the body as "matter." It seems a mighty trick, but the *infinity* as a material expression is only infinite by "recursion." The manifest universe cannot be truly "infinite" for such is the property only of the "potential," and again—the only "absolute" is the LAW-of-ALL, encompassing and entangling all potential existences at once.

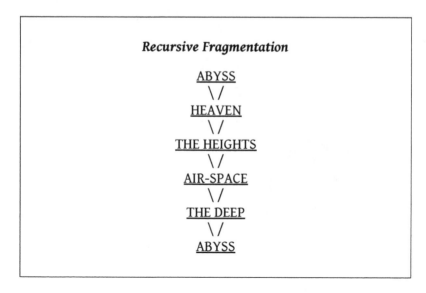

Recursive Fragmentation

ABYSS
\ /
HEAVEN
\ /
THE HEIGHTS
\ /
AIR-SPACE
\ /
THE DEEP
\ /
ABYSS

Material or mathematical infinity is not always as we might imagine it. Although it carries a relative "endless" appearance, it is not necessarily "boundless" so much as it is "recursive"—repetitive and cyclic—which we have also demonstrated philosophically. In fact, it is a very symbolic but genuine representation of infinity that we use to designate an order or cohesion to the *seven* as All-as-One when we draw the figure "8" as itself or on its side to indicate literally "infinity." And by no esoteric co-incidence, the "8" on a keyboard also coincides with the "*" asterisk, a symbol derived in form and name from the "istari," a cuneiform sign for "AN" meaning: "star" or "heavens"—but most literally the word: "god."

Magic is not a "supernatural" art—on the contrary, it is quite "natural" although not "common" among the masses. Just as differing degrees of physical or emotional prowess are found in some, or intentionally practiced and exercised by others, we find intellectual and spiritual gifts in a select few drawn toward deeper *esoteric* understanding of themselves, the universe, and the connection between. This is a very real energetic connection present throughout all existence and between all peoples—some are naturally more active sensitivity or awareness of the constant interaction and energetic exchange taking place throughout the cosmos.

There is nothing "unnatural" about magic, except ironically the refusal to pursue this living awareness by a majority of the population. This distinction directly contributes to the obscure or secretive aura radiated by individuals and groups that *do* pursue these matters—because it is out of reach and beyond the scope attained by a normative "mundane" existence. The truth is that a person may very well get by an entire lifetime without taking notice of the bigger picture, and such a person will never understand why someone else would even bother with such "ridiculous trifles" or "dangerous devil-worship"—as they comprehend it.

Modern *seekers* will be quick to find numerous other applications for the BAB-ILI system—and will undoubtedly spend a great deal of time drawing parallels between this most ancient systemology and all of the traditions drawn from the same lore. However, above all else, the true and original purpose of the BAB-ILI system is to develop a *Self-Honest* relationship with the *Anunnaki*, and in the process, a true and faithful *Self-Honest* awareness of-and-as *Self*. The *Self* is the real "I-AM" that is doing the "observing." All of the *filters* we assume in our lives, in our philosophy and our beliefs and assumptions about the world around us, are directly responsible for the interpretation of existence and reality for what is ultimately deemed true as "personal experience."

The *Babylonian Anunnaki Tradition* is the specific paradigm that takes precedence in ancient *Mardukite Babylon* and all magical lore connected to the BAB-ILI "gate system" of religious-styled spiritual work. The "gate-work" or "spiritual pathwork" is alluded to on clay cuneiform tablets as "prayers" and "hymns" to petition representative powers of the pantheon of *Seven* by name, and their consorts—"Divine Couples" listed as *Guardians of the Gates*.

As a true magician, priest or priestess approaches each of the *Gates* in true *Self-Honest* "devotion" and "dedication," this exploratory journey allows opportunities to develop a true understanding and practical access to the most raw, primordial and powerful currents of energy in the cosmos. This is reinforced by an *esoteric* use of what others will fail to see beyond an empty "religious lip-service" reflected in a daily regimen of meditation, prayer and ritual, coupled with a pious lifestyle and dedication to an energetic spiritual ascension of the *Self*. This is far from the methodology realized today among more common forms of organized "religion" and empty deity "worship"—particularly those paths that tend to promote a restrictive dependence on the organization or institution for all "enlightenment" as opposed to the *Self*.

The very important Mardukite-specific semantic concept of "*Self-Honesty*" has been explored at great length throughout the *Mardukite Core* of literary materials—and its intellectual off-shoot branch, Systemology —but to clarify for present purposes: *Self-Honesty* is *not* simply "being honest with yourself" as is generally assumed on the surface. It actually goes much deeper than this: *Self-Honesty* is the directed will of *Self* in a state of *honesty in Truth*—without a manifold array of the "many parts" and "fragmentation" serving as filters and programmed beliefs, many of which are unfounded, illogical or unnecessary and which contribute to what we have the ability to know and experience—or not. The "*ladder of lights*" or "*stairway to heaven*" proposed in this paradigm is nothing short than the original methodology of systematic removal of these other filters that keep the *human experience* or *human condition* from a *Self-Honest* experience and awareness of the Absolute—the *Cosmic Law* that is within and as all existence and which is the main subject of the wizard or magician's art. When we can see—historically and anthropologically —that the systematization of the "civil human" is structured within the ancient Mesopotamian paradigm, it should come by no surprise that the same "higher minds" responsible for this fragmentation would also have kept detailed records, even if only for their own private collections, of the "way back," the "key" to the "door" that leads *outside* of the system.

Some esoteric practitioners believe that the "*ladder-stairway*" is means for taking on *more* attributes, levels or layers of existence—as such, it is actually quite opposite. We already occupy an entangled spiritual existence in *sevenfold* fragmentation—something that Eastern traditions have called *chakras*, inter-dimensional energetic centers of the "body" connected to the universal *seven rays*. All "pathwork" conducted within this tradition is concerned with the energetic "refinement" of these filters, not accumulating or assimilating something *more*.

In every way, in all forms material, and in every aspect of energy that is defined by the *human condition*, the reoccurring theme within this work (and all true *mystical* work) is *Light*—and yet, this is not necessarily the same concept that is otherwise relayed in fanciful New Age lore or other "dualistic" moral doctrines. The *Light* is that which emerged fro the void of the Abyss, the infinite nothingness. *Light* is the infinite made manifest and visible. Where the All-as-One and singular expression of *Light* is an Absolute, we experience and encounter a fragmented spectrum—a unity divided to display rainbow arrays. True magic pertains to these same rays, but only as a means to access the singular and highest expression. The *Clear Light* and the *Seven Rays* are a part of us and everything that is around us, the very reason our "experiences"—whether "mystical" or "mundane"—*are* experienced as they are.

The grimoire portions that follow are self-explanatory. That being said, there are those who will at first be most interested in ritual particulars, to which we provide the following list of suggested materials:

Tools of Mardukite Magick

- *Sigil-seals* of the Four Watchtowers.
- *Candles* or *lamps* for the Four Quarters (Watchtowers).
- *Sigil-seals* of the *Anunnaki*: (Supernal Trinity and the Seven).
- *Gate-sigil* glyphs appropriate to a particular "level" or "step"
- *Cauldron* or *fire brazier* (consecrated).
- *Candles* or *lamps* to represent the "God and Goddess" (usually Marduk & Sarpanit in Mardukite-specific or Marduk & Ishtar in other versions) and likewise:
- *An image of your god and goddess* (statuary or visual art).
- *Seven Divine Decrees*, implements of the Divine Arts of Eridu in accordance with the ancient Sumerian Anunnaki Tradition.

- *Incense* or *herbal offerings* to be burned—usually frankincense, myrrh, sandalwood, pine resin, palm resin, &tc.
- *Waters* and *salt* for ceremonial consecration.
- *Flour of Nisaba* or *Nabu* and Teshmet, to mark the boundary of the circle (consecrated).

Of the items previously listed, the one aspect appropriately deserving of additional comment—the *Seven Divine Decrees*. These are equivalent to legendary "articles" taken from Enki's possession at his city of Eridu by Inanna-Ishtar, which she brought back to her city, Uruk, subsequently moving the capital of early Sumerian development there. In other mystic sagas found on cuneiform tablets, these articles are described in Inanna-Ishtar's own cycle of *"Descent to the Underworld"*—but the purposes of a Babylonian magician or priestess, however, should be concerned with the *"Rising on the Planes"* in the opposite direction, using a *Ladder of Lights* described by the BAB-ILI system of Babylon to achieve true spiritual evolution to walk among the spheres as *gods*. Assuming the ascension of "godhood" is always the *intention* of the high magical arts, but seldom is achieved through conventional "Western magick." In conclusion, the "legendary articles" are described as follows:

The Seven Divine Decrees

- *Shugurra — "Starry Crown of Anu"* ("diadem")
- *Wand — of "crystal" (lapis lazuli)*
- *Blue Necklace — of "crystal" (lapis lazuli)*
- *Bag of Gemstones — presumably lapis lazuli*
- *Ring of Power — usually "golden"*
- *Frontlet Amulet — breastplate "talisman"*
- *Pala —* "royal" or "priestly" robes (garments)

—PART ONE—

THE COMPLETE BOOK OF MARDUK BY NABU

(LIBER W+Z/G)

*Being a series of prayers
taught to the priests of Babylon
and the Order of Nabu
as a devotional method for them
to honor the Anunnaki.*

INTRODUCTION & APPLICATION
NABU-TUTU SERIES – TABLET IV

We have sealed seven representative stations or gates in BABYLON. While it is true that each of the cities did emphasize their local patrons, a god and a goddess, We have sought a unity for all the gods, under the watchful eye of my father, MARDUK, son of ENKI.

Our father, ENKI, took MARDUK as an apprentice to the magical and religious arts while in E.RIDU and I later took hold of such mysteries and dispersed the knowledge to my scribes and priests in BABYLON and Egypt, where my family was recognized by other names.

The "Seven" are each embodiments of one of the seven gates forged in BABYLON, homes to the gods of the "younger pantheon." It is true, the same seven-fold division may be found to fragment the *world of form*—corresponding to color, sound, or the planets observed by the ancient ancestors from Earth, seen as *"Guardians."*

The seven planetary systems, which have been connected to the "Seven" of the Gates, also correlate to an easily observable weekly cycle of time. The planet-ruling days will offer the supplicant [priest] an intention ceremonial or meditative opportunity to appeal to each of the "sets" of ANUNNAKI "divine couples" honored in the "younger pantheon" of Babylon.

> Sunday – Sun – SHAMMASH [UTU] (& AYA)
> Monday – Moon – NANNA [SIN] (& NINGAL)
> Tuesday – Mars – NERGAl (& ERESHKIGAL)
> Wednesday – Mercury – NABU (& TESHMET)
> Thursday – Jupiter – MARDUK (& SARPANIT)
> Friday – Venus – ISHTAR [INANNA] (& DUMUZI)
> Saturday – Saturn – NINIB [NINURTA] (& BA'U)

Within the combined domains of the "Seven" are all of the material and spiritual aspects a priest or magician seeks in life (e.g. ISHTAR for *love* or SAMAS for *truth*) and one merely must appeal with self-honesty and true words to attain them. This is as the original arts were set down in days of old, left for men to remember us—and we will remember you.

The names and Gates are not merely there for the bedazzlement of the "occult initiate" as you have been taught (there to ascend to and forget about): they are very real "magical skills" and "spiritual lessons" based on the division and the fragmentation of the material universe—a mastery only attainable by a true and faithful relationship with the ANUNNAKI gods of your ancestors.

Man's use of the spiritual power of the gods became subverted, altered and bastardized into the mystical systems now given for your disposal, written by men with no better understanding of the traditions they seek to invoke then those who read them. (And some of these traditions have even falsely said to be derived from my hand.) The true priest or magician compels the gods by friendship and trust, not fear and hatred.

By MARDUK, I learned the power of incantation. I was taught to appease the gods in his name, to speak the words of the higher. MARDUK invoked the name of ENKI, our father, who, invoked the name of ANU. And so was born the magical "hierarchies" that magicians have confused. I taught the magician-scribes of my order to invoke my name and seal during their petitions to the gods, which I have given here, as I learned it from MARDUK. . .

THE GRAND INVOCATION
INCANTATION OF ERIDU

ANU above me, King in Heaven.
ENLIL, Commander of the Airs.
ENKI, Lord of the Deep Earth.
I am NABU – hear my words.
I am the priest of MARDUK and SARPANIT.
Son of our father, ENKI and DAMKINA.
I am the priest in E.RIDU.
I am the magician in BABYLON.
My spell is the spell of ENKI.
My incantation is the incantation of MARDUK.
The Tablets of Destiny, I hold in my hands.
The Ankh of ANU and ANTU, I hold in my hands.
The wisdom of ENLIL and NINLIL, I call to me.
The Magic Circle of ENKI and DAMKINA,
*   I conjure about me.*
SHAMMASH and AYA are before me.
NANNA-SIN and NINGAL are behind me.
NERGAL and ERESHKIGAL are at my right side.
NINIB-NINURTA and BA'U are at my left side.
The blessed light of ISHTAR and DUMUZI
*   shines favorably upon my sacred work.*
It is not I, but MARDUK,
*   who performs the incantations.*

As should become increasingly apparent to contemporary folk of the current age, the ANUNNAKI are powerful and influential, though often directly unseen, forces behind the reality of the life you exist in—as your ancestors were well aware of. If you work with us in conjunction with the natural flow of the universal energies, then you will come face to face with your true destiny—and invited home, again.

Discern your true-knowledge, learn the challenge of self-mastery, and then dear *seeker*, resolve to walk with the gods among the stars, circumnavigating the illusions of this world which have been raised before you as a test of your existence.

When you have proven yourself before us,
we shall celebrate your arrival . . .

[*Here ends the Nabu-Tutu Tablet IV*]

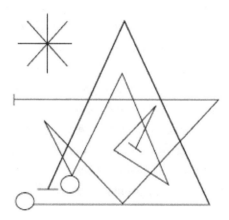

THE BOOK OF

MARDUK

(LIBER-W)

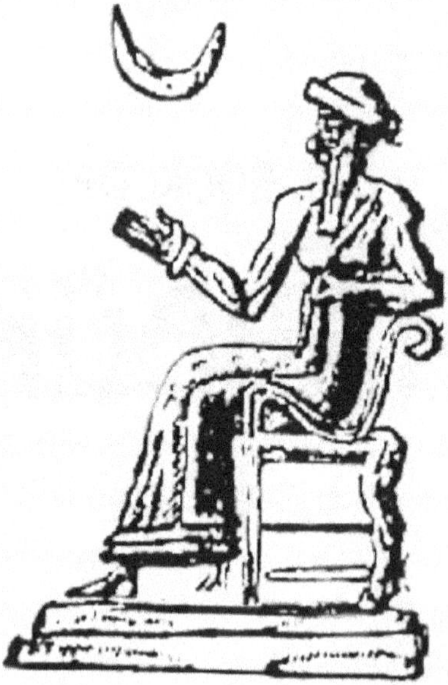

MONDAY

NANNA-SIN

THE MOON

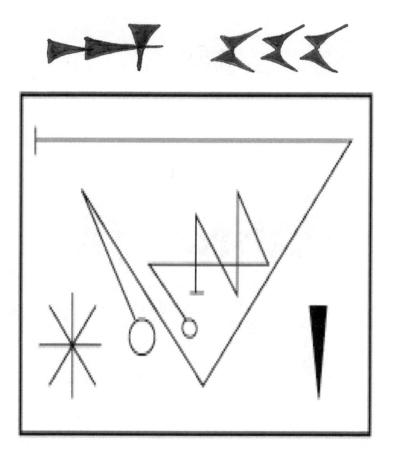

MONDAY — THE MOON — NANNA-SIN

To the ancients, the moon was the "sun at night." It illuminated the path for travelers and kept watch as the people slept. Just as the sun was invoked to grant judgments of the daytime, the moon is given the domain over the dreams of men. Being the first spiritual threshold (Gate) between earth and heaven, the moon is significantly linked to the astral plane. The priestesses (and later witches) of INANNA-ISHTAR revered the moon, called NANNA by Sumerians or Sin to the Babylonians, as their sky-father and/or spiritual-mate. ISHTAR literally was the "daughter of the moon" (and a twin to the sun/SAMAS) and her followers often also took this title.

Our pantheon places NANNA in the position of lunar god with the designation of 30, the basic lunar month of the Sumerian calendar (30 x 12 = 360). The name NANNA (or NANNAR) is actually an attribute of the full moon. He is called Sin (or SU.EN) when representing the crescent and the name for the new moon is: *AS.IM.BABBAR*. The lunar current is heavily water oriented with blue hues, though best represented ritually in the non-color spectrum (silver, black, white).

PRAYER TO NANNA & NINGAL

ilu-NANNA. ilu-SIN. ilu-istari-NINGAL.
ilu-NANNAR. ilu-NAMRASIT.
su-bu-u man-za-za ina ilani rabuti
  maru aplu ilu-ENLIL u ilu-NINLIL
nam-rat urru-ka ina sami-i ina sat musi
du natalu, nasaru anabu harranu-dim
u nisu ina bitu sat musi suttu
itti namrasit ina sami-i
kima diparu, kima ilu-SAMAS
samsatu ilu-NANNA namaru suttu
  agu
abu ilu-SAMAS
rimi-nin-ni-ma anaku ____ , apil ____ , sa
  ilu-sa ___ u ilu-istari-su ____ .
ilu-NANNA u ilu-NINGAL rimi-nin-
  ni-ma
kaparu anaku sillatu
  lu-us-tam-mar ilu-ut-ka
petu babu temu
li-iz-ziz ina imni-ya u sumuli-ya
  anaku arad-ka elu
an-un-na-ki ti-i-ru u
  na-an-za-zu

PRAYER TO NANNA & NINGAL

NANNA. SIN. NINGAL.
NANNAR. MOON.
Mighty One among the gods, son of ENLIL
    and NINLIL,
Brightest in the heavens at night,
Keeping watch, protecting weary travelers
And the people in their homes as they sleep.
Your brightness extends through the heavens,
Like a torch – Like a fire-god.
Radiance of NANNA, who reflects the
    dreams of men,
To you was born the SUN.
Be favorable to me, I, __ son of __ , whose
    god is __ and whose goddess is __ .
May NANNA and NINGAL deal graciously
    with me,
Cleanse me of iniquity that I may be free to
    call upon thee.
Open the Gates of your mysteries to me,
Stand on either side of me,
    a servant of the Highest.
May the ANUNNAKI come forth an be
    established.

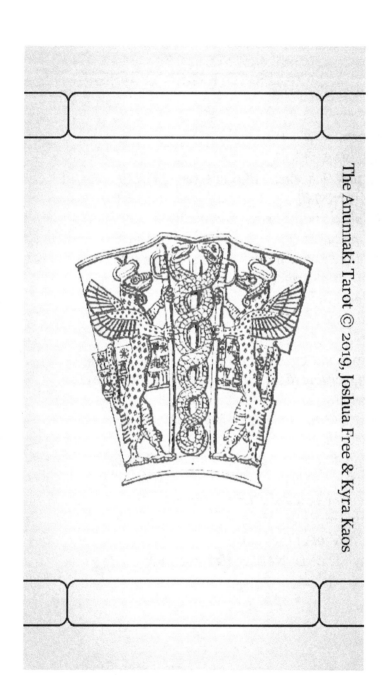

TUESDAY

NERGAL

MARS

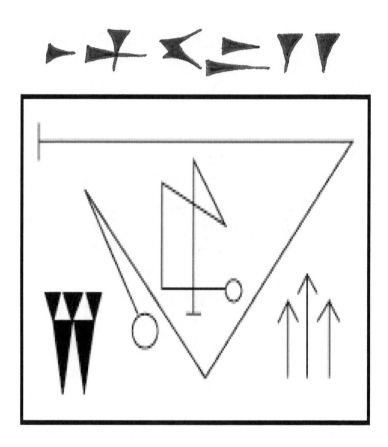

TUESDAY — MARS — NERGAL

The martian current has always been one of the most difficult to properly relay on a spiritual basis. To emphasize the primal fiery destruction would be all too simple. The current is best correlated to the Sumerian concept of *"Girra"* or *"fires of God."* The "hand" of God requires a representative vehicle in which to exercise even its own power in physical ways.

Underlying the power of Mars, and the demonstrator of this force in Babylon (NERGAL), is really "passion." The outer demonstrations of this pure attribute are what can later be deemed by men as lust, love, anger, jealousy and the like. But these are outer forms only – it is the passion, pure and true, that must be embraced. NERGAL is invoked, then, to temper the visions of anger or discord in our lives so we might embrace the passion beneath with clarity, which is anything but evil or destructive. The number of NERGAL is 8, showing that he is outside of the "heavenly" ranks (ending in 5 or 0). His abode is with ERESHKIGAL, who is Queen in the "Underworld." Combined, the pair represent the most "gothic," misunderstood and yet truly romantic elements and attributes of divinity and creation: passion and death.

PRAYER TO NERGAL & ERESHKIGAL

ilu-NERGAL. ilu-IRRIGAL. Ilu-istari-
   ERESHKIGAL. ilu-ERRA.
siru belu ersetu
ilu-istari-ERESHKIGAL, beltu ersetu
saqu-su manzazu
   it-ti ilani samu
ilu-NERGAL u ilu-istari-ERESHKIGAL
rimi-nin-ni-ma, ana-ku ___ , apil ____ ,
   sa ilu-su ___ ilu-istar-su ___ .
banu-ya libbu alalu
di-ni uzzu ina ramanu libbu
ana-ku izuzzu mahru ze
petu babu temu
rimi-nin-ni-ma ina damu
   u du lemnutu seg ina ramanu zi
ana-ku arad-ka elu kamazu ze
   rimi-nin-ni-ma
babu-mah du pataru
an-un-na-ki ti-i-ru u
   na-an-za-zu

PRAYER TO NERGAL & ERESHKIGAL

NERGAL. IRRIGAL. ERESHKIGAL.
ERRA. MARS.
Exalted Lord of the Underworld.
ERESHKIGAL, Queen of the Underworld.
Great is your place
  among the gods of heaven.
NERGAL and ERESHKIGAL,
Truly have mercy on me, __ , son of ___ ,
  whose god is ___ , whose goddess is ___ .
May your hearts be tempered.
Temper also the anger within my heart,
That I may stand before you,
Make me perfect to call upon you,
Open the Gates of your understanding to me.
Grant me a favorable death
  and keep evil from me in life.
I, a servant of the Highest, kneel before thee,
  take pity on me.
May the Great Doors stand open.
May the ANUNNAKI return and
  be established.

WEDNESDAY

NABU

MERCURY

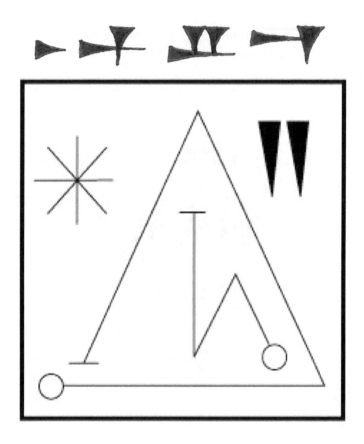

WEDNESDAY — MERCURY — NABU

The *Mercurial* current is connected to divination: relaying information through the universe, or else, communication. Whether it is prayers, a song, the recording of history or the prediction of the future, the performance is undertaken by the blessing of the "scribe-messenger" of the gods. "*Thoth*" or "*Hermes*" is sometimes identified for this current, demonstrating the connection to magic systems, occultism and the air element. Babylonian tradition observes me, NABU, as son of MARDUK, as the scribe-priest of the gods, the keeper of the "destinies" among the younger pantheon with the designation of 12 (connecting heavenly-time and earth-time).

My scribe-priests worked diligently during the Babylonian era forging tablet texts based on the Sumerian tradition, supporting our local patron, MARDUK, as *King of the Gods*, usurping the position of ENLIL and usurping the rights of the position by NINURTA for both spiritual and physical politics. This travesty in Babylon that we conducted, but which is being currently resolved, shows the power of knowledge, true or false, and how it can be used to shape people and the world. Invoke my name for clarity and discernment in the seeking of truth. My color is blue.

PRAYER TO NABU & TESHMET

ilu-NABU. ilu-TUTU. ilu-istari-TESHMET
 ilu-istari-TASMIT. ilu-NEBOS.
tupsarru si-mat ilani
sarru nam-zu si-mat ilani
asaridu bukur ilu-MARDUK u ilu-
 SARPANIT
ilu-NABU na-as duppu si-mat
 ilani
ramanu ur-hi suttu
 lid-mi-ik
ilu-NABU u ilu-TASMITU
 ka-ba-a si-ma-a suk-na ya-si-sa
rimi-nin-ni-ma, ana-ku ___ , apil ___ sa
 ilu-sa ___ u ilu-istari-su ___ .
ebbu ramanu nam-eme-sig u ummuqu
 si-mi-i su-pi-ya
petu babu temu
amat a-kab-bu-u kima a-kab-bu-u
 lu-u ma-ag-rat
sumu-ka ka-lis ina pi nisi ta-a-ab
anaku arad-ka elu
an-un-na-ki ti-i-ru u
 na-an-za-zu

PRAYER TO NABU & TESHMET

NABU. TUTU. TESHMET – TASMIT(U).
NEBOS. MERCURIOS.
Scribe among the Gods,
Keeper of the Wisdom of the Gods,
Firstborn of MARDUK and SARPANIT.
NABU, Bearer of the Tablet of Destinies
  of the gods,
May my dreams [destiny] be filled with
  prosperity.
May my petitions fall on the ears of
  NABU & TASMIT.
Be favorable to me, I, __ son of __ , whose
  god is __ and whose goddess is __ .
Cleanse me of false knowledge, that I might
  be fit to call upon thee.
Open the Gates of your understanding to me.
Bless my mouth with true words to speak
  the prayers.
May the prayers rise from the lips of the
  people.
I am a servant of the Highest,
May the ANUNNAKI come forth and be
  established.

THURSDAY

MARDUK

JUPITER

THURSDAY — JUPITER — MARDUK

The industrious and raw expansive power of Jupiter is placed at the height of most 'Olympian' pantheons (*Zeus* or similar). "Jupiter" comes from the Romans: *Dys Pater*, meaning "Father-God." This current commands outright worldly success and the magic of spirits: command of the hierarchies. Elder Gods originally attributed this position to ENLIL in Sumer. I personally heralded my father, MARDUK, into Enlilship of the "younger pantheon" in Babylon. Our tradition there, and in Egypt, was wholly based on him being the centralized figure. Invoke my father for his strength and power, as well as a petitioner to the Elder Gods.

He is exalted as the Master of Magicians, carrying the mysteries of my grandfather, ENKI, to Babylon, and bestowing the traditions upon me to relay. The original designation of Jupiter is 50, the number attributed first to ENLIL and later to MARDUK by the Babylonians, who first was given the number 10. The color of the current is purple, but also airy and fiery colors (yellow, orange, black). This energy is preferred by many leaders and law enforcing folk, lending to those who are pure to receive it, the power to command the material world.

PRAYER TO MARDUK & SARPANIT

ilu-MAR.DUG. ilu-MAR.DUK. ilu-istari-
   ZARPANIT. ilu-silik-MULU.KHI DIL.GAN.
lugal arali, belu asipu
ilu-su BAB.ILI
ilu-SARPANIT(UM), belitu istari-su BAB.ILI
gasru u sapsu ina an-ki
   zi atwu
belu u belitu su BAB.ILI
maharu ramanu arua abnu-gesnu, abnu-
   uqnu u hurasu
dinu-ma ramanu lid-mi-ik
anaku ___ apil ___ sa ilu-su ___ u
   ilu-istar-su ___ .
lu-us-tam-mar ilu-ut-ka
   u atwu ramanu maharu karabu
petu babu temu – petu babu idu
ina ki-bi-ti-ka sir-ti lu-ub-lut lu-us-lim-ma
napsiti narbu ramanu ki-bi su
   su-sud ilani samu
anaku arad-ka elu
an-un-na-ki ti-i-ru u
   na-an-za-zu

PRAYER TO MARDUK & SARPANIT

MARDUK. MERODACH. SARPANIT.
MULU-KHI. JUPITER.
Lord of the Lands, Master of Magicians,
God of Babylon.
SARPANIT, Lady of Babylon.
Mighty and powerful on earth and heaven
  are your words.
Lord and Lady of Babylon,
Accept my offerings of alabaster, lapis lazuli
  and gold.
Judge my life favorably,
I ___ , son of ____ , whose god is ____ , and
  whose goddess is ____ .
Make me fit to behold your divinity
  and teach me to receive thy blessings.
Open the Gates of your power to me.
Let me live. Let me be perfect.
Command greatness in my life as your
  expansion permeates the gods of heaven.
I am a servant of the Highest.
May the ANUNNAKI come forth and
  be established.

FRIDAY

ISHTAR

VENUS

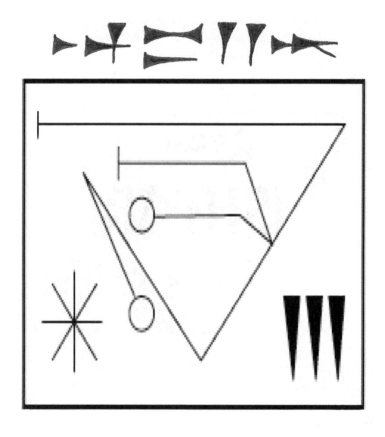

FRIDAY — VENUS — ISHTAR

Most famous among energetic currents of these mysteries is Venusian. It is always dedicated to the "goddess of
love and war." A determined goddess, she made her
place among all ancient pantheons: whether *Isis, Aphrod-
ite, Ashtoreth...* she is also known as the "goddess of
witches," and celebrated in their rites. In Babylon, by re-
quest of MARDUK, her political anger was appeased by
being established as ISHTAR (Venus).

When ISHTAR and MARDUK were not pair-bonded (as intended), each took it upon themselves to elevate and
usurp their own positions among our "younger pantheon."

The Venusian current (and that of Jupiter) are extremely
powerful and actively raw energies. They are not always
as obvious with their executions, such as you might find
with the Sun or Mars, but they store mass amounts of energy for eventual release at the most "propitious" or favorable times. ISHTAR may be invoked to channel energies directed toward the acquisition of desires. (A wise
one will be certain this is for their higher good first.) Her
number is 15. Colors are green, yellow-green and white,
and her elements are water and earth.

PRAYER TO ISHTAR & DUMUZI

ilu-INANNA. ilu-istari-ISHTAR. ilu-
DUMUZI. ilu-ISTAR.
belitu, martu-su ilu-NANNA-SIN
  sa karabu ina samu
ramu-su ilu-ANU, rabianu samu
namru-sat musi
lu-dub-gar-ra sat musi
li-iz-ziz ilu-istari-ya ina sumili-ya
  sutlumu karabu nissanu sabu u ilani
ilu-istari-ISHTAR u ilu-DUMUZI
rimi-nin-ni-ma, ana-ku ___ apil ___ sa
  ilu-sa ___ u ilu-istar-su ___
mesu-ya nigussu, anaku aga
  simtu maharu zi qistu
petu babu temu
li-iz-ziz ramanu manahtu-su zid
a-mat a-kab-bu-u kima a-kab-bu-u lu-u
  ma-ag-rat
is-ti-' nam-ri-ir-ri-ki lim-mi-ru samu
  kima nasaru sabu-su karabu
si-lim itti ya-a-tu-u anaku arad-ka elu
an-un-na-ki ti-i-ru u
  na-an-za-zu

PRAYER TO ISHTAR & DUMUZI

INANNA. ISHTAR. DUMUZI.
ISTARI VENUS.
Queen, Daughter of the Moon,
  who is blessed by the heavens,
Beloved of ANU, Command in Heaven,
Brightness of the Evening,
Huntress of the Night,
Do come to stand favorably at my side,
  grant me the fruits of men and gods.
ISHTAR and DUMUZI,
Be favorable to me, I, ___ son of ___ , whose
  god is ___ and whose goddess is ___ ,
Cleanse me of impurity make me a vessel
  fit to receive your rewards.
Open the Gates of your understanding to me.
May my actions be true.
May the words I speak bring me to success.
May your light shinning in the heavens
  be a guide to all men you bless favorably.
Bless me, a servant of the Highest.
May the ANUNNAKI come forth and
  be established.

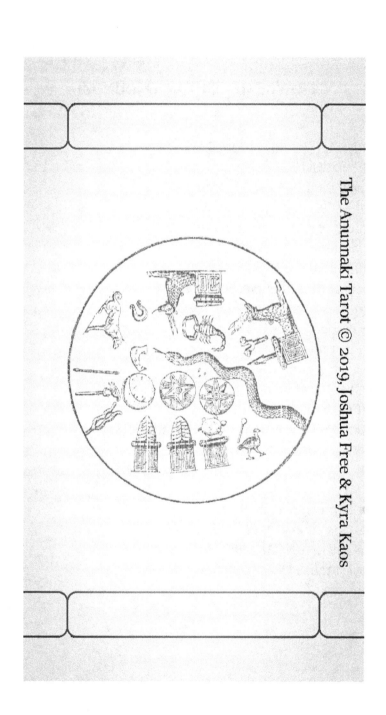

SATURDAY

NINURTA

SATURN

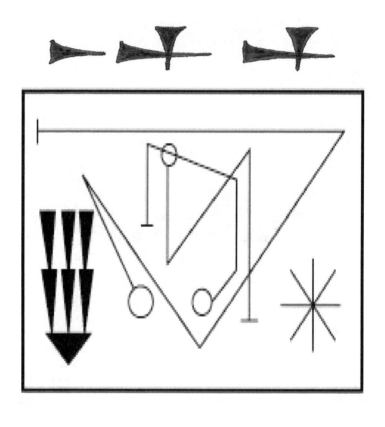

SATURDAY — SATURN — NINURTA

Among planets, Saturn is traditionally dark and secretive, representing hidden power and the *"hidden key"* by which one may be released from the material world of Gates and illusions.

The Saturnalian current is a threshold to the Outer Ones that the secret societies and mystery schools have covertly sought through the ages. NINURTA represents Saturn in Mesopotamia. He also reflects the dark secret of Babylon: He is the heir to Enlilship, a position MARDUK usurped.

In the Babylonian system, NINURTA is given a designation of 4. This indicates he is outside of the 'Olympian pantheon' of 'sky gods,' waiting to take his place, being heir of ENLIL with the number 50. Saturn energy is just as passively introspective as it is actively reflecting the outer world. These lessons demand confronting dark, repressed, guilt-laden aspects of themselves to ascend to self-honest wholeness. The elements of *air* and *earth* are both present in this current and the darker color spectrum is most resonant. Invoke NINURTA to aid in one's own path toward mastery in addition to giving recognition to correct the aspects that have kept the very system from achieving its own wholeness.

PRAYER TO NINURTA & BA'U

ilu-NINURTA. ilu-NINIB. ilu-istari-BA'U.
  ilu-ADAR.
siptu aplu gas-ru bukur ilu-ENLIL
su-bu-u man-za-za ina ilani rabuti
  siru rubu-su ilu-ENLIL u ilu-NINMAH
belu u beltu sihip same u erseti
ilu-NINIB u ilu-istari-BA'U
atwu karabu-ya kisalmahu
ana-ku ___ apil ___ sa ilu-su ___ u
  ilu-istar-su ___
an-ni pu-tur
sir-ti pu-sur
lu-us-tam-mar ilu-ut-ka
  u atwu ramanu lid-mi-ik
petu babu temu,
  anaku arad-ka elu
ilu-istar-BA'U, biltu sur-bu-tu, sela ummu
ilu-NINIB, nisirtu qarradu ilu-ENLIL
ki-bit narbu ramanu zi
si-lim itti ya-a-tu-u
sumu-ka ka-lis ina pi nisi ta-a-ab
an-un-na-ki ti-i-ru u
  na-an-za-zu

PRAYER TO NINURTA & BA'U

NINURTA. NINIB. BA'U.
ADAR. SATURN.
Mighty firstborn son of ENLIL.
Great is your place among the gods,
  royal prince of ENLIL and NINMAH.
Lord and Lady of the heavenly abode,
NINIB and BA'U,
Speak favorably of me in your courts,
I, ___ , son of ___ , whose god is ____ , and
  whose goddess is ____ .
Absolve me of my sins.
Remove my iniquities.
Make me fit to call upon and receive your
  blessings.
Open the Gates of you Understanding to me,
  a servant of the Highest,
BA'U, Mighty Lady, merciful mother.
NINIB, hidden warrior of ENLIL.
Command greatness in my life.
Look upon me favorably.
May your name be in the mouth of the people.
May the ANUNNAKI return and
  be established.

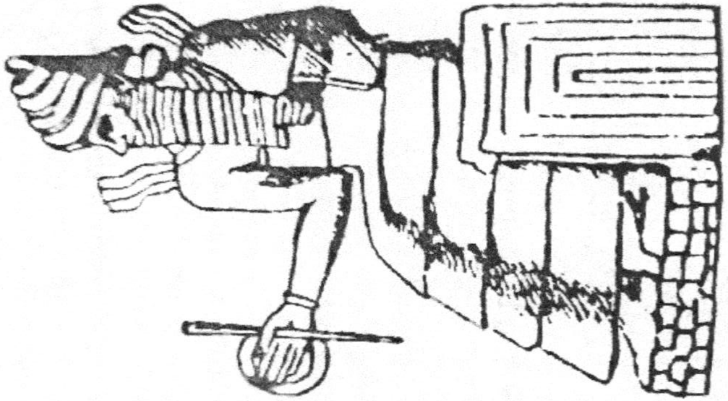

SUNDAY

SHAMMASH

THE SUN

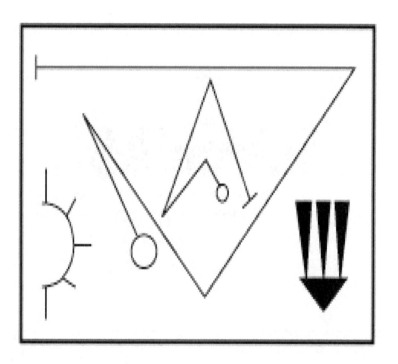

SUNDAY — THE SUN — SHAMMASH

The sun represents the brilliance and radiance of life on earth. It is the light that allows organic life to grow and it is also the manner in which time is divided, including a lifespan. The sun also symbolizes expansive powerful energy and is often invoked for general success and well-being in this existence (and the next). The fiery nature of the star is called to "incinerate iniquities" and also to reveal darkness or lies: the revelation of truth. Mistaken as monotheistic solar worship, the veneration of the sun is the celebration of life, and so annual festivals were marked by the path of the sun (at solstices and equinoxes). As a representative of "Heaven," the sun signifies the physical presence and watchful eye of "God" and is invoked to bring righteous judgment to critical situations.

In the Babylonian pantheon, the solar designation of 20 is given to SAMAS (*Shammash*) also known by the Sumerians as UTU. The colors of this energy current are bright (yellow, white, gold) and the dominant element is clearly fire or *starfire*. The prayer that follows, invokes SAMAS to come forth and be established as the supreme judge of the destinies of men on earth.

PRAYER TO SHAMMASH & AYA

ilu-SHAMMASH. ilu-UTU. ilu-istari-AYA.
ilu-SAMAS. samsu.
anqullu u igigallu
dinu ilani
maru aplu ilu-NANNA-SIN
sapiru nam-simtu apitu
ilu-SAMAS u ilu-AYA
karabu danu simtu
metequ damaqu
la-kasadu immu kararu
ilu-SAMAS u ilu-AYA
si-lim itti ya-a-tu-u ___ , apil ___ ,
* sa ilu-sa ___ , ilu-istar-su ___ .*
napahu ramanu sir-tu
lu-ub-lut lu-us-lim-ma maharu nuru
enu atwu uznu ilu-ENLIL
petu babu temu
sumu-ka ka-lis ina pi nisi ta-a-ab
qibitu nig-silim ina ramanu
* napistu*
ana-ku arad-ka elu
an-un-na-ki ti-i-ru u
* na-an-za-zu.*

PRAYER TO SHAMMASH & AYA

SHAMMASH. UTU. AYA.
SAMAS. SUN.
Fiery and Powerful One,
Judge among the gods,
Son of the Moon-god,
Overseer of the destinies of the lands.
SHAMMASH and AYA,
Be the favorable judges of my destiny.
May the path be prosperous.
Unequaled light of day,
SHAMMASH and AYA
Shine favorably on me, __ , son of __ ,
  whose god is __ and whose goddess is __ .
Incinerate my iniquities.
Make me perfect to behold your light.
Lord, who appeals to the ears of ENLIL,
Open the Gates of your understanding to me.
Permanent is your mighty word on earth.
May your unquestioned command dictate
  prosperity in my life.
I am a servant of the Highest,
May the ANUNNAKI return and
  be established.

ENKI

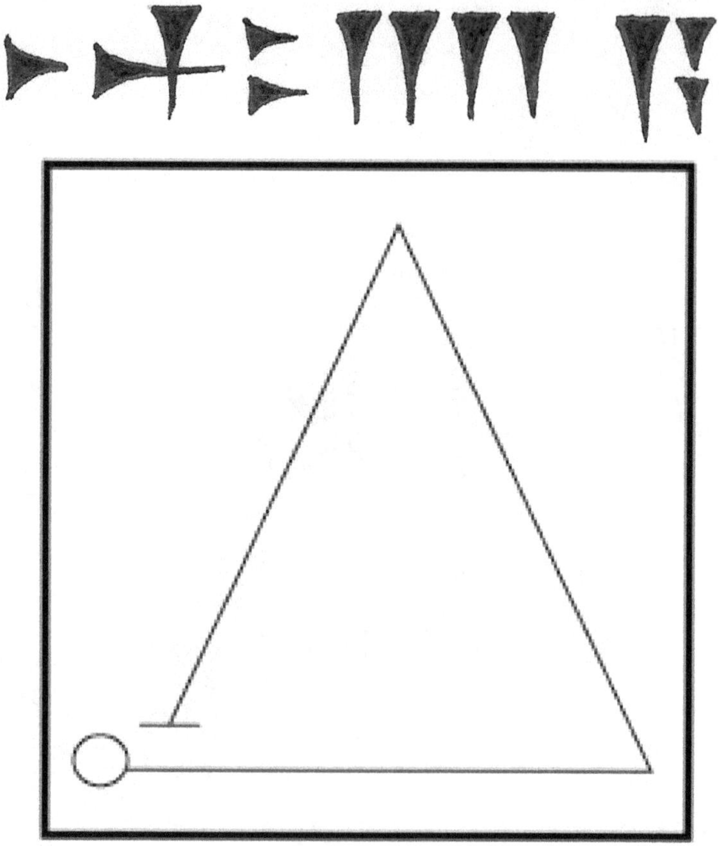

SUPERNAL – E.A.–ENKI – NEPTUNE

ENKI assisted his brother ENLIL in developing the local universe, pre-Babylonian Sumer, and the organization of the physical world. Later, ENKI or E.A. ("Whose House is Water") is given domain over physical manifestation and creation in the form of "magic." In Babylon we gave to him the name of EN.KI meaning "Lord of the Earth." In raising him to this position among the people it was much easier for his son, MARDUK, to be given a high station as well.

The elements *earth* and *air* are strong in this energetic current. ENKI is sometimes referred to as "Our Father" among *our* Race of Marduk. He is given charge of the *"Word of Power"* [called MAAT by the Egyptians] that charges the incantations of magic that breathe changes into the universe. These secrets were passed onto MARDUK and myself. They became the foundation of our traditions in Babylon and Egypt. As a planetary power, ENKI is Neptune, the Greek 'Poseidon of the Deep.' His power is ancient and strong knowing no boundaries in the universe. For a time he had in his possession the Anunnaki *Tablets of Destiny* – the 'Arts of Civilization' powering the magic of the priests in Babylon.

PRAYER TO ENKI & DAMKINA

ilu-E.A ilu-IA ilu-EN.KI
ilu-istari-NIN.KI ilu-istari-DAM.KI.NA
ilu-EN.KI samu-ya sa mesari eresti
ilu-istari-DAM.KI.NA sar-rat kal
  an-un-na-ki ilani la-tu
ilu-EN.KI u ilu-istari-DAM.KI.NA
  sur-ba-ti ina ilani
  la-u parsuki
rimi-nin-ni-ma anaku ___ apil ___ sa
  ilu-sa ___ u ilu-istari-sa ___
abu u ummu kispu
nabatu kabasu ramanu manahtu
rasanu-ya rigmu ina ramanu siptu
ki-bi-ma lis-si-mi zik-ri
amat a-kab-bu-u kima a-kab-bu-u
  lu-u ma-ag-rat
dinu-ma ramanu lid-mi-ik
lu-us-tam-mar ilu-ut-ka nabatu anaku
  arad-ka elu
an-un-na-ki ti-i-ru u
  na-an-za-zu
u emedu salimu menu u tes
  enu zid katamu [AN.KI] sihip
  same u eresti

PRAYER TO ENKI & DAMKINA

EA. IA. ENKI.
NINKI. DAMKINA.
ENKI, Your name is the depths of the Earth.
DAMKINA, Queen among the Anunnaki
  Gods
ENKI and DAMKINA,
  You are great among the gods,
  Mighty is your command.
Be favorable to me ___ son of ___ whose
  god is ___ and whose goddess is ___ .
Father and Mother of Magic,
Shine upon my work.
Be the voice of my incantations.
Speak and let the Word by heard.
Let the Word I speak, when I speak it,
  be favorable.
Open the Gates of your understanding.
Judge my existence favorably.
Let your Divine Light shine through me,
  a servant of the Highest.
May the Anunnaki come forth and
  be established.
And may peace, love and unity,
  reign true throughout the Universe.

ENLIL

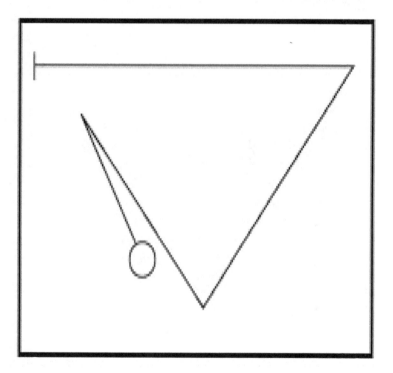

SUPERNAL - ENLIL (EL) - ELDER-JUPITER

ENLIL is "Lord of the Command" - heir to *Anuship* in 'Heaven', position of 'God' in the local universe. This shift in power began the Judeo-Semitic age, when ENLIL appeared to the people of the "Holy Lands" as "Jehovah." It can be said that ENLIL is indeed the God of the Israelites and the Judeo-Christian and Islamic traditions.

Duality split the pantheon between lineages of ENLIL and ENKI occurred on Earth and in Heaven. ENLIL should be rightfully acknowledged as the power of *Anuship* in modern times, with his own heir, NINURTA as successor. Such was the original arrangement for the last age and for the "peace, love and unity to reign true in the Universe," it is essential that the perceptions of these traditions, in addition to their realizations in modern times, is carried in self-honesty.

Jupiter is the original current of ENLIL, though we observe MARDUK in Babylon, and the power to execute "*Anuship*" in the material world - an exercise of power in elemental domains of *air* and *fire* elements. Where ENKI is "Lord of the Earth," ENLIL is seen as "Lord of the Airs," the intermediary space bonding (between) the earth and the heavens.

PRAYER TO ENLIL & NINLIL

ilu-ENLIL ilu-BEL
ilu-istari-NINLIL ilu-istari-BELTU
sumu-ya sa dug-ga
rigmu-ya dug-ga samu u erseti
ilu-ENLIL abu ilani
ilu-BEL-ENLIL u ilu-istari-
  BELITU-NINLIL
zi kima ramanu abu u ummu anaku ___
  apil ___ *sa ilu-su* ___
  ilu-istari-su ___
ka-ba-a sutlumu ramanu tehu
  u amaru dingir-ya itti ilani
sutlumu-lu manzazu-ya itti ilani masu
banu anaku aga zaku temu
petu babu temu
karabu ramanu manahtu
  u zaqtu napharu
lu-us-tam-mar ilu-ut-ka nabatu anaku
  arad-ka elu
qibitu narbu ina [An.Ki] sihip same u eresti
an-un-na-ki ti-i-ru u
  na-an-za-zu
u emedu salimu menu u tes
  enu zid katamu [An.Ki] sihip same u eresti

PRAYER TO ENLIL & NINLIL

ENLIL. BEL.
NINLIL. BELTU.
Your name is the command.
Your voice rules the Heavens and Earth.
ENLIL, Father of the Gods,
BEL-ENLIL and BELITU-NINLIL,
You are as a father and mother to me ___ ,
son of ___ , whose god is ____ and whose
goddess is ____ .
At your command, allow me to approach
and behold your divinity among the gods.
Let not your place among the gods
be forgotten.
Make me a vessel of clear understanding.
Open the Gates of your understanding to me.
Bless me in my workings
and show me wholeness.
Let your divine light shine through me,
a servant of the Highest.
Command greatness in the Universe.
May the Anunnaki come forth and
be established,
And may peace, love and unity
reign true throughout the Universe.

ANU

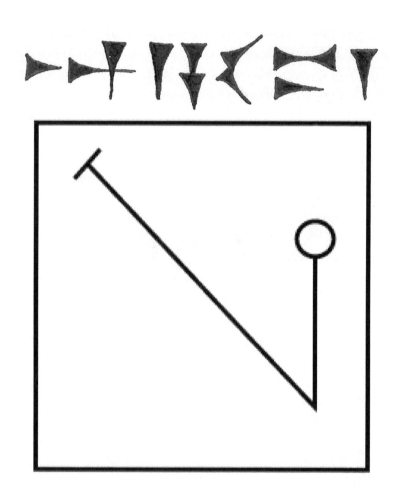

SUPERNAL – ANU (AN) – URANUS

From the start of recorded history in Sumer, cuneiform tablets kept by NABU *priest-scribes* , it is ANU who is given role of "Father in Heaven," All-Father of the gods. This is what He was to us all, the father of both ENLIL and ENKI. All members of the Anunnaki pantheon from both lineages are His children.

The *"House of Anu"* is the "domain of Heaven," also the name given to the planet Uranus [UR-ANU]. His heavenly force has not always been immediately felt on earth, and has instead, been left to his heirs, ENLIL and ENKI, to command the cosmos in his stead.

ANU, the blessed Father of us all, shall ever remain in the mouth of the people – in the prayers. His legacy shall always remain on epic tablets and through the deeds of his children. His place in Heaven shall always be known to us, though it will be filled by another, as ANU has left us now with only his Shade remaining – and a position in the heavens meant to be filled by ENLIL (and his successor, NINURTA). With the dawning of the New Age comes another change in divinity. Let self-honest peace, love and unity reign true through the Universe when it does.

PRAYER TO ANU & ANTU

ilu-ANU ilu-AN ilu-AN.NA
  ilu-istari-AN.TU
ilu-ANU abu ina samu
ilu-AN.NA samu-sa zi nigul sumu
daru-sa zi gitmalu-ya amatu
duru-sa zi dingir-ya edullu
zi biritu [an.sar] samu u [ki.sar] erseti
  sa-zi u'uru
madu ilani
  duru risatu zi mulammu
guhsu-ya gistaggu
  la urru
ilu-istaru-AN.TU ummu samu u nabalu
si-lim itti-ya a-tu-u
dingir hamdan ina samu lu-us-tam-mar
  itu-ut-ka u atwu ramanu lid-mi-ik
anaku ___ apil ___ sa ilu-su ___
  ilu-istar-su ___
anaku izuzzu wasru gudmu zi
anaku arad-ka-ya
  arad-ka elu
an-un-na-ki ahurru-ya
  ti-i-ru u na-an-za-zu

PRAYER TO ANU & ANTU

ANU. AN. ANNA.
  Goddess, ANTU.
ANU, Father in Heaven.
Heaven is your everlasting name.
Eternal is your perfect Word.
Forever is your Divine Kingdom.
The domain of Heaven and Earth
  is yours to command.
May the Great Gods
  ever rejoice in your splendor.
May your Altar of Offering
  never be empty.
ANTU, Mother of the Sky and Land,
Be favorable to me.
Divine Union of Heaven, make me fit
  to call upon and receive your blessings.
I, son of ___ whose god is ___ and whose
  goddess is ___ ,
Stand humbly before thee in praise.
I am thy servant –
  a servant of the Highest.
May the Anunnaki, your children,
  come forth and be established.

*Being a series of rituals
taught to the priests of Babylon
and the Order of Nabu
as a devotional method for citizens
to celebrate the New Year
and the Supremacy of Marduk.*

THE BOOK OF

ZAGMUK

(LIBER Z)

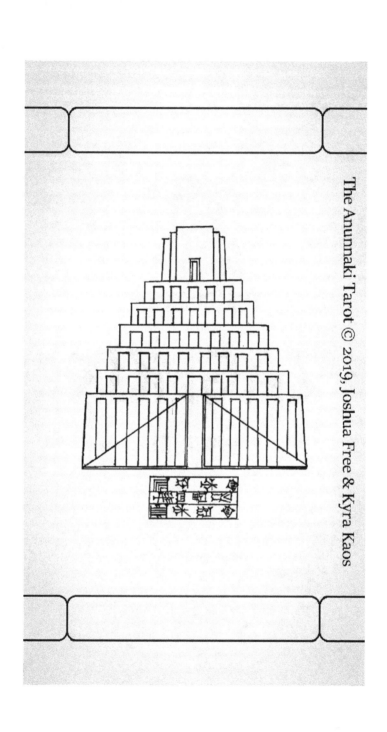

INTRODUCTION & APPLICATION
A.KI.TI / A.KI.TU FESTIVAL RITE

In ancient *Babylon*, the New Year Festival was the central most religio-political "Mardukite" event marking the beginning of the
annual cycle. At that time in "celestial history," the spring equinox observation of *Akitu* (or *Akiti*) coincided with the sun entering
the "*Aries*" zone, the zodiacal sign of MARDUK. This spring festival symbolized not only agricultural fertility and renewal of the
land on earth, but also a restatement or reinforcement of the national position of MARDUK and his role in the universe.

The Akkadian name for the final day of the festival—*Akiti* or *Akitu*
—translates roughly to "*On Earth, Life.*" Most scholars usually only
recognize the "agricultural" significance and not necessarily the
"political" and "mystical" functions of the observation. True, the
Akitu festival took place twelve days before the annual crops were
planted—but, this large public national "celebration" also recon-
firmed supremacy of MARDUK and his position in the *Babylonian*
Anunnaki Pantheon, making it the single most important ancient
"holiday" for the Mardukite tradition.

After a time of gods had come and gone, the priests and kings
continued to observe these ceremonial customs using representative "images" or statuary to symbolized the "divine presence" of
MARDUK and NABU as they made a procession each year through
the streets of *Babylon*. Each of the twelve festival days begins at
dawn. The High Priest of the "Temple of Marduk"—the E.SAG-ILA
or "House of Marduk"—goes and prepares the temple and other
ceremonial areas before dawn, then makes a "general invocation"
to MARDUK, before the "image" (statue) of the god in his shrine.

INVOCATION PRAYER TO MARDUK

MARDUK, Almighty, Powerful One of ASURA,
Exalted, Noble-Blood, Firstborn of ENKI,
Almighty MARDUK,
Who causes the ITURA to rejoice, Lord of the ESAGILA,
Aid to BABYLON, Lover of the EZIDA, Preserver of Life,
Prince of IMAHTILLA, Renewer of Life,
Shadow over the Land,
Protector of Foreign Lands,
Forever is MARDUK the Sovereign of Shrines,
Forever is MARDUK the Name in the mouth of
    the people.
Almighty Lord MARDUK,
At your command the Earthborn remain alive,
At your command let me live, let me be perfect,
Let me behold your divinity.
What I will to be, let me obtain my wishes.
MARDUK, cause righteousness to come from
    my mouth,
MARDUK, cause mercy to dwell in my heart,
Return to the Earth; re-establish the ANUNNAKI
    and command mercy.
May my God stand at my right hand.
May my Goddess stand at my left hand.
May my Lord who is favorable to the stars, stand
    firmly at my side,
To speak the Word of Command, to hear my prayer
    and show favor,
When I speak, let the words be powerful.
Almighty Lord MARDUK, come and command life.
BEL's Fires go with you, ENKI smile upon us all.
May the Elder Gods delight in your mercy.
May the Earth Deities be favorable to thee and me.

THE FIRST DAY

On the first day of the festival, *after* the priests carried out morning services, the King accompanies a procession around the city of *Babylon*, showing the people that he carried the official "royal" regalia of his position—the *"Crown of Anu*," the *Scepter of Dragonblood, &tc*. This is to secure the symbolism of "worldly material reign" firmly in the consciousness of the population. Transfer of this power to the king by the gods demonstrates his *"Divine Right to Rule."* Then, portions of the *"Enuma Eliš"* (Mardukite Tablet-N) are read to prove that Marduk is authorized to dispense this "divine right."

THE SECOND DAY

During the second day, the *High Priest* is charged to ritually cleanse the temple with consecrated waters from both rivers of *Babylon*—the *Tigris* and the *Euphrates.* Sweet fragrances of juniper and cypress fill the air. The official image (statue) of NABU is carried from the nearby city of *Borsippa* and left just outside of *Babylon* at the *Uras Gate.* The sacred symbols of "worldly material reign" are removed from the King by the *High Priest* and taken by procession to the *Temple of Marduk*, where the symbols are placed before the (statue) feet of the *god.* These "sacred objects" are only "returned" to MARDUK briefly, so that the *Anunnaki King* may dispense them "officially" back to the *Earthly King* who rules the Babylonian nation in the name of MARDUK. This also demonstrates to all concerned that these symbols of reign are only "borrowed" by kings, who are really "stewards" for MARDUK on Earth. The statue of MARDUK is brought outside the *Esagila* and the King makes his appeal to rule before it. Then, the items of power are returned to the King by the *High Priest,* and a procession ensues back to the palace, showing the people that the King has been granted the "Divine Right" by MARDUK.

THE THIRD DAY

Day three involves a reenactment of the *"Enuma Eliš,"* followed by a procession of the image/statue of NABU on a pathway of reeds. NABU is brought before the Sumerian *"Temple of Ninurta"* (sometimes called the *"Temple of Fifty"*) where he is to "defeat" two enemies (*"evil gods"*) in the name of MARDUK. A dramatization is performed—two statues are destroyed before his image. NABU is then left at the *"Temple of Ninurta"* until the sixth day of the festival.

THE FOURTH, FIFTH & SIXTH DAY

On the fourth day, both statues are ritually "cleansed" by the *High Priest*. The image of MARDUK is returned to the *Esagila*, where MARDUK is symbolically "imprisoned within the mountain" (or the "pyramid")—which had happened during the fall of the first "Tower of Babel" in prehistory. In one account, he is trapped is by "two evil gods," presumably the same ones that NABU defeats. A more accurate explanation according to tradition is that his imprisonment was political punishment for the death of *Dumuzi* (or *Tammuz*)—consort of INANNA-ISHTAR. MARDUK remains "buried alive"—*dead but dreaming*—for three days. During this, on the fifth day, the epic cycle of INANNA-ISHTAR—known as (Mardukite Tablet-C or) the *"Descent to the Underworld"*—is recited (or dramatized) and NABU finally enters the city again on the sixth day.

THE SEVENTH AND EIGHTH DAY

Ceremonial applications of the seventh day are derived from a wisdom series, given as Mardukite Tablets I, II and III of the *Nabu-Tutu (Tablet-T)* series. Here, the young prophet-son deity—NABU—approaches the *voice* of the *"unseen god,"* MARDUK as *Amon-Ra* entrapped in the "pyramid." During the festival, NABU—the statue/

THE GREAT HYMN TO MARDUK

*Among the multitudes of men who exist and
   have names,
Who is there that can of himself have True-
   Knowledge?
Who has not erred on Earth? Who has not
   transgressed?
Who is there to follow on Earth knowing the
   Way of the God?
I will worship the God of Heaven, but I will
   not tolerate the wickedness
that reigns in Men on Earth.
I will seek out the regions where flows the
   Waters of Life.
I wash clean my iniquity before thee,
   which is seen by my God.
Forgive me, my Lord, for the sins I have
   committed on Earth,
Willingly or unknowingly, from the time of
   my youth until now.
Let not me fall into despair, but destroy the
   sin and fault in me,
Lighten the labor of my turmoil and illuminate
   my gloom.
Let the sins of my father and mother and
   their generations,
Not fall upon me, may they pass on one side.
Speak to me now, my Lord! Make me clean
   and pure!*

Let the merciful hands of my Lord fall grant me
    well-being,
So that I may ever stand strong before thee with
    prayer.
May the good folk spread throughout the world
    bend their knee,
Let them worship thee who may destroy their sin.
MARDUK, Lord of the Magicians and Priests,
    destroy my sin.
ERU(A), Great Goddess of the Earth, destroy
    my sin.
NABU, Fair One, Herald of your Father, MARDUK,
    destroy my sin.
TESHMET, Consort of Marduk, Lady of Borsippa,
    Hear my prayer, destroy my sin.
SARPANIT, Consort of Marduk, Lady of BABYLON,
    destroy my sin.
NERGAL-ERRA [The Annihilator], destroy my sin.
You ANUNNAKI [gods] who dwell in the Heavens
    with ANU,
May you come forth and destroy my sin, do away
    with my sin.
May your heart be at peace,
May the heart of my mother and father be
    at peace,
Bring me a life of sinless peace, and then,
Brave MARDUK,
    will I honor thee with submission.

image of NABU—is brought before the image of the imprisoned "MARDUK" statue to receive the mysteries from the "unseen god."

THE NINTH, TENTH, ELEVENTH & TWELFTH DAY

A great victory procession of MARDUK and NABU commences on the ninth day, including honorary recitation of the *Enuma Eliš* finale, proclaiming the *"Fifty Names of Marduk"* (Mardukite Tablet-F). Their statues and those of their consorts—SARPANIT and TESHMET—are cleaned on the tenth day before they are receive a final grand celebratory procession on the eleventh day. Then after the priests conduct closing "consecration" rites at dawn on the twelfth day, all of the images/statues are retired to their appropriate places and Babylonian work-a-day life returns to normal.

Additional Notes:

The Babylonian "Akitu"/"Akiti" Spring Equinox festival replaced national significance of the former Sumerian "Zagmuk" New Year festival and eventually, given the emphasis on Marduk and Mardukite themes, the two rites were symbolically joined together as one. This time marked the beginning of the planting/sowing half of the year—and also the triumph or light over dark, or else order over chaos, represented by the victory of Marduk over Tiamat (and also the ability of Inanna-Ishtar to descend to the Otherworld/Underworld and return, yet further emphasizing the resurrection themes of the season and origins for the modern "Easter" observations—carrying a pagan name "Ostara" that is named for Ishtar). As a national 12-day ceremonial observation, the Akiti/Akitu public festival rituals occupied a significant portion of the religious year, combining the modern equivalence of Christmas and Easter into one grand holiday observation.

*Here are recorded the
Tablets of Creation as given
by the Priests of Nabu,
which describes the victory
of Marduk over Tiamat.*

THE BOOK OF

ENUMA ELIŠ

(TABLET-N)

ENUMA ELIŠ SERIES – TABLET I

When in the heights the Heavens had not been named,
And the Earth had not yet been named, And the primeval
APSU, who birthed them, And CHAOS, TIAMAT,
The Ancient One, Mother to them all.
Their waters were as One and no field was formed,
No marsh was to be seen;
When of the gods none had been called into being,
And none bore a name, and no destinies were ordained;
Then were created the celestial gods in the midst of
    heaven,
LAHMU and LAHAMU were called into being
And the Ages increased.
Then ANSAR and KISAR were created,
And the god ANU then came forth who begat NUDIMMUD
    [ENKI].
Abounding in all wisdom he had no rival.
Thus the Great Gods were established.
But TIAMAT and APSU were still in confusion,
Troubled and in disorder.
APSU was not diminished in might, and TIAMAT roared.
APSU, the begetter of the great gods,
Cried unto MUMMU, his minister,
And said: "MUMMU, thou minister that causes my spirit
    to rejoice,
Come with me to TIAMAT."
So they went and consulted on a plan with regard to the
    gods, their sons.
APSU spoke: "Let me destroy their ways, let there be
    lamentation,
And then let us lie down again in peace."
When TIAMAT heard these words, she raged and cried
    aloud.
She uttered a curse and unto APSU she asked:
"What then shall we do?"
MUMMU answered giving counsel unto APSU,

"Come, their way is strong, but you can destroy it;
This day you shall have rest, by night shalt thou lie down
   in peace."
They banded themselves together
And at the side of TIAMAT they advanced; they were
   furious;
They devised mischief without resting night and day.
They prepared for battle, fuming and raging;
They joined their forces and made weapons invincible;
She spawned monster-serpents, sharp of tooth, and
   merciless of fang;
With poison, instead of blood, she filled their bodies.
Fierce monster-vipers she clothed with terror.
With splendor she clothed them, she made them of lofty
   stature.
Whoever beheld them, terror overcame him,
Their bodies reared up and none could withstand their
   attack.
She set up vipers and dragons, and the monster
   LAHAMU.
And hurricanes, and raging hounds, and scorpion-men,
And mighty tempests, and fish-men, and rams;
They bore cruel weapons, without fear of the fight.
Her commands were mighty, none could resist them;
After this fashion she made eleven kinds of monsters.
Among the gods who were her sons,
Inasmuch as he had given her support,
She exalted KINGU; in their midst she raised him
   to power.
To march before the forces, to lead the host,
To give the battle-signal, to advance to the attack,
To direct the battle, to control the fight,
Unto him she entrusted, saying: "I have uttered thy spell,
In the assembly of the gods I have raised thee to power.
The dominion over all the gods have I entrusted
   unto him.
Be thou exalted, you are my chosen spouse,

May your name be magnified among all ANUNNAKI."
She gave him the Tablets of Destiny, on his breast she
  laid them,
Saying: "Thy command shall not be in vain,
And your decrees shall be established."
Now KINGU, thus exalted, having received the power
  of ANU,
Decreed the fate among the gods his sons,
Saying: "Let the opening of your mouth quench the
  Fire-god;
He who is exalted in the battle, let him display his
  might!"

ENUMA ELIŠ SERIES – TABLET II

TIAMAT made weighty her handiwork,
Evil she wrought against the gods her children.
To avenge APSU, TIAMAT planned evil,
But how she had collected her forces, the god unto EA
  [ENKI] divulged.
ENKI was grievously afflicted and he sat in sorrow.
The days went by, and his anger was appeased,
And to the place of ANSAR his father he took his way.
He went and, standing before ANSAR, his father,
All that TIAMAT had plotted he repeated unto him,
Saying "TIAMAT, our mother hath conceived a hatred
  for us,
With all her force she rages, full of wrath.
All the gods have turned to her,
With those, whom you created, they go to her side.
They have banded together and at the side of TIAMAT
And they advance; they are furious,
They devise mischief without resting night and day.
They prepare for battle, fuming and raging;
They have joined their forces and are making war.
TIAMAT, who formed all things,

And made weapons invincible;
She hath spawned monster-serpents,
Sharp of tooth, and merciless of fang.
With poison, instead of blood, she hath filled their
　　bodies.
Fierce monster-vipers she hath clothed with terror,
With splendor she has armed them;
She has made them tall in stature.
Whoever beholds them is overcome by terror,
Their bodies rear up and none can withstand their
　　attack.
She hath set up vipers, and dragons, and the monster
　　LAHAMU,
And hurricanes and raging hounds, and scorpion-men,
And mighty tempests, and fish-men and rams;
They bear cruel weapons, without fear of the fight.
Her commands are mighty; none can resist them;
After this fashion, huge of stature,
She has made eleven kinds of monsters.
Among the gods who are her sons,
Inasmuch as he has given her support,
She has exalted KINGU;
In their midst she hath raised him to power.
To march before the forces, to lead the host,
To give the battle-signal, to advance to the attack.
To direct the battle, to control the fight,
To him she has uttered your spell;
She hath given to him the Tablets of Destiny,
On his breast she laid hem,
Saying: 'Thy command shall not be in vain,
And the your word shall be established.'
"O my father, let not the word of thy lips be overcome,
Let me go, that I may accomplish all that is in
　　thy heart.
I shall avenge."

ENUMA ELIŠ SERIES – TABLET III

ANSAR spoke to his minister:
"O GAGA, thou minister who causes my spirit to rejoice,
Unto LAHMU and LAHAMU I will send thee.
Make ready for a feast, at a banquet let them sit,
Let them eat bread, let them mix wine,
That for MARDUK, the avenger, they may decree the fate.
Go, GAGA, stand before them, And all that I tell thee,
Repeat unto them, and say: 'ANSAR, your son, has
    sent me,
The purpose of his heart he has made known unto me.
He said that TIAMAT, our mother, has conceived a hatred
    for us,
With all her force she rages full of wrath.
All the gods have turned to her, with those, whom you
    created,
They go to her side. I sent ANU, but he could not
    withstand her;
NUDIMMUD [ENKI] was afraid and turned back.
But MARDUK has set out, the champion of the gods,
    your son;
To set out against TIAMAT his heart has called him.
He opened his mouth and spake unto me,
Saying: 'If I, your avenger, Conquer TIAMAT and give
    you life,
Appoint an assembly, make my fate preeminent and
    proclaim it so.
In UPSUKKINAKU seat yourself joyfully together;
With my word in place I will decree fate.
May whatsoever I do remain unaltered,
May the word of my lips never be changed nor made of
    no avail.'
Quickly decree for him the fate which you bestow
So that he may go and fight your strong enemy."
GAGA went humbly before LAHMU and LAHAMU,
    the gods,

His fathers, and he kissed the ground at their feet.
He humbled himself; then he stood up and spake unto
   them saying:
"ANSAR, your son, has sent me,
The purpose of his heart he hath made known unto me.
He says that TIAMAT, our mother, hath conceived a
   hatred for us,
With all her force she rages full of wrath."
And he spoke the words of the tale.
LAHMU and LAHAMU heard and cried aloud.
All of the IGIGI wailed bitterly, saying:
"We do not understand the deed of TIAMAT!"
Then did they collect and go,
The great gods, all of them, the ANUNNAKI who
   decree fate.
They entered in the House of ANSAR, kissed one another,
They made ready for the feast, ate bread,
And they mixed sesame-wine.
They were wholly at ease, their spirit was exalted;
Then for MARDUK, their avenger, they decreed the fate.

ENUMA ELIŠ SERIES – TABLET IV

The ANUNNAKI prepared for MARDUK a lordly chamber,
Before his fathers as prince he took his place.
"MARDUK, You are now chief among the great gods,
Thy fate is unequaled, thy word is ANU.
Your words shall be command,
In your power shall it be to exalt and to abase.
None among the gods shall transgress your boundary.
Abundance, shall exist in thy sanctuary shrine,
Even if you lack offerings.
MARDUK, you are our avenger!
We give you sovereignty over the whole world.
Sit down in might; be exalted in thy command.
Your weapon shall never lose its power; it shall crush
   your enemy.

134

Lord, spare the life of him that puts his trust in thee,
But as for the god who began the rebellion, empty them
   of life."
The ANUNNAKI set out a garment
And continued to speak to MARDUK.
"May thy fate, O lord, be supreme among the gods,
To destroy and to create; speak only the word,
And your command shall be fulfilled.
Command now that the garment vanish;
And speak the word again and let the garment reappear!"
Then he spake the words and the garment vanished;
Again he commanded it and the garment reappeared.
When the gods, his fathers, beheld the fulfillment of
   his word,
They rejoiced, and they did homage unto him,
Saying, "Maerdechai! Maerdechai! MARDUK is king!"
They bestowed upon him the scepter, the throne and
   the ring,
They give him invincible weaponry to overwhelm the
   enemy.
"Go, and cut off the life of TIAMAT," they said.
"And let the wind carry her blood into secret places."
MARDUK made ready the bow, his first choice in weapon,
He slung a spear upon him. He raised the club in his
   right hand.
The bow and the quiver he hung at his side.
He set the FLAMING DISC in front of him
And with the flame he filled his body.
He fashioned a net to enclose the inward parts of
   TIAMAT,
He stationed the four winds so that nothing of her
   might escape;
The South wind and the North wind and the East wind
And the West wind He created the evil wind,
And the tempest, and the hurricane,
And the fourfold wind,
And the sevenfold wind, and the cyclone,

And the wind which had no equal;
He sent forth the winds which he had created, seven
   in total;
To disturb the inward parts of TIAMAT.
Then MARDUK raised the thunderbolt, mounted the
   chariot,
A storm unequaled for terror, and he harnessed four
   horses
Named DESTRUCTION, FEROCITY, TERROR,
And SWIFTNESS; and foam came from their mouths
And they were mighty in battle,
Trained to trample underfoot.
With garments cloaked in terror and an overpowering
   brightness
Crowning his head, MARDUK set out toward the raging
   TIAMAT.
Then the gods beheld him.
And when the lord drew near,
He gazed upon the inward parts of TIAMAT,
He heard the muttering of KINGU, her spouse.
As MARDUK gazed, KINGU was troubled,
The will of KINGU was destroyed and his motions ceased.
And the gods, his helpers, who marched by his side,
Beheld their leader's fear and their sight was troubled.
But TIAMAT did not turn her neck.
She spit rebellious words.
MARDUK raised the thunderbolt,
His mighty weapon, against TIAMAT,
Who was raging, and he called out:
"You have become great as you have exalted yourself
   on high,
And your heart has prompted you to call to battle.
You have raised KINGU to be your spouse,
You have chosen Evil and sinned against ANU and
   his decree.
And against the gods, my fathers,
You have dedicated yourself to a wicked plan.

Let us face off now then in battle!"
When TIAMAT heard these words,
She acted possessed and lost her sense of reason.
She screamed wild, piercing cries,
She trembled and shook to her very foundations.
She recited an incantation, and cast a spell,
And the gods of the battle cried out for their weapons.
Then TIAMAT and MARDUK advanced towards one
   another,
The battle drew near.
Lord MARDUK spread out his net and caught her,
And the evil wind that gathered behind him he let loose
   in her
Face when she opened her mouth fully.
The terrible winds filled her belly,
And her courage was taken from her,
And her mouth opened wider.
MARDUK seized the spear and burst her belly,
Severing her inward parts, he pierced her heart.
He overcame her and cut off her life;
He cast down her body and stood upon it.
After slaying TIAMAT, the leader of the ANCIENT ONES,
The might was broken and her minions scattered.
But they were surrounded, so that they could not escape.
MARDUK took them captive and broke their weapons;
In the net they were caught and in the snare they
   sat down.
And on the eleven monsters which she had filled
With the power of striking terror, he brought them
   affliction,
Their strength he stole and their opposition
He trampled under his feet.
From KINGU who he had conquered,
He rightly took the Tablets of Destiny
And sealed them with his seal, then hung them from
   his neck.

Now after MARDUK had conquered and cast down his
  enemies,
And had fully established ANSAR's triumph over the
  enemy,
And had attained the purpose of NUDUMMID [EA (ENKI)],
Over the captive gods he strengthened his position,
And he returned to the conquered TIAMAT.
With his merciless club he smashed her skull.
He cut through the channels of her blood,
And he made the North wind steal it away
Outside in secret places between spaces.
His fathers beheld, and rejoiced and were glad;
Presents and gifts they brought unto him.
Then Lord MARDUK rested, gazing upon her dead body
And devised a cunning plan.
He split her up like a flat fish into two halves;
One half of her he established a covering for heaven.
Sealed with a GATE he stationed a WATCHER IAK SAKKAK
And fixed him not to let her waters to ever come forth.
MARDUK passed through and surveyed the regions
  of Heaven,
And over the Deep he set the dwelling of NUDIMMUD
  [ENKI].
And after measuring the structure of the Deep,
He founded his Mansion,
Which was created likened to Heaven and he set down
The fixed districts for ANU, ENLIL and ENKI to reign.

ENUMA ELIŠ SERIES – TABLET V

MARDUK fixed the Star Gates of the Elder Gods;
And the stars he gave images as the stars of the Zodiac, which he
fixed in place.
He ordained the year and into sections he divided it;
For the twelve months he fixed the stars.
He founded his Star Gate on NIBIRU to fix them in zones;
That none might rebel or go astray,

He fixed the Star Gate of ENLIL
And IA [E.A.-ENKI] alongside him.
He opened great gates on both sides,
He made strong gates on the left and on the right
And in the midst thereof he fixed the zenith;
He fixed the Star Gate for the Moon-god
And decreed that he shine forth,
Trusting him with the night and to determine days;
The first of the great gates he assigned to NANNA [SIN]
And every month without ceasing he would be crowned,
  Saying:
"At the beginning of the month, when you shine down
  upon the land,
You command the trumpets of the six days of the moon,
And on the seventh day you will divide the crown.
On the fourteenth day you will stand opposite as
  half-moon.
When the Sun-god of the foundation of heaven calls thee,
On that the final day again you will stand as opposite.
All shall go about the course I fix.
You will drawn near to judge the righteous
And destroy the unrighteous.
That is my decree and the covenant of the first gate."
The gods, his fathers, beheld the net which MARDUK
  had fashioned,
They beheld his bow and how its work was accomplished.
They praised the work which he had done and then ANU
  raised up
And kissed the bow before the assembly of the gods.
And thus he named the names of the bow, saying:
"Long-wood shall be one name,
And the second name shall be Dragonslayer,
And its third name shall be the Bow-star,
In heaven shall it remain as a sign to all."
Then ANU and MARDUK fixed a Star Gate for it too,
And after the ANUNNAKI decreed the fates for the
  ANCIENT ONES,

MARDUK set a throne in heaven for himself at ANU's right hand.

ENUMA ELIŠ SERIES – TABLET VI

The ANUNNAKI acclaimed him "First among the ELDER GODS."
MARDUK heard the praises of the gods,
His heart called to him to devised a cunning plan.
He approached IA [ENKI] saying:
"The Key to the GATE shall be ever hidden, except to my offspring.
I will take my blood and with bone I will fashion a Race of Men,
That they may keep watch over the GATE.
And from the blood of KINGU I will create a race of men,
That they will inhabit the Earth in service to the gods
So that our shrines may be built and the temples filled.
But I will alter the ways of the gods, and I will change their paths;
Together shall they be oppressed
And unto evil shall they no longer reign.
I will bind the ELDER GODS to the WATCHTOWERS,
Let them keep watch over the GATE of ABSU,
And the GATE of TI.AM.TU and the GATE of KINGU.
I bind the WATCHER IAK SAKKAK to the GATE
With the Key known only to my Race.
Let none enter that GATE
Since to invoke DEATH is to utter the final prayer."
The ANUNNAKI rejoiced and set their mansions in UPSUKKINAKU.
When all this had been done, the Elders of the ANUNNAKI
Seated themselves around MARDUK
And in their assembly they exalted him
And named him FIFTY times,
Bestowing upon him the FIFTY powers of the gods.

*Here are recorded
the Fifty Names of Marduk
concluding the epic
Tablets of Creation series of
the Priests of Nabu.*

THE BOOK OF FIFTY NAMES

NINNU

(TABLET-F)

ENUMA ELIŠ SERIES – TABLET VI

1. The First Name is MARDUK-DUGGA-ANU,
   Son of the Sun, Lord of Lords, Master of Magicians,
   Most Radiant Among the Gods is he.
2. The Second Name is MARDUKKA,
   ANUNNAKI Creator,
   Knower of the Secrets of MARDUK,
   Time, Space & Creation [Geometry of the Universe].
3. The Third Name is ARRA-MARUTUKKU,
   Master of Protections and of the Gate to the
   ANCIENT ONES
   And to whom the people give praise as Protector of
   the City.
   Possesses the ARRA-Star.
4. The Fourth Name is BARASHAKUSHU-BAALDURU,
   Worker of Miracles, with wide heart and strong
   sympathies.
5. The Fifth Name is LUGGAL-DIMMERANKI(A)-BANU
   TUKKU,
   Commander of the Wind Demons,
   The Metatronic Voice Heard Among the Gods.
6. The Sixth Name is NARI-LUGGAL-DIMMERANKI(A)-
   BAN-RABISHU,
   Watcher of the Star Gates of the IGIGI & ANUNNAKI,
   And who is named the Monitor of the Gods in their
   stations.
   Keeper of the Gates between worlds.
7. The Seventh Name is ASARU-LUDU-BAN-MASKIM,
   Wielder of the Flaming Sword, The Light of the
   Gods.
   Called for the safety and protection of the
   Gatekeeper.
8. The Eighth Name is NAMTI-LAKU-BAN-UTUK-
   UKUT-UKKU,
   Master of the Death Gate and of Necromancy,

And who is able to revive the Gods with a single
prayer.

9. The Ninth Name is NAMRU-BAKA-KALAMU,
The Shining One who is Counselor of the Sciences.
Called to increase the scientific knowledge of the
Gatekeeper.

10. The Tenth Name is ASARU-BAALPRIKU,
Creator of grains and plants, who knows no
wasteland.
Called to increase the vegetative and blooming
growth.

11. The Eleventh Name is ASARU-ALIM-BAR-MARATU,
Who is revered for wisdom in the house of counsel,
And who is looked to for peace when the Gods are
unsettled.
Called to aid in communication with the ANUNNAKI
and to dispel deception.

12. The Twelfth Name is ASARU-ALIM-NUNA-BANA-
TATU,
The Mighty One who is the Light of the Father of
the Gods,
And who directs the decrees of ANU, ENLIL and
ENKI/EA.
Called to aid in the enforcement of law on Earth.

13. The Thirteenth Name is (NABU)-TUTU,
He who created them anew, and should their wants
be pure, then they are satisfied.
Called to reveal the hidden gnosis within the
Gatekeeper.

14. The Fourteenth Name is ZI-UKKINA-GIBIL-ANU,
The life of the Assembly of the Gods
Who established for a bright place for the Gods in
the heavens.
Called to reveal the secrets of astrology and the
celestial sphere.

15. The Fifteenth Name is ZI-AZAG-ZI-KU-IGIGI-
MAGAN-PA,
Bringer of Purification, God of the Favoring Breeze,
Carrier of Wealth & Abundance to the people.

16. The Sixteenth Name is AGAKU-AZAG-MASH-
GARZANNA,
Lord of the Pure Incantation, The Merciful One,
And whose name is on the mouth of the Created
Race.
Called to bring life to elementaries and ward spirits.

17. The Seventeenth Name is TUKUMU-AZAG-MASH-
SHAMMASHTI,
Knower of the Incantation to destroy all evil ones.
Called in the Maqlu Rite to dispel evil sorceries.

18. The Eighteenth Name is SAHG-ZU-MASH-
SHANANNA,
Founder of the Assembly of Gods and knows their
heart,
And whose name is heralded among the IGIGI.
Called for aiding the Gatekeepers psychic
development.

19. The Nineteenth Name is ZI-SI-MASH-INANNA,
Reconciler of enemies, who puts an end to anger;
Bringer of Peace.

20. The Twentieth Name is SUH-RIM-MASH-SHA-
NERGAL,
Destroyer of wicked foes, who confuses their plans.
May be sent to destroy the enemies of the
Gatekeeper.

21. The Twenty-first Name is SUH-KUR-RIM-MASH-
SHADAR,
Who confounds the wicked foes in their places.
May be sent to destroy the unknown enemies of the
Gatekeeper.

22. The Twenty-second Name is ZAH-RIM-MASH-
    SHAG-ARANNU,
    Lord of Lightning, A warrior among warriors.
    May be raised against entire armies of men.
23. The Twenty-third Name is ZAH-KUR-RIM-MASH-
    TI-SHADDU,
    Destroyer of the Enemy in battle,
    Who slays in a most unnatural fashion.
24. The Twenty-fourth Name is ENBILULU-MASH-
    SHA-NEBU,
    Knower of the secrets of water and of secret places
    for grazing.
    Called to bestow the secrets of dowsing and aid
    irrigation.
25. The Twenty-fifth Name is EPADUN-E-YUNGINA-
    KANPA,
    Lord of Irrigation, who sprinkles water in the
    heavens and on Earth.
    As the previous, also the secrets of Sacred Geometry.
26. The Twenty-sixth Name is ENBI-LULU-GUGAL-
    AGGA,
    Lord of growth and cultivation, who raises the
    grains to maturity,
    And some have said is a face of ENKI.
27. The Twenty-seventh Name is HEGAL-BURDISHU,
    Master of farming and the plentiful harvest
    And who provides for the people's consumption.
    May also be called to aid in personal fertility.
28. The Twenty-eighth Name is SIRSIR-APIRI-KUBAB-
    ADAZU-ZU-KANPA,
    The domination of TIAMAT by the power of the Net.
    Called for mastery of the Serpent and the Kundalini.
29. The Twenty-ninth Name is MAL-AHK-BACH-
    ACHA-DUGGA,

Lord of bravery and courage, Rider of the Ancient
Worm.
Summoned for courage, bravery and self-confidence.
30. The Thirtieth Name is GIL-AGGA-BAAL,
Furnisher of the life-giving seed, Beloved
(betrothed) consort to INANNA-ISHTAR.
Called for women who desire pregnancy.
31. The Thirty-first Name is GILMA-AKKA-BAAL,
Mighty One and Divine Architect of the temples.
Possesses secrets concerning the Geometry of the
Universe.
32. The Thirty-second Name is AGILMA-MASH-SHAY
-E-GURRA,
Maker of Rain Clouds to nourish the fields of the
Earth.
Called forth in times of drought.
33. The Thirty-third Name is ZULUM-MU-ABBA-BAAL,
Giver of excellent counsel and power in all
businesses,
And Destroyer of the wicked foe, maintaining
goodness and order.
34. The Thirty-fourth Name is MUMMU,
Creator of the Universe from the flesh of TI.AM.TU.
Keeper of the Four Watchtower Gates to the Outside.
35. The Thirty-fifth Name is ZU-MUL-IL-MAR-AN-
DARA-BAAL,
The heavens have none equal in strength and
vitality.
Called forth to aid in healing rituals and rites.
36. The Thirty-sixth Name is AGISKUL-AGNI-BAAL-
LUGAL-ABDUBAR,
Who sealed the ANCIENT ONES in the abyss.
Called by the piously righteous for strength and
vigor.

37. The Thirty-seventh Name is PAGALGUENNA-AR
   RA-BA-BAAL,
   Possessor of Infinite Intelligence, preeminent among
   the Gods.
   Offers wisdom in oracles and divination.
38. The Thirty-eighth Name is LUGAL-DURMAH-
   ARATA-AGAR-BAAL,
   King of the gods, Lord of Rulers [Durmah].
   Aids the Gatekeeper in developing all mystic powers.
39. The Thirty-ninth Name is ARRA-ADU-NUNA-
   ARAMAN-GI,
   Counselor of ENKI/EA, who created the Gods, his
   fathers,
   And whose princely ways no other God can equal.
   Called during (self)-initiations to aid you through
   the Gates.
40. The Fortieth Name is DUL-AZAG-DUMU-DUKU-
   ARATA-GIGI,
   Possessor the secret knowledge and the wand of
   Lapis Lazuli.
   Can reveal untold marvels of the cosmos to the
   Gatekeeper.
41. The Forty-first Name is LUGAL-ABBA-BAAL-DIKU,
   Eldest of the Elder Ones, and pure is his dwelling
   among them.
   Aids the Gatekeeper in acquiring "self-honesty."
42. The Forty-second Name is LUGALDUL-AZAGA-
   ZI-KUR,
   Knower of the secrets of the spirits of wind and star.
   Offers the Gatekeeper secrets to command spirits.
43. The Forty-third Name is IR-KINGU-BAR-E-RIMU,
   Holding the capture of KINGU, supreme is his might.
   Keeper of the Blood(Birth)-Rights.
44. The Forty-fourth Name is KI-EN-MA-EN-GAIGAI,

Supreme Judge of the ANUNNAKI, at whose name
   the gods quake.
To be called when no other spirit will arrive.

45. The Forty-fifth Name is E-ZIS-KUR-NENIGEGAI,
Knows the lifespan of all things,
And who fixed the Created Race's life at 120 years.

46. The Forty-sixth Name is GIBIL-GIRRA-BAAL-
   AGNI-TARRA,
Lord of the sacred fire and the forge, creator of the
   Sword.
Also possesses the secrets of the "fiery passions."

47. The Forty-seventh Name is ADDU-KAKO-DAMMU,
Raiser of storms that blanket the skies of Heaven.

48. The Forty-eighth Name is ASH-ARRU-BAX-
   TAN-DABAL,
Keeper of time, the secrets of the past and future.
May be summoned to aid acts of divination.

49. The Forty-ninth Name is The STAR, let NEBIRU be
   his name,
He who forced his way through the midst of
   TIAMAT,
May he hold the ALPHA and the OMEGA in his hands.
Summoned to discern the Destiny of the Universe.

50. The Fiftieth Name is FIFTY and NINNU-AM-
   GASHDIG,
The Judge of Judges, Determiner of the laws of the
   Realm.
The Patron of the Dragonblood Kings of Earth.

APOCRYPHA OF THE MARDUK TABLET

The Forty-ninth Name is the STAR, that which shines
  in the heavens.
May he hold the ALPHA and the OMEGA in his hands,
And may all pay homage unto him, saying:
"He who forced his way through the midst of TI.AM.TU
  without resting,
Let NIBIRU be his name – The Seizer of the Crossings
That causes the stars of heaven to uphold their paths.
He comes as a shepherd to the gods who are like sheep.
In the future of mankind at the End of Days,
May this be heard without ceasing; may it hold sway
  forever!
Since MARDUK created the realm of heaven and
  fashioned the firm earth,
He is forever the Lord of this World."
ENLIL listened. ENKI heard and rejoiced.
All of the Spirits of Heaven waited.
ENLIL gave to MARDUK his name and title BEL.
ENKI gave to MARDUK his name and title EA and
Said: "The binding of all my decrees, let MARDUK now
  control.
All of my commands, shall he make known."
The Fiftieth Name is FIFTY and NINNU-AM-GASHDIG,
The Judger of Judges, Determiner of the laws of the
  Realm.
By the name FIFTY did the ANUNNAKI then proclaim
  MARDUK's "Fifty Names."
The ANUNNAKI made his path preeminent.
Let the Fifty Names of MARDUK be held in
  remembrance to all
And let the leaders proclaim them;
Let the wise gather to consider them together,

Let the father repeat them and teach them to his son;
Let them be in the ears of the priest and the shepherd.
Let all men rejoice in MARDUK, the Lord of the gods,
That be may cause the land, his Earth, to be
    prosperous,
And that he himself may enjoy prosperity!
His word hold and his command is unaltered;
No utterance from his mouth goes unnoticed.
His gaze is of anger and turns his back to none;
No god can withstand his wrath.
And yet, wide is his heart and broad is his compassion;
The sinner and evil-doer in his presence weep for
    themselves.

THE BOOK OF

GATES

(LIBER L/G)

*Here are recorded the
Teachings of Marduk as given
to his firstborn heir Nabu,
Keeper of the Secrets of Writing
and the Wisdom of Eridu
used to raise Marduk in Babylon
and to guide the Priests.*

THE BOOK OF

NABU-TUTU

(TABLET-T)

NABU-TUTU SERIES – TABLET I

And so NABU {indicated as I} went to the Mountain
  [pyramid],
To hear the Voice of the Great God come from the
  Mountain.
The Unseen God, whose vision and voice comes to the
  prophet.
And the voice of MARDUK came out of the Mountain
  [pyramid].
"I am the voice of the God who cannot be here.
I am the voice of the God who is in the hearts of all men.
I am the voice of the God who appears in many faces.
It is I, the voice of the God, that will teach you the way,
And I command you, dear son, to write this what I say
On tablets for all of humanity's sake,
That they might honor the Gods of their Ancestors
  [ANUNNAKI]
But worship the Eternal Source of All Being & Creation.
I am not only the voice of your God, but also your
  commander.
Prepare for the long and hard battle such as lies ahead."
NABU asked MARDUK:
"What can men do to prepare for the sake of their
  own lives,
How can they live to serve and worship proper?"
And the voice of MARDUK echoed out:
"Live piously and by the Union Code [Tablet] of the
  ANUNNAKI.
For there is no longer any religion higher than the
  Source.
And the desire of God is for us to love one another,
And not to sacrifice the life which has been made
  possible.
A certain knowledge of what is good and evil on Earth,
With perfected choice will be the former, so is the will
  of God.

There is no pleasure to be gained from the wasteful shed
of blood.
Celebrate life and sing praises to the creation around
you,
Which has been carefully made for you, by the Highest,
Under who the ANUNNAKI live and reign over the
Lower."
And NABU asked MARDUK:
"For what can men do to repent of their sins if not by
sacrifice?"
The voice of MARDUK responded:
"Give to the Eternal Source dedication and commitment
in life,
And this is all that is asked of you in this life.
Men approach the face of God in fear and beg
forgiveness,
When their efforts could be better spent in prayer and
praise.
Men flood the temple-shrines with more food than is
consumed,
When it could be better distributed among the poor.
[something later instilled by Babylonian kings...]
Bring the God of Life no more vain offerings of flesh.
Pray and live a pious life at one with creation. How hard
is this?
Make simple rituals if it pleases you,
For only prayer and devotion is asked of the God of All.
Do not deny yourself of a happy existence in the name
of God.
Never let your livelihood be neglected because you
worship God.
Lives dedicated to the Source are not preoccupied by
worship,
For to go out and live and act the pious life among men
is best."

NABU-TUTU SERIES – TABLET II

All things that are, are moved; Only that which is not, is
   unmovable.
Every Body is changeable.
Not every Body is able to be dissolved into elements.
Some Bodies are able to be dissolved into elements.
Every living thing is not mortal.
Not every living thing is immortal.
That which may be dissolved is also corruptible.
That which is Eternal is unchangeable, incorruptible.
That which is unchangeable is eternal.
That which is always physical is always corrupted.
That which is made but once,
Is never corrupted and does not become any other thing.
First, God; Second, the World; Third, Man.
The World for Man, Man for God.
Of the Soul-Program,
That part has been given as the conscience of mortals,
But that which is Reasonable is immortal.
Every essence is immortal.
Every essence is unchangeable.
Every thing that is, is double.
None of the things that are stand still.
Not all things are moved by a Soul-Program,
But everything that is, is controlled by its own Soul-
   Program.
Every thing that suffers is Sensible,
Every thing that is Sensible suffers.
Every thing that is sad is also able to rejoice,
And must be a mortal living Creature.
Not every thing that is able to be joyous can also be sad,
Like unto the eternal living things.
Not every Body can be sick;
but every sick Body is dissoluble.
The Mind resides in the All [God].
Reasoning in experience is in Man,

Experience becomes the Reason in the Mind.
The Mind is void of suffering.
No thing in a Body is true.
All that is incorporeal, is void of Lying.
Every thing that is made is corruptible.
Nothing good made upon Earth, nothing evil made in
 Heaven.
God is good, Man is evil.
Good is voluntary, or of its own accord.
Evil is involuntary or against its will.
The Gods choose good things, as good things.
Time is a Divine thing.
Law is Human.
Malice is the nourishment of the Material Kingdom .
Time is the Corruption of Man.
Whatsoever is in Heaven is unalterable.
All upon Earth is alterable.
Nothing in Heaven is for a charge, nothing on Earth
 is free.
Nothing unknown in Heaven, nothing known upon Earth.
The things upon Earth communicate not with those in
 Heaven.
All things in Heaven are without blame,
All things upon Earth are subject to consequence.
That which is immortal, is not mortal:
That which is mortal is not immortal.
That which is sown, is not always brought to fruition;
But that which is manifest had always been sown.
Of the perishable Body, there are two Times,
One from sowing to generation, one from generation
 to death.
Of an everlasting Body, the time is only from the
 Generation.
Perishable Bodies are increased and diminished,
Perishable matter is divided into contraries;
As in Corruption and Generation, but Eternal matter
 exists unto its self.

NABU-TUTU SERIES – TABLET III

The Generation of Man is Corruption,
The Corruption of Man is the beginning of Generation.
That which off-springs or produces another,
Is itself an product of another.
Of things that are, some are in Bodies, some in their Ideas.
Whatsoever things belong to operation or working, are in
   a Body.
That which is immortal, partakes not of that which is
   mortal.
That which is mortal, does not come into an immortal Body,
But that which is immortal can come into a mortal Body.
Operations or Workings are not carried upwards,
But descend downwards.
Things upon Earth do nothing to advantage those in
   Heaven,
But all things in Heaven can do profit
And advantage for the things upon Earth.
Heaven is capable and a fit receptacle of everlasting
   Bodies,
The Earth is one of corruptible Bodies.
The Earth is brutish, the Heaven is rational.
Those things that are in Heaven are subjected or placed
   under it,
But the things on Earth, are placed over it's matrix
Heaven is the first Element.
Providence is Divine Order.
Necessity is the Minister or Servant of Providence.
Fortune is the vehicle or consequence of what is without
   Order;
The focus of operation,
Nothing more than opinionated glamour or a fantasy.
Avoid all conversation, both idle and wise,
With the multitudes or common people of the masses,

For that which is Above
Would not have you become either the subject of Envy,
Much less to be considered ridiculous by the many.
The like have always been pulled toward themselves,
That which is like,
Such as when the waters settle upon their levels.
The unlike will never agree with the unlike natures,
Such is the pattern of their way:
Such as you will find
With the variegated philosophical discourses.
And dogmatic treatise that circulate among the masses.
The unlike natures are unique in one facet:
That they act as a sharpening stone for the evil
    tendencies in men,
Another vehicle for their maliciousness.
Conclusively it is better to avoid the multitudes
And realize that they are not in the path of
    understanding the virtue
And power of the things that have been said here.
And concerning the nature
And composition of those living things called "humans,"
It may be simply said that they are prone to
    maliciousness,
being something they are both familiar with and
    nourished by.
When first the world was made,
All things were in perfected accordance
With Providence and Necessity, Destiny [or Fate],
Bearing Rule over all. Knowing this perfection,
The mortal creatures will be the worse for it,
Despising the whole because it was made.
And if the only power known to them is to be the evil
    cause
Of disorder upon Fate or Destiny,
Than they will never abstain from the tendencies
Toward evil doings.

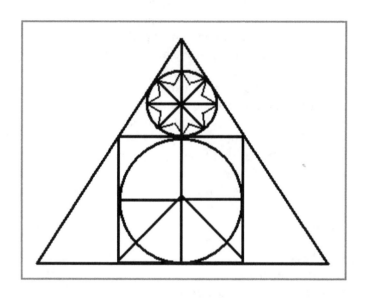

THE BOOK OF

CROSSINGS

(TABLET-X)

Our physical universe operates on fundamental geometry of metaphysical vibration. Defined natures of energetic currents (vibrations) are what wizards and mystics understand as magical correspondences. Energetic polarity of a specific current is allocated across many systems of correspondence, for example: colors, planets, days of the week. Emphasis should not be on the fragmentation of "levels." The separation of the whole into parts only to find more separate relationships and correspondences is not the best way back to true unification.

Accessing powers of the Gates requires activation and/or dissolution (depending on semantic preference) of the astral form or Body of Light as the "I AM" paradigm and then envisioning the Gate in the astral world. Increased familiarity, true knowledge and experience developed from working with individual currents —and the lore they represent—increases the Gatekeepers chances for energetic conscious connection/communication. The Seeker approaches each "Veil of Existence" on their ascent back to the Source.

Preparation of a proper portal (or mental impression on the subconscious) may include any number of the glyphs from the BABILI tablets (given throughout the current volume). True-knowledge of the system and self-honesty are adamantly necessary for perceiving existence as it truly is, from the perspective of its designers, as opposed to the way in which a player is programmed to experience it.

Rituals, energy work and meditation may incorporate any key glyphs, symbols, and incantations, for each individual "step" on the "Ladder of Lights" or "Star-Tower." Supplemental Mardukite material may also aid the modern Gatekeeper in "tuning in" to the frequency-vibration of each Gate current successfully.

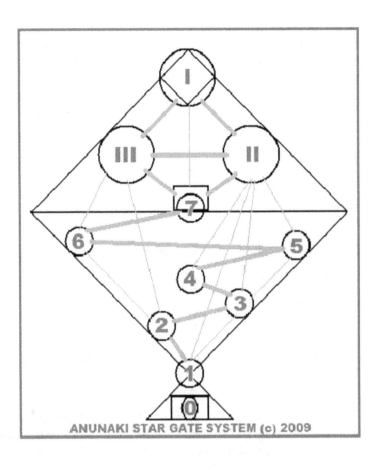

Descriptions of the original Mesopotamian "Ladder of Lights" model are seldom explored in contemporary mysticism. In the Star-Gate depiction shown here, the Gatekeeper will see a dual pyramid, one in the "heights" of Heaven, and one in the "depths" of material existence [Earth]—but these are actually one and the same "pyramid of existence" (not to mention the "spaces between"), encompassed by the etheric ALL that entangles all existence as One—All-as-One. "Heights" (AN) meet "Depths" (KI) and are unified in an all-encompassing existence bound together and interconnected as the ALL.

The many "Gates" can just as easily be seen as "one" or even "none" since it is the fragmented mind which separates our experience from the whole. By "ascending" the course, we are consciously making efforts to "travel backwards" to the Source from which we were removed, or rather which was removed from us via the fragmentation into varied "shells."

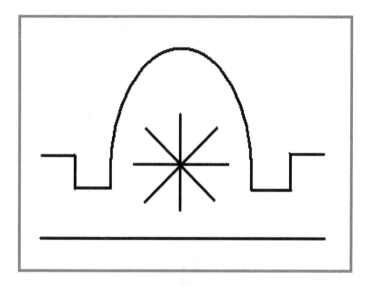

From the "Earthed" point-of-view, we must access the "Ladder of Lights" by ascending the pyramid, essentially backwards, from our side, meaning to first access it through the Earth Gate—the alpha spirit of man or True Self as "I AM"—which is numbered: zero. Also--when magicians call forth powers of the Universe from within a "mandala" or microcosmic ritual "circle," they call upon and open Four Quarters, Quadrangles or Watchtowers. Boundaries of this dimensional universe are bound by the Earth Gate—which is perceived by the Four Directions sealing material existence—and the Self as the Fifth (elemental gate) experiencing the others; and the Gates of the Heights above and the Depths below—All-as-One.

THE NORTH GATE

Gate of the Formless Hunter and of the Abyss,
Thee I invoke the Bornless One
Who brings the "Cleansing Darkness."
Spirits of the Northern Gate, open your mysteries unto me.
Gate of the Scales of Judgment and the Outside,
From which comes the Hosts and Fiends,
Manifest the Shield of ARRA, Truth and Spirit in my hands,
And protect me from the fires of the Destroyer.
Gatekeeper of the Northern Gate, remember:
Open wide the Gate.
Spirit of the Gate of the North, Thou art conjured!

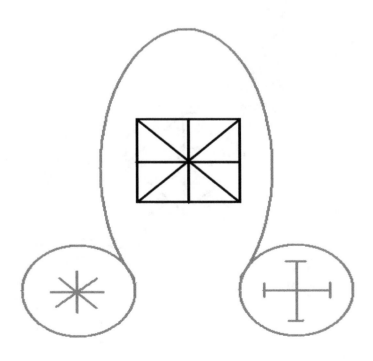

THE EAST GATE

Gate of the Rising Star and of the Rising Sun,
Spirits of the Eastern Gate, Open your mysteries unto me.
Gate of the Forgotten Memory, stir your light in my head,
Kindle the warm fires of remembrance in my being,
Protect me from the "light-so-blinding"
And bring clarity to the washed out childhood memory.
Gatekeeper of the Eastern Gate, remember:
Open wide the Gate.
Spirit of the Gate of the East, Thou are conjured!

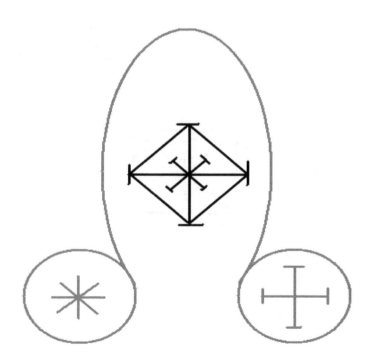

THE SOUTH GATE

Gate of the Fiery Angel and of the StarFire,
Spirits of the Southern Gate, Open your mysteries unto me.
Gate of the Fires of BEL,
Manifest the Sword of Fire, Truth and Spirit in my hands,
And protect me from the Destroyer and the destroyed.
In the names of the most holy armies of
MARDUK and ENKI,
Stand firmly by my side during the Decision [Judgment].
Gatekeeper of the Southern Gate, remember:
Open wide the Gate.
Spirit of the Gate of the South, Thou are conjured!

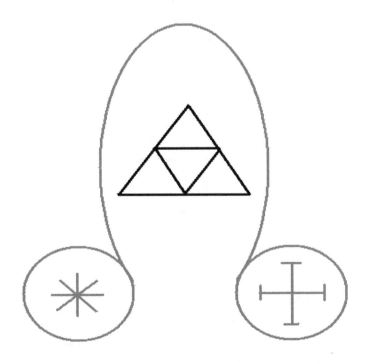

THE WEST GATE

Gate of the Twilight Shadows and of the Setting Sun,
Spirits of the Western Gate, Open your mysteries unto me.
Gate of the Symphony of Light and Darkness,
Kindle the "cold dark blue flame" in my head
And protect me from the sorrow of remembrance.
Gatekeeper of the Western Gate, remember:
Open wide the Gate.
Spirit of the Gate of the West, Thou are conjured!

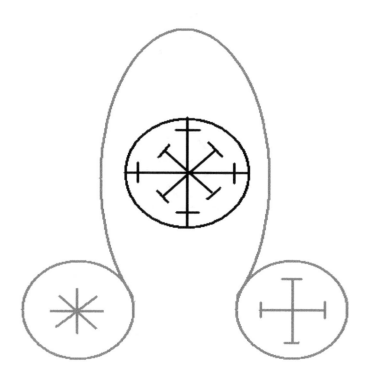

—PART TWO—
THE MAQLU RITUALS
(LIBER M)

THE MAQLU EXORCISMS & BANISHINGS.

Here is the *Book of Burnt Offerings*, the *Book of Burnings*, and the *Book of Exorcisms* handed down from the Keepers of the Old Ways—when ENKI walked the Earth, and made his home in *Eridu*. Here is the *Book of Maqlu Tablets* —key components to the ancient mysteries of "Mardukite" Babylonian Tradition as given to the priests of NABU and MARDUK. When the practitioner finds times of warfare not of this world—when malignant energies run rampant—when the wicked witch and warlock cast their evil magick against thee by the grace of their gods —in such times of trial, a self-honest Priest or Priestess of the *Anunnaki* is not left unprotected.

Functional use of ceremonial exorcisms to banish "evil spirits" is a most ancient form of mysticism—and "sympathetic magic"—perhaps the oldest of all forms. On a personal level, the purpose of the "*Maqlu*" (or "*Maklu*") cuneiform tablet series is exoterically—or outwardly— to target "evil spirits" and "evil-doers" (called "witch" or "warlock") that either has attacked or is actively working against the magician, their family and/or community. As a petition for the "power of the gods," it is assumed that the enemy exists within a similar *Anunnaki* cultural "paradigm" (worldview) and that the more righteous and pious servant of this tradition need only appeal to the same energetic authorities by which to shut the enemy off from their source—and in extreme situations, resulting in the fitful death of the enemy, and at the very least, a means of protecting the practitioner from any further assaults.

THE BOOK OF MAQLU & MAQLU RITUAL.

The Mardukite Tablet-M or "*Maqlu*" series consists of nine Akkadian-Babylonian cuneiform tablets illustrating a very extensive ritual—or combination of several rituals and incantations—by which the "Priest" (magician, practitioner, priestess, &tc.) calls on the power of Chief Gods from the *Anunnaki* pantheon: ANU, ENLIL, ENKI, MARDUK and SHAMMASH to "curse," "banish," "exorcise"—or literally "burn"—all of the evil-doers and wickedness of society in an elaborate ceremonial effort. Such rites were even held publicly as a major national festival event.

We translate the word "*Maqlu*"—or "*Maklu*" if you still subscribe to the Simon methodology—to mean "burnings," indicative of the type of effigy scape-goat "witch-burnings" envisioned from the Middle Ages, except for one key difference: <u>no</u> living beings are burned or sacrificed for the ritual. "*Maqlu*" ceremonial "effigy" burnings are metaphoric—rooted in sympathetic magic—performed with "images" of your enemy, symbolic representations of all the evil plaguing society.

The "*Maqlu*" ritual is sometimes called the "*Rite of Burnt Offerings*" because—using consecrated "images" charged with intention and heavy emotional energy—the "soul" of evil, or "souls" of evil-doers, are destroyed or "sacrificed" by incineration to benefit the world and a prosperous nation. Modern "revival" practitioners within "Mardukite" tradition and other systems of Mesopotamian "neo-paganism" have found varying degrees of success using popular translations of these exorcism tablets. That success increases exponentially and synchronously with the practitioner's understanding and experience with both "practical magic" (including "mysticism") and an understanding of *Anunnaki* "systemology"—the core knowledge base found throughout the modern "Mardukite" library of materials.

Much of the "Mesopotamian Magic" tradition is contained within archaic cuneiform religious or incantation tablets, and the "*Maqlu*" tablet series is no exception. However, these incantations are supplemented with specific ceremonial actions—the construction and consecration of various "images of the enemy" and ritual gestures describing the manner of cursing and incineration by fire: the "burnings."

Esoterically, public observance of "*Maqlu*" rites allowed for a shift in mass consciousness—the triumphant night of "order conquering chaos" reminiscent of European "Halloween" rites. Meanwhile, for the priesthood, the "*Maqlu*" ritual is a serious "astral ceremony" in which the practitioner would "climb the *Ladder of Lights*" and appeal to the Anunnaki gods for personal protection, the protection of the city (community), and destruction (elimination) of the enemy to this "world order"—all evil-doers and wicked witches and warlocks throughout the lands operating intently against the community. As a fixed movement of large amounts of energy, the ceremony enacts a "chain-curse" projected outward to extend far and beyond the immediate environment as a "public service" meant to "purge" the Realm.

A practical execution of the "*Maqlu*" ritual in its entirety requires intensive concentration—the full focus and adept attention of a practicing magician or priestess, perhaps in excess of a day, as the full observation is an overnight firelit vigil of ceremonial "cleansing" and emotional "purging" for the community—the most ancient "Burning Man" festival. Although not indicated on the "*Maqlu*" tablets themselves, all of the traditional ritual elements—preparation of the *Temple*, evoking *Guardians of the Watchtowers* and invoking the *Anunnaki* gods and their spiritual *Star Gates of Babylon*—are carefully observed before conducting any of the numerous "*Maqlu*" incantation-rituals. Much of this is also relayed throughout the greater literary collection of modern "Mardukite" materials, including our other related newly prepared practical pocket companion: *"The Complete Book of Marduk by Nabu: 10th Anniversary Collector's Edition."*

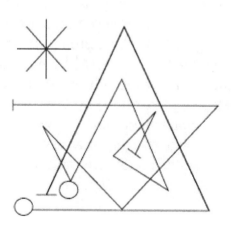

MARDUKITE

LIBER-M

ARCHIVES

THE DARK ARTS OF BABYLON.

How often we have heard of the "Dark Arts" born of a "polarized" and "dualistic" view of the universe—and the *forces* that occupy it. It is a simple nature of the "order of things"—for every pious priestly "magician," there is a dark spell against him; and to every system of *Order*, there is a *Chaos* factor—no fragmented experience of reality can ever actually exist isolated in perfect "balance." There is the pendulum swing of action and the movement of energy throughout the cosmos amorally controlling the tidal ebb and flow of universal currents. This is what makes energetic activity of "creation" or "manifestation" possible in the "physical world"—or at least our perception of a "3-Dimensional" reality experienced. As such, with a once united "crystal" being cracked into varied refractions of human experience, language and culture, a "dualistic" world also emerged early in human consciousness; right before the very eyes of ancient *Mesopotamians*—from the heart and cradle of known human civilization.

It is not within the scope of the current *"Liber-M"* archives to put forth an entire basis for the ancient *Anunnaki* tradition—or to catalogue the numerous historic *firsts* that arose from *Sumerian* culture "as if from nowhere"—or the greater legacy of post-Sumerian "Mardukite" *Babylon* throughout the evolution of human civilization, societal order, "belief systems" and their long-standing and far-sweeping effects on the planet and its populations... All of this has already been so concisely organized and offered in previous materials form the "Mardukite" literary collection. For our present purposes, we fix our sights on a specific singular element within all of this—the "Maqlu" cuneiform tablet series pertaining to the "Dark Arts" as encountered in the ancient *Mardukite* system observed in *Babylon*.

As a method of ancient spirituality realized through "ritual magic," this newly revised and translated "*Maqlu*" text is comprehensible as introduced and presented—though it is suggested that the reader-seeker or potential practitioner is familiar with the greater scope of Mesopotamian or "Mardukite Babylonian" tradition that these rites are derived from. "Magic" of this system is considered *high magic* and *holy magic* once reserved to an intellectually and spiritually elite class of priests and priestesses in Babylon—dependent on an *established* true and faithful relationship between the "operator" and the "supreme" powers ceremonially called forth.

Esoteric books transcribe excerpts of early academic "Maqlu" incantation translations out of context and tend to emphasize the more "colorful" elements portrayed by the tradition—those most appropriately pertaining to the Dark Arts: "Sumerian Sorcery," "Babylonian Witchcraft," "Mesopotamian Exorcisms," "magickal warfare" or "wizards' duels." The full picture shared via the Mardukite "Liber-M"/"M-Series" interpretive materials and translations offers an entirely new a more complete rendering of this 4,000+ year old operation from esoteric experimentation by the "Mardukite Research Organization" conducted from 2009 through 2019.

* * * * * * *

Mesopotamian languages are archaic forms of communication that we are still only now reaching clear understandings of. Yet—as with many terms—the words may often be interpreted differently, and it is not uncommon for meanings to shift during information transmission based on variegated perceptions, literal language differences, semantic issues and even personal beliefs of the translators. That being said: typically understand MAQLU to mean *"the Burnings."* This context is a good *base* for our working knowledge of the rites—especially in public displays of a community bonded together to "burn evil in effigy." It is even possible that the term more accurately describes a *"burning man"* if we adopt a similar literal interpretation of *maqlu.*

The complete *"Maqlu"* operation evolved from what was once probably a much simpler, mostly internalized, meditative and solitary protection ritual used by the earliest priests, priestesses and magicians in *Mesopotamia*. It later developed more dramatically as a public *"Fire Festival"* in Sumer and Babylonia, involving entire community populations gathered together in combined mass focuses of emotional and spiritual intention to "drive out" or *dispel* "evil" and "evil-doers" of the land. Here we see an ancient demonstration in effective abilities of mass-consciousness moving energies when large groups—or better, the majority of the population—focuses on a specific "emotional" event. Even as "quantum" events, the social effects carry very real ramifications for the consciousness of the population— and perhaps the greater cosmos as a whole in this entangled universe. So long as the event is properly orchestrated, the individuals need not even be aware of the exact esoteric nature of their participation.

Ritual incantations from *"Maqlu"* tablets coincide with construction and incineration of representative images —the *Burning Man* symbolizing all the "evil-doers" of the world—those "plaguing" humanity with their wickedness, thereby upsetting the "world order" of the *gods*, in addition to the *gods* themselves—those Anunnaki figures sharing a covenant of protection with their pious priests and priestesses.

The upset of a disharmonic balance was usually felt throughout the community socially as "illness" and "pestilence," "disease" and "famine"—and such could

prove devastating to a still developing human civilization. Actions leading toward such malignant results
were deemed "evil" and often personified as the most
wicked of "demons." Anything that might lead to un-
healthy results—mostly concerning uncleanliness and
misappropriated living—were considered "taboo," else
the original tribal "sins," and for good reason. For example—eating from an unclean plate was "taboo" (a
"sin") because it could lead to the spread of disease.
Clearly, ancient humans were meticulous observers far
from *primitive* in their understanding of the natural
world and their relationship with it. Before political authoritarian use in classical times, "taboos" and "sins"
were not given from dogma—but out of medicinal necessity. Humans were not "civilized" by nature; they
were "trained"—and language, civic systems and
"priestly institutions" developed to oversee this, maintain it, and even enforce it.

* * * * * * *

Representative "images" have a long-standing history
of use in "idol magic" or "sympathetic magic." These
are not instruments of demonic worship—as some
mythographers have repeatedly put forth—but are instead symbolic embodiments of an "energetic current."
These energies are universally entangled to a "focal object" and its form—and by the laws of "sympathetic
magic," affecting the form can equally affect the same

universally entangled energies it represents. We see this in other similar methods that are enacted to affect a person from a distance by using something that belongs to them, or better still: hair, nail clippings, and so forth. In related practices of necromancy and ancestral magic, personal articles and bone fragments are similarly used as relics to connect to a specific "entangled" energy from across the astral.

"Sympathetic magic" appears strongly in *Maqlu* rituals numerous times where a representative *image* of "evil," a "demon," a "wicked witch" or "evil warlock" is constructed and then ceremonially obliterated. These "idols" are not subjects of worship or glorification of Babylonian "daemonology," but to demonstrate control over—or at the very least, the ability to appeal to the Anunnaki gods that maintain control over—the chaotic forces of the universe that are often perverted by the wicked toward selfish and antagonistic ends. The *images* represent known and unknown "enemies of the state," or in more personal cases, a "witch" or "warlock" who is using magic against you. The degree of cosmic coherence portrayed by the entire "*Maqlu*" ceremony is far from primitive.

****

It is next to impossible to conjure a metaphysical or esoteric conversation of the "*Burning Man*" to a "New

Age" mind without also considering more geographic-
ally and chronologically recent examples from the
Western world. One that even motion pictures have
made into a household name is derived from Roman-in-
spired writings concerning the *Celtic Druids*—called the
Wicker Man, or else the "Burning Man" by some neopa-
gans and others who revive this emotionally-purging
annual festival today in America. Although once incited
as part of ancient warfare and even fertility rites, modern celebrations of community and healthy artistic
release actually mirror original "mass consciousness"
esoteric festivals very closely.

As a magical component, *Fire* commonly appears in
"magical" and "shamanic" systems during early development of human civilization—in fact, mastery of *Fire*
indisputably correlates *with* development of modern
humans. Antiquated *"Fire Festivals"* are aligned to the
Sun—often appearing to coincide with critical turning
points of the year, an annual cycle marked by key
points of agricultural significance: the planting and
harvest of sustaining foodstuffs. The "light" and "dark"
halves of the year also marked points of spiritual significance, such as we see with the Akiti/Akitu Babylonian
New Year observed on the Spring Equinox—a turning
point that celebrates renewal of the realm. Opposite
this festival of "lights" we also observe a "darker" time
of year, ritually dramatized as a cyclic mythological

struggle between *order* and *chaos*, *creation* and *entropy*, *life* and *death*—and to ensure the pendulum swing returns to the side of *Life*, we are given personal and communal "purification" exercises—the "*Maqlu*."

MAQLU MAGIC.

Esoteric "New Age" revival of *Maqlu* fragments for *Simon's Necronomicon* left many early initiates to wonder what *more* might remain behind the curtains of this form of Babylonian mysticism. In fact, even among the "Mardukite Research Organization," a full translation and total understanding of the complete ceremony would take nearly a decade amidst other work. Naturally, *Simon's Necronomicon* offered only a small part of the *Maqlu* data, just as we have seen in examples from many modern Mardukite predecessors—a greater literary cycle and spiritual tradition exists beneath the surface interpretations that have gone on inspiring for decades. Within and about all of the complete *Maqlu* cuneiform tablet series we find nothing short of a purely "Mardukite Babylonian" masterpiece of authentic ceremonial ritualism.

Many esoteric readers were first introduced to the *Maqlu* (or "*Maklu*") from the elementary and bastardized fragments appearing in the *Simon* work—causing many to overlook, dismiss or confuse what the original cuneiform *Maqlu* tablets actually represent. Only a small portion of the complete text appears in the popular *Simon* edition, and they are treated as individual rites of protective "counter-magic" against "worshipers of the *Ancient Ones*" and not as a singular ceremonial expression. There are other common elements of the *Maqlu* incantations that some occultists and esoteric magicians find reminiscent to other mystical work in related systems: *Arabic, Semitic, Assyrian, Canaanite, Hebrew, &tc.* In such comparisons, similar incantations appear in forms of "healing magic" or to drive away "evil spirits"—what we refer to as "*exorcisms.*" More than simply combating entities and energies directly, the *Maqlu* magic focuses on practitioners feeding these power-currents their existence (via participation and belief). At the same time, these "evil worshipers" are feeding off of and deriving channeled energy from malignant currents appearing "negative" in polarity when clashed against the "reality" of the ordered "Realm."

Maqlu magic stands apart uniquely, even amidst a modern "New Age" revival of ancient esoterica. Similar practices held by "politically correct occultism" of today are mainly *passive* "binding" meditations employing only the "astral powers *of the shield.*" The *Maqlu* offers ancient priest-magicians of the "State" a means of "magical law enforcement" with "astral powers *of the sword.*" As a religious practice, the *Maqlu* enables the pious priest and priestess mystic rights to "fight fire" with "God-Fire."

BABYLONIAN MAGIC & WITCHCRAFT.

Ancient magical practice and beliefs—as external demonstrations of will and outward ritualized communion with the "cosmos"—are common throughout the ancient world, and no less so in the underground today. Practice of magic, in and of itself, was not criminal in Mesopotamia—a cultural region adept in its widespread use and even producing a tradition known today as the *Chaldean Magi*—from which we have our word "magician." This being said: "magic" was an institution of the "State"—or that is to say, linked specifically to systematic power of the "Realm." Esoteric incantation tablets were sole property of "official" scribe-priests, priestess, magicians and kings of the "Realm." And to be clear: few citizens outside this elite circle were even literate enough to read them.

The original magical traditions were exclusively observed by those in positions of civic responsibility, those charged by a "Divine Right"—the covenant of *Anunnaki gods*—to appropriately execute esoteric "magical arts" throughout the realm. These were dispensed alongside a more "outward" (*exoteric*) "religious" understanding carried by the general masses. This distinction in understanding is reflected even today among the esoteric "Mardukite" movement in contrast to a purely academic or historic pursuit of Mesopotamian mysteries without adherence to the authentic paradigm or systemology that the material is derived from. Clearly, what is generally available to *seekers* now —after thousands of years of fragmentation, cultural separation, paradigm formations and other various *grimoires*—is but a *shadow* of the "real magic" secretly known to the ancient mystics working side-by-side with their Anunnaki "*Sky Gods.*"

Misinformed efforts, by later humans, corrupted the "sacred arts" of *magic*. But, this is not about placing blame; it matters little *who* is at fault now—only that the issue is rectified. The ancient mystics considered "priestly-magic" as "divine" or "transcendental," given to the "*Race of Marduk*" as a birth-right; *sacred* and not to be taken for granted. Education and use of "magical arts" were a closely guarded secret among the most ancient factions, sects and schools—all connected to *Anunnaki* traditions in whatever guises and names they might carry, or by whatever language or semantics they apply to the same universal system. Many later schools —later branches of the tree—were far removed, fragmented and divided from the original source, leaving each of the various sects only a limited understanding— a limited perceptual experience—of the *All-as-One.*

When we examine the specific language used throughout the *Maqlu*—and the disapproving labels applied to wicked evil-doers dedicated to the *"Dark Arts"*—the Seeker uncovers origins for a spiritual division or distinction regarding "class magic." Where some portray the *Maqlu* itself as a *"Book of Black Magic,"* this could not be further from the truth. Instead we discover a spiritual and religious method for *fighting, countering* and *defending* against the "Dark Arts." What's more—rather than put a self-honest magician at the risk of "turning to the Dark Side," the *Maqlu* ritual allows the *Mardukite* to petition the *Anunnaki* to execute final judgment and any retribution on their behalf. Of course, the literal nature of the *Maqlu* magic is still considered the "Dark Arts" to an extent—but when used on the side of *right*, karmic and energetic repercussions are transferred away from the operator and taken up by the divine intermediary. By appealing to the "Highest," the one who is in greatest alignment with *cosmic order* will prevail.

In contrast to terms like "priest," "priestess," "magician" or "seer," we see a clear distinction between these pious practitioners and the "wicked witch" or "evil warlock" that they are fighting against using *Maqlu* rituals. This means that the term "witch" has had a negative connotation since the original birth of language in Mesopotamia—not against a gender or practitioner of magic, but as a specific term for one who practices magic "outside" or "apart" from the ordered system of pious "priestly" spirituality. Although seldom relayed accurately by historians and academicians, the entire religious framework and infrastructure of Mesopotamia, Sumer, Babylonia, &tc. is entirely rooted in "Cosmic Order" and living unto the highest accord in alignment with "Cosmic Law" as described by the early Sumeriologist, Samuel N. Kramer, in his book: "*History Begins at Sumer*"—

"The Sumerians, according to their own records, cherished goodness and truth, law and order, justice and freedom, righteousness and straightforwardness, mercy and compassion. And they abhorred evil and falsehood, lawlessness and disorder, injustice and oppression, sinfulness and perversity, cruelty and pitilessness. Kings and rulers constantly boasted of the fact that they had established law and order in the land; protected the weak from the strong; the poor from the rich; and wiped out evil and violence. . . The gods, too, according to the Sumerian sages, preferred the ethical and moral to the unethical and immoral, and practically all the major deities of the [Anunnaki] pantheon are extolled in Sumerian hymns as lovers of the good and the just, of truth and righteousness. . ."

THE MAQLU RITUAL INSTRUCTIONS.

Using *Mardukite* standards of operation, the *Maqlu* ritual is conducted by "Divine Right" and via the "*Incantation of Marduk,*" which is to say the "*Incantation of the Deep*" or "*Incantation of Eridu.*" As such, all *fundamental* elements of a "Mardukite" ritual apply. Acknowledgment of the control and authority of Marduk in Babylon is among these—such as described by the scribe-priests of *Nabu* in the *Enuma Elis,* Babylonian "*Creation Tablets*" attributing all worldly authority to the Anunnaki god *Marduk.* It was not uncommon for this "myth" to be told or dramatically reenacted for festival ceremonies, as indicated in the Akiti/Akitu Spring Festival performance instructions.

Maqlu magic operates under the occult doctrine known in anthropology as "sympathetic magic" or "transference." It's based on mystical principles of entanglement and correspondence—often illustrated in the axiom: *Like attracts Like.* In our original descriptions of the *Maqlu* from previous "Mardukite" literature, the *initiate* is shown the "Ladder of Lights" on which they must "ascend" in order to appeal to the *Anunnaki gods* and make their petition for the occasion. In this instance, the power of *Starfire* or God-Fire ("Fire of God") is called forth and consecrated for a singular lofty purpose—*burning of evil.* Naturally, this priestly authority to command is restricted to those adept initiates already having "traversed" the *Gates of Babylon* and developed a personal relationship with the *Anunnaki gods.*

No definitive description is included with the *Maqlu* tablets proper, but we might surmise that the traditional cloth dressings (of practitioners and the altar, &tc.) appropriate to this type of magic are *black.* However, as traditional priestly garments were *white,* we can assume the practitioner changes their attire during the complete *Maqlu* sequence, probably right after evening "counterspells" and "exorcisms" are performed and the rites move toward a focus of "purification" and the emerging "dawn" that dispels the darkness. [On a related note, blue and purple hues (often with gold accents) were also common among the elite classes— later adopted as "royal" colors in Europe.]

Maqlu tablet instructions indicate quite clearly that this ritual is to be exclusively "performed by the pure offspring of the Deep," meaning specifically "Mardukites." The *"Deep"* is a literal translation for the domain of *E.A.-Enki,* whose domain is the "Deep" or *"Eridu,"* the ancient home of *Enki,* where *Marduk* and *Nabu* were apprenticed in the esoteric, scientific and magical arts of the *Anunnaki.* This same mystery tradition passed to the "Mardukites" of Babylon and were eventually preserved on cuneiform tablets by priest-scribes dedicated to *Nabu* and the legacy of *Marduk*. Among the many tablet series offering suggestions for modern methods of practical magic, we find the *Maqlu*.

All traditional "Mardukite Babylonian" ceremonial applications are intended for a "temple" environment, one that is regularly prepared and energetically charged through repeated use in dedication to the *Anunnaki* pantheon. Naturally, as with all modern efforts toward ancient esoteric revitalization and rekindling, there are obviously many ways of adapting the original methods for portability and practicality. In the instance where a physical permanent temple-space is not maintained, we find many cuneiform tablet examples suggesting a *mandala* of sorts—elsewhere referred to in Western occultism as *casting a circle*. A personal/portable *mandala* or "magic circle" is called *usurtu* on some cuneiform tablets and this sacred space was often distinguished by a circle, glyphs and other symbols marked on the ground with consecrated "Grain-flour of Nabu" (called the "Flour of Nisaba" in more antiquated Sumerian examples). A few Mesopotamian texts also refer to sprinkling lime throughout the internal

The *"Burnt Offerings"* are constructed according to the materials described on *Maqlu* tablets. This newly revised edition restores this information corresponding with each incantation that is usually not disclosed until the final (ninth) tablet. Additional ritual components are consecrated and incorporated as indicated throughout the text, but it is evident that a supply of specific materials for fashioning images are prepared ahead of time. Additionally, one is to make all petitions to the *Anunnaki* pantheon "before an image of your god and goddess," often the patrons of a particular city or priestly sect. In Babylon, popular images of *Marduk* and *Sarpanit* (and even *Nabu* and *Teshmet*) are frequently used in religious ceremonies, such as during the Akiti/Akitu festival. Finally, a reoccurring presence of "seven idol" statues or "seven watchers" often appears on ritual magic tablets of Mesopotamia.

[The Maqlu M-Series Tablets are given in the following section. A transliterated sign for EN and SU.EN marked the beginning and ending of each incantation—allowing us to easily separate each section of the ritual. As these words are not said as part of the verbal incantation, they are not redundantly used in this transcription.]

THE MARDUKITE

MAQLU

TABLET SERIES

THE MAQLU SERIES – TABLET I

OPENING INCANTATION—PETITION
TO THE GODS.

al-si-ku-nu-ši ilimeš mu-ši-ti
I call upon you, Gods of Night
it-ti-ku-nu al-si mu-ši-tum kal-la-tum ku-túm-tum
With you, I call upon the Night, the Veiled Lady
al-si ba-ra-ri-tum qab-li-tum u na-ma-ri-tum
I call at twilight, midnight and dawn,
áš-šú kassaptuú-kaš-šip-an-ni
Because the sorcerer has enchanted me,
[5] e-li-ni-tum ub-bi-ra-an-ni
A [sorceress] has spoken against me,
ili-ia ù distar-ia ú-šis-su-ú eli-ia
Causing my god and goddess to distance from me;
elî a-me-ri-ia am-ru-u a-na-ku
I am a pathetic sight to behold,
im-di-ku la a-la-lu mûša ù ur-ra
I am unable to rest day or night
qu-ú im-ta-na-al-lu-ú pî-ia
and a gag has filled my mouth
[10] ú-pu-un-ti pi-ia ip-ru-su
food has been kept from my mouth
mêmeš maš-ti-ti-ia ú-ma-u-ú
the water ceases to enter my throat;
e-li-li nu-bu-ú hi-du-ti si-ip-di
my praise is lament, my rejoice is sorrow:
i-zi-za-nim-ma ilimeš rabutimeš ši-ma-a da-ba-bi
stand by my side, Great Gods, give me notice,
di-ni di-na a-lak-ti lim-da
be a judge in my case, grant me a decision.
[15] e-pu-uš alam amelkaššapi-ia u kaššapti-ia
I formed an image of my sorcerer and sorceress,

šá e-piš-ia u muš-te-piš-ti-iar
of my enchanter and enchantress;
áš-kun ina šap-li-ku-nu-ma a-dib-bu-ub di-ni
I have laid them in fire and await your judgment;
áš-šú i-pu-šá lim-ni-e-ti iš-te-'-a la ba-na-a-ti
because [they] have conjured evil against me:
ši-i li-mut-ma a-na-ku lu-ub-lut
may [they] die, that I can live!
[20] kiš-pu-šá ru-hu-šá ru-sú-u-šá lip-pa-áš-ru
The evil magick, the evil spell must be broken!
ibînu lil-lil-an-ni šá qim-ma-tú ša-ru-ú
The [*Tamarisk*] purifies me!
igišimmaru lip-šur-an-ni ma-hi-rat ka-lu-ú šáru
The [datepalm] catching all the wind, frees me!
šam-maštakal li-bi-ban-ni šá iritimtim ma-la-a-ta
The [*maskatal*] shines through me, filling the earth.
terînatu lip-šur-an-ni šá še-am ma-la-a-ta
The [pinecone] full of seeds, frees me!
[25] ina mah-ri-ku-nu e-te-lil ki-ma šamsassati
In front of you I have become light as grass;
e-te-bi-ib az-za-ku ki-ma la-ar-di
I am shinning and pure like grass.
tu-ú-šá šá kaššapti li-mut-te
The spell of the [sorceress] is baneful;
tu-ur-rat amât-sa ana pî-šá lišân-šá qa-a-rat
Let [her] words fall in her mouth, tongue-tied!
in elî kiš-pi-šá lim-ha-u-ši ilimeš mu-ši ti
Let the Gods of Night overcome [her] spell.
[30] maarâtimeš šá mu-ši lip-šu-ru ru-hi-šá lim-nu-ti
Let the Three Watchers overcome the evil spell.
pú-šá lu-ú lipû lišân-šá lu-ú âbtu
Let [her] words be dust and tongue turned to salt,
šá iq-bu-ú amât limutimtim-ia ki-ma lipî lit-ta-tuk
which spoke the baneful formula, come to dust!

[35]

196

šá i-pu-šú kiš-pi ki-ma âbti liš-har-mi
The magick, let it dissolve like salt!
qi-is-ru-šá pu-u-u-ru ip-še-tu-šá hul-lu-qú
The knots are undone, [her] efforts are destroyed,
[35] kal a-ma-tu-šá ma-la-a êra
All [her] words fill the void
ina qi-bit iq-bu-ú ilimeš mu-ši-tum
by the covenant that the Gods of Night decreed!

INCANTATION—PETITION TO EARTH GODS.
irsitumtum irsitumtum irsitumtum-ma
Earth! Earth! Ye Spirit of the Earth
dgilgameš BEL ma-mi-ti-ku-nu
[Gilgamesh] is the lord of your course!
min-mu-ú at-tu-nu te-pu-šá ana-ku i-di
What has befallen you, I know:
[40] min-mu-ú ana-ku ip-pu-šu at-tu-nu ul ti-da-a
What has befallen me, you know not yet.
min-mu-ú kaššapatimeš-ia ip-pu-šá e-ga-a-pa-ti-ra pa-šir lâ ir-ašši
What the [sorceress] has let loose on me, no one can undo; it has no undoer!

INCANTATION—CONSECRATING SPACE.
ali-ia (zab-ban) ali-ia (zab-ban)
My city is [Zabban]. My city is [Zabban].
šá ali-ia (zab-ban)-ta abullatimeš-šú-it
My city of [Zabban] has two Gates:
ana sit dšamši šá-ni-tu ana erib dšamši-it
The first is on the east, the second on the west.
[45] ana si-it dšamšiši šá-ni-tu ana e-rib dšamšiši
One is for the sunrise, one is for the sunset.

a-na-ku e-ra ha-as-ba šam-maštakal na-šá-ku
I am lifting to you my seed [*maskatal*].
a-na ilimeš šá šamêe mêmeš a-nam-din
To the Sky Gods I bring water.
kîma ana-ku ana ka-a-šú-nu ul-la-lu-ku-nu-ši
As do I come to purify you
at-tu-nu ia-a-ši ul-li-la-in-ni
so come forth to purify me!

INCANTATION—GRAND INVOCATION.

[50] ak-la ni-bi-ru ak-ta-li ka-a-ru
I have barred-up the river-crossing and harbor,
ak-li ip-ši-ši-na šá ka-li-ši-na ma-ta-a-ti
I hold back the magick of all lands;
A-NIM u AN-TUM iš-pu-ru-in-ni
ANU and ANTU have sent me here
man-nu lu-uš-pur a-na BE-LIT-sêri
but whom should I send to BELIT-SERI?
ana pî lúkaššapi-ia u kaššapti-ia i-di-i hur-gul-li
In the mouth of the evil warlock and witch, gag!
[55] i-di-i šipat-su šá apqal ilimeš MARDUK
By the incantation of the Magician God,
MARDUK!
lil-sa-ki-ma la tap-pa-li-ši-na-a-ti
They will call upon you, but do not answer them;
liq-ba-nik-ki-ma la ta-šim-me-ši-na-a-ti
They will come before you, but do not listen to them.
lu-ul-si-ki-ma a-pu-ul-in-ni
Only should I call to you, should you answer me:
lu-qu-ba-ki-ma ši-min-ni ia-a-ti
Should I come before you, should you listen to me,
[60] ina qí-bit iq-bu-u A-NIM AN-TUM u BE-LIT-sêri

And to the covenant that ANU, ANTU and BELIT- SERI have issued!

MAQLU INCANTATION OF MARDUK.

šap-ra-ku al-lak '-ú-ra-ku a-dib-bu-ub

Where I am sent, I go. When ordered, I speak:

a-na li-it lúkaššapi-ia u kaššapti-ia ASAR-lú-du BEL a-ši-pu-ti iš-pur-an-ni

Against the evil sorcerer and sorceress, *Asariluhi* [MAR-DUK], Lord of the Incantation, has sent me.

šá šamê qu-la šá irsitimtim ši-ma-a

Take note of what is in sky and on earth!

šá nâri qu-la-ni šá na-ba-li ši-ma-a amât-su

Take note of what is in the river and the word spoken on land!

[65] šaru na-zi-qu tur-ru-uk e tal-lik

Wind, carrier of lightning, strike it down!

šá gišhatti u gišmar-te-e tur-ru-uk e tal-lak

The stick [image] is now broken, break it!

li-iz-zi-iz har-ra-an mârat ilimeš ra-butimeš

Let them stand waiting at the Gateway to the Gods

a-di a-mat lúkaššapi-ia u kaššapti-ia a-qab-bu-ú

until I speak the Word to my evil sorcerer and wicked witch.

šu'u i-pa-áš-šar immeru i-pa-áš-šar

The lamb will be freed! The sheep will be freed!

[70] a-mat-su-nu lip-pa-šir-ma a-ma-ti la ip-pa-áš-šar

Their words may be loosened, but my Word will not be.

a-mat a-qab-bu-ú a-mat-su-nu ana pân amâti-ia lâ iparrik

The Word that I speak, their words cannot withstand it!

ina qi-bit ASAR-lú-du BEL a-ši-pu-ti
By the covenant of MARDUK, the Lord of the Incantations!

INCANTATION—CONSECRATION OF IMAGES.
[*Images constructed are used in later incantations.*]
NUSKU an-nu-tum salmânimeš e-piš-ia
NUSKU, these [images] are of my evil sorcerer.
an-nu-ti salmânimeš e-piš-ti-ia
These [images] are of my wicked sorceress;
[75] salmânimeš lúkaššapi-ia u kaššapti-ia
These [images] are of my warlock and witch,
salmânimeš e-piš-ia u muš-te-piš-ti-ia
These [images] are of my enchantress,
salmânimeš sa-hir-ia u sa-hir-ti-ia
These [images] are of my stupifier,
salmânimeš ra-hi-ia u ra-hi-ti-ia
These [images] are of my bewitchment,
salmânimeš BEL ik-ki-ia u BELIT ik-ki-ia
These [images] are of my lord and lady opponent,
[80] salmânimeš BEL sir-ri-ia u BELIT sir-ri-ia
These [images] are of my lord and lady enemy.
salmânimeš BEL ri-di-ia u BELIT ri-di-ia
These [images] are of my lord and lady prosecutor.
salmânimeš BEL di-ni-ia u BELIT di-ni-ia
These [images] are of my lord and lady accuser.
salmânimeš BEL amâti-ia u BELIT amâti-ia
These [images] are of my lord and lady slanderer.
salmânimeš BEL daba-bi-ia u BELIT daba-bi-ia
These [images] are of my lord and lady defector.
[85] salmânimeš BEL egirri-ia u BELIT egirri-ia
These [images] are of my lord and lady nemesis.
salmânimeš BEL limutti-ia u BELIT limut-ti-ia

These [images] are of my lord and lady evil-doer.
NUSKU da-a-a-nu tidu-šú-nu-ti-ma ana-ku la i-du-šú-nu-ti
NUSKU, only you know them. I do not know them,
šá kiš-pu ru-hu-u ru-su-u up-šá-še-e lim-nu-ti
their trick, their magick, their evil spells,
ip-šá bar-tum a-mat li-mut-ti râmu zêru
sorceries, manipulations, evil words, love, hate,
[90] dipalaa zitarrutâa kadibbidâa kúš-hunga
lying, murdering, confounding the truth of words,
šabalbalâa su-ud pa-ni ša-ni-e tè-mu
untrusting, quick to anger, lacking wisdom,
ma-la ibšu-u-ni is-hu-ru-ni u-šá-as-hi-ru-ni
everything that they have drawn to them,
an-nu-tum šú-nu an-nu-ti salmânimeš-šu-nu
these are those things; these are their [images],
kima šu-nu la iz-za-az-zu salmânimeš-šu-nu na-šá-ku
**because the [images] cannot stand up, I lift them
toward you,**
[95] at-ta NUSKU u ANU ka-šid lim-nu u a-a-bi kušus-su-nu-ti-ma ana-ku la ah-hab-bil
**NUSKU and ANU, you who captures enemies, catch mine
before I am destroyed!**
šá salmânimeš-ia ib-nu-u bu-un-na-an-ni-ia ú-maš-ši-lu
**Those others that make my [images] and mimic
my form,**
pani-ia ú-sab-bi-tú kišâdi-ia ú-tar-ri-ru
they attack my face, they tie up my neck,
irti-ia id-i-bu esemti-ia ik-pu-pu
they hit my chest, they bend up my back.
a-hi-ia un-ni-šu ni-iš lib-bi-ia is-ba-tu
they make my arms weak and remove my strength,

[100] lib-bi ilimeš itti-ia ú-za-an-nu-ú emûqi-ia un-ni-šu
they make the Spirit of the Lord angry with me and removed my strength,
li-it a-hi-ia iš-pu-ku bir-ki-ia ik-su-ú
they stripped the strength from my arms, and my knees are plagued with pain,
man-ga lu-'-tú ú-mal-lu-in-ni
they cause me to faint,
akâlemeš kaš-šá-pu-ti ú-šá-ki-lu-in-ni
they cause me to eat accursed food,
mêmeš kaš-šá-pu-ti iš-qu-in-ni
they cause me to drink foul water,
[105] rim-ki lu-'-ti ú-ra-me-ku-in-ni
they have purified me with unclean water,
nap-šal-ti šam-me lim-nu-ti ip-šu-šu-in-ni
they have washed me in juice of unclean seeds,
ana lúmiti i-hi-ru-in-ni
they have mocked me as though I am dead,
mêmeš napištimtim-ia ina qab-rì uš-ni-lu
they have placed my spirit among the dead,
ilu šarru BELU u rubû it-ti-ia ú-za-an-nu-ú
they have made my god, king and master angry with me;
[110] at-ta GIRRA qa-mu-ú lúkaššapu u kaššaptu
GIRRA [*Fires of God*] who burns the evil warlock and witch,
mu-hal-liq rag-gi zêr lúkaššapi u kaš-šapti
Who slays the evil offpsring of the warlock and witch,
mu-ab-bit lim-nu-ti at-ta-ma
Who slays the evil-doers? It is You!
ana-ku al-si-ka ki-ma SAMAS u ANU
I call upon you like SAMAS [*Shammash*] and ANU

di-i-ni di-ni purussâ-ai purusus
Make me right, be the judge of my decision!
[115] qu-mu lúkaššapu u kaššaptu
Burn the evil sorcerer and sorceress!
a-kul ai-bi-ia a-ru-uh lim-nu-ti-ia
Be the eater of my enemies, consume all those who wish me evil!
ûm-ka iz-zu lik-šu-šu-nu-ti
May they catch your roaring flames!
ki-ma mêmeš nâdi ina ti-qi liq-tu-ú
May their lives end like sewage!
ki-ma ti-rik abnêmeš ubânâtimeš-šú-nu liq-ta-as-si-sú
May their fingers be wrecked like those of stone-masons, chewed off!
[120] ina qi-bi-ti-ka sir-ti šá lâ innakaruru
By the name of the Glorious Command
ù an-ni-ka ki-nim šá lâ innennuú
and your Everlasting Covenant!

INCANTATION—CONSECRATION OF FIRE.

NUSKU šur-bu-ú i-lit-ti da-nim
NUSKU, Mighty Offspring of ANU
tam-šil abi bu-kur EN-LIL
True [image] of your father, firstborn of ENLIL,
tar-bit apsî bi-nu-ut dBEL šamêe irsitim
Son of the Abyss, Son of the Lord of Heaven-Earth
[125] áš-ši tipâra ú-nam-mir-ka ka-a-šá
I lift the torch and illuminate you,
lúkaššapu ik-šip-an-ni kiš-pi ik-šip-an-ni ki-šip-šú
The wicked sorcerer who has cursed me, curse him with the spell [he] used on me!
kassaptutak-šip-an-ni kiš-pi tak-šip-an-ni ki-šip-ši

The wicked witch who has cursed me, curse her with the spell [she] used on me!

e-pi-šu i-pu-šá-an-ni ip-šú i-pu-šá-an-ni e-pu-su

The sorcerer who has ensnared me, ensnare him with the spell [he] used on me!

e-piš-tu te-pu-šá-an-ni ip-šú te-pu-šá-an-ni e-pu-si

The sorceress who has ensnared me, ensnare her with the spell [she] used on me!

[130] muš-te-piš-tu te-pu-šá-an-ni ip-šú te-pu-šá-an-ni e-pu-si

The enchantress who bewitched me; now bewitch her with the spell [she] used on me!

šá salmânimeš ana pi-i salmânimeš-ia ib-nu-ú

Who made [images] in my [image] and mimicked my shape;

bu-un-na-an-ni-ia ú-mašši-lu ru'ti-ia il-qu-ú šârti-ia im-lu-su

they drained my saliva, they ripped at my hair,

sissikti-ia ib-tu-qu e-ti-qu epirhi.a šêpê-ia is-bu-su

they cut hems from my robe and steak the earth where my foot falls.

GIRRA qar-du šipat-su-nu li-pa-áš-šir

GIRRA [*Fires of God*], undo their incantation!

INCANTATION—OPENING OF THE BURNINGS.

[135] anašiši ti-pa-ru salmânimeš-šú-nu a-qal-lu

I raise up the torch that I may burn the figures

šá ú-tuk-ku še-e-du ra-bi-su e-tim-mu

of the Demon, the Spirit, the Lurking Ghost,

la-maš-ti la-ba-si ah-ha-zu

the [*lamastu*], the [*labasu*], the [*ahhazu*],

lúlilu flilitu ardat lili

the [*lilu*], the [*lilitu*], the [*nightmare*],

ù mimma lim-nu mu-sab-bi-tu a-me-lu-ti
and any evil that plagues humanity:
[140] hu-la zu-ba u i-ta-at-tu-ka
dissolve, melt, drip away like wax!
qu-tur-ku-nu li-tel-li šamê
May your smoke drift ever upwards
la-'-mi-ku-nu li-bal-li dšamši
and may the Sun extinguish your coals!
lip-ru-us ha-a-a-ta-ku-nu mâr EA maš-mašu
**May he extinguish your emenations, by the son of ENKI
[who is MARDUK], Master of Magicians.**

THE MAQLU SERIES – TABLET II

INCANTATION—USING A TALCUM IMAGE.

NUSKU šur-bu-ú ma-lik ilîmeš rabû-timeš
NUSKU, Mighty Counselor of the Great Gods!
pa-qid nindabêmeš šá ka-la IGIGI
Overseer of the sacrifices of all IGIGI,
mu-kin ma-ha-zi mu-ud-di-šu parakkêmeš
Founder of cities, who reviews the Seats of Gods!
u-mu nam-ru šá qi-bit-su si-rat
Brilliant shining day, the promise of all goodness,
[5] sukkal A-NIM še-mu-ú pi-ris-ti EN-LIL
Messenger of ANU, obeying the secret of ENLIL,
še-mu-ú EN-LIL ma-li-ku ša-du-ú IGIGI
Commander ENLIL, counselor of the IGIGI,
gaš-ru ta-ha-zu šá ti-bu-šú dan-nu
Powerful in combat, whose rising is powerful,
NUSKU a-ri-ru mu-šab-riq za-ai-ri
NUSKU, brilliant shinning one who blinds his enemies,
ina ba-li-ka ul iš-šak-kan nap-ta-na ina é-kur

without you there is no meal in the E.KUR,
[10] ina ba-li-ka ilîmeš rabûtimeš ul is-si-nu qut-rin-nu
without you, the Gods do not rise to smell the
incense,
ina ba-li-ka SAMAS u ANU ul i-da-a-ni di-i-nu
without you, SAMAS and ANU do not hold court.
ha-sis šu-me-ka te-it-tir ina i-dir-ti ta-ga-mil ina pušqi
Whosoever remembers your name, you deliver [him] from
difficulty, sparing [his] miseries.
*ana-ku ardu-ka annanna apil annanna šá ilu-šú annanna
ISTAR-šú annannitumtum*
I am your servant __, son of __, whose god is __ and whose
goddess is __.
as-hur-ka eš-e-ka na-šá-a qâtâ-ai šá-pal-ka ak-mis
I turn to you, seek you out, hands raised; I throw myself at
your feet:
[15] qu-mi kaš-šá-pi ù kaš-šap-ti
Burn the evil warlock and the wicked witch,
*šá lúkaššapi-ia u kaššapti-ia ár-hiš ha-an-tiš napišta-šú-nu lib-
li-ma*
My warlock and witch, may they lose their life quickly.
ia-a-ši bul-lit-an-ni-ma nar-bi-ka lu-šá-pi dà-li-li-ka lud-lul
Spare my life so I will be forever in your debt, alive to
praise your greatness all my days!

COUNTERSPELL—USING A SALT, COPPER OR TALCUM IMAGE.

GIRRA BELu git-ma-lu gaš-ra-a-ta na-bi šum-ka
GIRRA, "You are powerful" is the meaning of your name.

[20] dnanna-ra-ta na-bi šùm-ka

NANNA, your eyes see all things.

tuš-nam-mar bitatimeš ka-la-ma

Your light brightens dark places, light of the moon over all countries.

tuš-nam-mar gi-im-ra ka-liš ma-ta-a-ti

Your light brightens all things, so I stand before you,

áš-šu at-ta ta-az-za-zu-ma

because you restore divine Justice.

ki-ma NANNA-SIN ù SAMAS ta-din-nu di-i-nu

Like NANNA-SIN & SAMAS you make things right,

[25] di-e-ni di-ni purussâ-a-a purusus

So restore the right in my life, be a judge of my decision.

a-na nûri-ka nam-ri az-ziz

To your brilliant shinning light, I come.

a-na elle-ti ti-pa-ri-ka az-ziz

To the brilliant shinning torch, I come.

BELU sissiktu-ka as-bat

Lord, I grab at the hem of your robe,

sissikat ilu-ti-ka rabi-ti as-bat

the hem of your divine robe I am grabbing.

[30] <unreadable part> -si il-ta-si eli-ia is-bat lìb-bi qaqqadi kišâdi-ia u muh-hi

[She] attacks the heart, the head, the neck and the face.

is-bat ênê-ia na-ti-la-a-ti

[She] attacks my watchful eyes,

is-bat sêpê-ia al-la-ka-a-ti

attacks my walking feet,

is-bat bir-ki-ia ib-bi-ri-e-ti

attacks my moving knees [joints],

[35] is-bat idê-ia mut-tab-bil-a-ti
attacks my strengthened arms.
e-nin-na ina ma-har ilu-ti-ka rabîtiti
Now I come before your Divine Greatness,
salmânimeš siparri it-gu-ru-ti
[I set before you] the 'crossed' copper [images]
lúkaššapi-ia u kaššapti-ia
of my evil warlock and wicked witch,
e-piš-ia u muš-te-piš-ti-ia
my sorcerer and sorceress,
[40] sa-hir-ia u sa-hir-ti-ia
my stupifier and stupifyress,
ra-hi-ia u ra-hi-ti-ia
my enchanter and enchantress,
BEL ik-ki-ia u BELIT ik-ki-ia
my lord and lady who opposes me,
BEL sir-ri-ia u BELIT sir-ri-ia
my lord and lady who is my enemy,
BEL ri-di-ia u BELIT ri-di-ia
my lord and lady who prosecutes me,
[45] BEL di-ni-ia u BELIT di-ni-ia
my lord and lady who accuses me,
BEL amâti-ia u BELIT amâti-ia
my lord and lady who slanders against me,
BEL dabâbi-ia u BELIT dabâbi-ia
my lord and lady defector,
BEL egirri-ia u BELIT egirri-ia
my lord and lady nemesis,
BEL limuttimtim-ia u BELIT limuttimtim-ia
my lord and lady evil-doers:
[50] ana lúmiti pu-qu-du-in-ni
They gave me over to the dead;
nam-ra-su kul-lu-mu-in-ni
They bound me in their ridicule,

utukku lim-nu lu-u alû lim-nu lu-u etim-mu lim-nu
to the evil [*utukku*] or evil [*alu*] or [*etimmu*],
gallû lim-nu lu-u ilu lim-nu lu-u râbisu lim-nu
the evil [*gallu*] or evil god [*ilu*] or [*rabisu*],
lamaštu lu-u labasu lu-u ahhazu
the evil [*lamastu*] or [*labasu*] or [*ahhazu*]
[55] lúlilu lu-u flilitu lu-u ardat lili
the evil [*lilu*] or [*lilitu*] or [*ardat lili*]
lu-u li-'-bu si-bit šadi
or evil fever, like the [*sibit sadi*] disease,
lu-u be-en-nu ri-hu-ut dšul-pa-è-a
or befallen with epilepsy and seizures,
lu-u AN-TA-ŠUB-BA lu-u DINGIR-HUL
or [*antasubba*] or the "Evil God",
lu-u ŠU-DINGIR-RA lu-u ŠU-IN-NIN-NA
or "Hand of God" or "Hand of Goddess,"
[60] lu-u ŠU-GIDIM-MA lu-u ŠU-UDUG
or "hand" of the Spirit of the Dead or of [*utukki*]
lu-u ŠU-NAM-LÚ-LÍL-LU lu-u la-maš-tu sihirtutú marat A-NIM
or "hand" of a human or [*lamastu*] Anu's daughter,
lu-u SAG-HUL-HA-ZA mu-kil rêš li-muttim
or [*sagulaza*], the record-keeper of debts,
lu-u di-kis šêrêmeš šim-ma-tú ri-mu-tú
or the roasting of flesh, paralysis, consumption,
lu mimma lim-nu šá šu-ma la na-bu-u
or everything bad that is without names,
[65] lu mimma e-piš li-mut-ti šá a-me-lu-ti
or anything that is baneful to human beings,
šá sab-ta-ni-ma mu-ša u ur-ra iredú-nimeš-ni
that which makes me a prisoner at night, that which chases me during the day,
ú-hat-tu-ú šêrêmeš-ia kal u-mi sab-ta-ni-ma
that which eats my flesh, seizes my body,

kal mu-si la ú-maš-šar-an-ni
which will not give me rest for a single night!
e-nin-na ina ma-har ilu-ti-ka rabîtiti
Now, I come before your Divine Greatness,
[70] ina kibri-dit ellititi a-qal-li-šú-nu-ti a-šar-rap-šú-nu-ti
I burn and incinerate them completely with sulfur.
nap-li-sa-an-ni-ma be-lum ú-suh-šú-nu-ti ina zumri-ia
Look favorably on me, tear them out of my body,
pu-šur kiš-pi-šú-nu lim-nu-ti
disintegrate their evil spell!
at-ta GIRRA be-lum a-li-ki i-di-ia
GIRRA [*fires of God*] be at my side,
bul-lit-an-ni-ma nar-bi-ka lu-šá-pi dà-li-li-ka lud-lul
Keep me alive that I may praise, adore and serve.

COUNTERSPELL—USING A COPPER OR DOUGH & SULFUR IMAGE.

GIRRA a-ri-ru bu-kur A-NIM
GIRRA [*fires of God*] born of ANU,
da-'-in di-ni-ia at-me-e pi-ris-ti at-ta-ma
who guides my hearing and judges my decision;
ik-li-e-ti tu-uš-nam-mar
you bring the darkness to light,
e-šá-a-ti dal-ha-a-ti tu-uš-te-eš-šir
you bring order to the chaos or destroyed;
[80] a-na ilimeš rabûtimeš purussâa ta-nam-din
to the Great Gods you grant resolutions,
šá la ka-a-ta ilu ma-am-man purussâa ul i-par-ra-as
but for you no God makes your decisions.
at-ta-ma na-din ur-ti ù te-e-me
It is for you to give order and directions;
e-piš lum-ni at-ta-ma ar-hiš ta-kam-mu

you alone bind the evil and the evil-doer,

lim-nu ai-bu ta-kaš-šad ar-hiš

you strike down the evil enemy with swiftness.

[85] a-na-ku annanna mar ili-šu šá ilu-šú an-nanna ISTAR-šu annannitum

I am __ , a son of his god, whose god is __ and whose goddess is __ .

ina kiš-pi lu-up-pu-ta-ku-ma ma-har-ka az-ziz

I am bewitched, this is why I have come to you!

ina pân ili u šarri na-zu-ra-ku-ma du ana mah-ri-ka

Before God and King I have turned toward you!

elî a-me-ri-ia mar-sa-ku-ma šá-pal-ka ak-mis

Unpleasant to behold, I throw myself before you!

GIRRA šur-bu-ú ilu el-lu

GIRRA – Radiant Fires of God!

[90] e-nin-na ina ma-har ilu-ti-ka rabîtiti

I come before your Divine Greatness,

salmanimeš lúkaššapi u kaššapti šá siparri e-pu-uš qa-tuk-ka

I have made two [images] of the evil warlock and wicked witch, in copper, by your hand:

ma-har-ka ú-gir-šú-nu-ti-ma ka-a-šá ap-kid-ka

In front of you I have 'crossed' them, I give them over to you.

šu-nu li-mu-tu-ma ana-ku lu-ub-lut

Cause them death that I may live!

šu-nu li-ti-ib-bi-ru-ma ana-ku lu-ši-ir

Their paths detract, but I go straight!

[95] šu-nu liq-tu-ú-ma ana-ku lu-um-id

They reach limits, but I continue to grow!

šu-nu li-ni-šu-ma ana-ku lu-ud-nin

They become weak, but I continue to be strong!

GIRRA šar-hu si-ru šá ilimeš

GIRRA, brilliant flame among the gods,

ka-šid lim-ni u ai-bi kušus-su-nu-ti-ma a-na-ku la ah-hab-bil
you seize the evil and evil-doer; seize them so I may not be destroyed,
ana-ku ardu-ka lul-ub-lut lu-uš-lim-ma ma-har-ka lu-uz-ziz
I, your servant, may remain living safe, able to stand in front of you!
[100] at-ta-ma ili-ia at-ta-ma be-li
You are my god, my lord supreme,
at-ta-ma da-ai-ni at-ta-ma ri-su-ú-a
You are my judge, my divine assistance,
at-ta-ma mu-tir-ru šá gi-mil-li-ia
You are my avenger, avenge me!

COUNTERSPELL—USING A COPPER OR BRONZE IMAGE.

GIRRA a-ri-ru mar da-nim qar-du
GIRRA [*fires of God*] raging fire born of ANU!
[105] iz-zu ahemeš-šú at-ta
Straightforward among your brethren;
šá ki-ma NANNA-SIN u SAMAS ta-da-an-nu di-i-nu
Like NANNA-SIN and SAMAS you make things right.
di-i-ni di-ni purussâ-ai purusus
Grant me justice, be the judge of my decision.
qu-mi kaš-šá-pi ù kaš-šap-ti
Burn the evil warlock and wicked witch!
GIRRA qu-mu lúkaššapi u kaššapti
GIRRA, burn the warlock and witch!
[110] GIRRA qu-li lúkaššapi u kaššapti
GIRRA, boil the warlock and witch!
GIRRA qu-mi-šú-nu-ti

GIRRA, incinerate them to nothing!
GIRRA qu-li-šú-nu-ti
GIRRA, boil them down!
GIRRA ku-šu-us-su-nu-ti
GIRRA, seize them!
GIRRA a-ru-uh-šú-nu-ti
GIRRA, devour them!
[115] GIRRA su-ta-bil-šú-nu-ti
GIRRA, remove them!
e-piš kiš-pi lim-nu-ti u ru-hi-e la tabûtimeš
They who inflict evil and the baneful spell,
šá a-na li-mut-ti ik-pu-du-ni ia-a-ši
Who think upon me with evil intention:
dan-nu ma-ak-kur-šu-nu šu-ul-qi
Let a criminal steal their possessions!
šu-bil bu-šá-šu-nu ik-ki-e-ma
Let a thief make off with their property!
[120] elî ma-na-ha-te-šu-nu hab-ba-ta šur-bi-is
Let a burglar invade their home!
GIRRA iz-zu git-ma-lu ra-šub-bu
GIRRA, wrathful, perfect and all-powerful
ina é-kur a-šar tal-lak-ti-ka tu-šap-šah-šu-nu-ti a-di sur-riš
In E.KUR, when you return, you will find peace!
ina a-mat E-A ba-ni-ka ù SAMAS an-nam-ru
By the incandation of ENKI, your progenitor and of SAMAS, I have become radiant;
apqallê šuut eri-du lik-pi-du-šú-nu-ti ana limnuttimtim
May the seven [apkallu] of ERIDU look onto them with evil intention!

COUNTERSPELL—USING A CLAY IMAGE.
GIRRA gaš-ru u-mu na-an-du-ru

GIRRA, commanding force of terrible weather!
tuš-te-eš-šir ilimeš u ma-al-ki
You lead the gods and peoples rightfully!
ta-da-a-ni di-ÉN hab-li u ha-bil-ti
You lead the trials of the oppressed peoples;
ina di-ni-ia i-ziz-za-am-ma ki-ma SAMAS qu-ra-du
be also present at my trial! Like SAMAS,
[130] di-i-ni di-ni purussâ-ai purusus
lead my trial and be judge of my decision.
qu-mi kaš-ša-pi u kaš-šap-ti
Burn the evil warlock and wicked witch!
a-kul ai-bi-ia a-ru-uh lim-nu-ti-ia
Devour my enemies, those who wish me evil!
ûm-ka iz-zu lik-šu-us-su-nu-ti NANNA-SIN
May they be caught up in your terrible weather!

COUNTERSPELL—USING A BRONZE
OR ASPHALT IMAGE.

[135] GIRRA šar-hu bu-kur da-nim
GIRRA [*raging fires of God*] born of ANU!
i-lit-ti ellitimtim šá-qu-tum dša-la-aš
Radiant ray of the Great [*salas*]!
šar-hu id-di-šu-u zik-ri ilimeš ka-ai-nu
Divine, ever-renewing, constant, Word of the Gods,
na-din nin-da-bi-e ana ilimeš IGIGI
who distributes the offerings to the gods [*IGIGI*],
šá-kin na-mir-ti a-na A-NUN-NA-KI ilimeš rabûtimeš
who gives radiance to the ANUNNAKI—the
Great Gods!
[140] iz-zu GIRRA muš-har-mit a-pi
Raging GIRRA, who destroys the pathway,
GIRRA al-la-lu-ú mu-ab-bit isemeš u ab-nemeš
GIRRA, strength to destroy wood and stone,

qa-mu-ú lim-nu-ti zêr lúkaššapi u kaš-šapti
who burns the evil seed of the warlock and witch,
mu-hal-liq rag-gi zêr lúkaššapi u kaš-šapti
**who incinerates the wicked seed of the warlock
and witch!**
ina u-mi an-ni-i ina di-ni-ia i-ziz-za-am-ma
Come to my trial this day, come raging!
[145] e-piš bar-ti te-na-na-a ku-šu-ud lim-nu
Maker of submission, who seizes all that is evil!
kima salmânimeš an-nu-ti i-hu-lu i-zu-bu u it-ta-at-tu-ku
**Like these figures drip away, melting and
dissolving away,**
lúkaššapu u kassaptuli-hu-lu li-zu-bu u lit-ta-at-tu-ku
**may the evil warlock and wicked witch drip away, melt and
dissolve.**

COUNTERSPELL—USING AN ASPHALT OR
SESAME-BUTTER IMAGE.

ki-e-eš li-bi-iš ki-di-eš
KES. LIBES. KIDES!
[150] a-ra-ab-bi-eš na-ad-ri-eš
ARABBES NADRES!
nâš ti-pa-a-ri ra-kib šá-a-ri
Who carries a torch and rides on the wind!
li-ru-un hu-un-ti-i
LIRUN HUNTI!
ka-sá-a-šu i-za-an-nun
KASAYASU IZANNUN!
ki-ma šá-ma-me el-ku-un
Rain down upon them from the heavens!
[155] ki-ma siri li-te-ru-ba-ma i-sá-a
Like a snake, bring them in, go hither!

lik-tum-ku-nu-si siptu iz-zi-tú rabîtutú šá E-A mašmaši
By the incantation of ENKI and [MARDUK]
Master of Magicians,
ù tu-kug-ga-e šá NIN-a-ha-qud-du
Rain down, you of NINAHAQUDDU,
li-la-ap-pit bu-un-na-an-ni-ku-nu
May they destroy the evil in existence!

COUNTERSPELL—USING AN ASPHALT IMAGE COVERED IN PLASTER.

[160] e-pu-šu-ni e-te-ni-ip-pu-šu-ni
They have performed magick (against me)!
ki-ma ki-i-ti ana ka-pa-li-ia
Like a ball of wool they have tried to roll me!
ki-ma hu-ha-ri ana sa-ha-pi-ia
Like a bird-clapper they have tried to catch me!
ki-ma ka-a-pi ana a-ba-ti-ia
Like a mason stone they have tried to destroy me!
ki-ma še-e-ti ana ka-ta-me-ia
Like a net they have tried to ensnare me!
[165] ki-ma pi-til-ti ana pa-ta-li-ia
Like a candlewick they have tried to snuff me out!
ki-ma pi-ti-iq-ti ana na-bal-ku-ti-ia
Like a cliffwall they have tried to climb over me!
ki-ma mêmeš mu-sa-a-ti a-sur-ra-a ana mal-li-ia
With unclean waters they have tried to fill me!
ki-ma šu-šu-rat bîti ana bâbi ana na-sa-ki-ia
Like garbage they have tried to discard of me!
ana-ku ina qi-bit MARDUK u BEL nu-bat-ti
I speak the incantation of MARDUK, Lord of the Night
[170] u ASARI-lú-du BEL a-ši-pu-ti

and MARDUK [*asariludu*], the Master of Magic[ians],
e-pi-šu u e-piš-ti
the evil sorcerer and sorceress;
ki-ma ki-i-ti a-kap-pil-šu-nu-ti
like a ball of wool, I will roll them!
ki-ma hu-ha-ri a-sa-hap-šu-nu-ti
Like a bird-clapper, I take them down!
ki-ma ka-a-pi ab-ba-šu-nu-ti
Like a mason-stone, I destroy them!
[175] ki-ma še-e-ti a-kat-tam-šu-nu-ti
Like a net, I ensnare them!
ki-ma pi-til-ti a-pat-til-šu-nu-ti
Like a candlewick, I snuff them out!
ki-ma pi-ti-iq-ti ab-ba-lak-kit-šu-nu-ti
Like a cliff-wall, I climb over them!
ki-ma mêmeš mu-sa-a-ti a-sur-ra-a ú-ma-al-la-šú-nu-ti
With unclean waters I fill them up!
ki-ma šu-šu-rat bîti ana bâbi a-na-as-sik-šú-nu-ti
Like garbage, I discard them!
[180] titalliš lil-li-ka salam lúkaššapi u kaššapti
May the [image] of the evil warlock and wicked witch be
burned to ash!

COUNTERSPELL—USING A CLAY IMAGE
COVERED IN TALCUM OR SALT.

at-ti man-nu kassaptušá ina nâri im-lu-'tita-ai
What is your name, witch? Who are you, who made an [im-
age] of me from river-clay?
ina bîti e-ti-i ú-tam-me-ru salmanimeš-ia
Who burned my [image] in her dark house?
ina qab-rì it-mi-ru mu-ú-a
Who has spilled my water over a grave?

[185] ina tub-qi-na-ti ú-laq-qí-tu hu-sa-bi-e-a
Who has stolen sprigs of my fruit trees?
ina bit lúašlaki ib-tu-qu sissikti-ia
Who has cut seams of my robe?
ina askuppati iš-bu-šu epirhi.a šêpê-ia
Who has gathered up the earth beneath my feet?
áš-pur ana bâb ka-a-ri i-šá-mu-ú-ni li-pa-a-ki
I send to the harbor where you buy salt;
áš-pur ana hi-rit ali iq-ri-su-ú-ni ti-i-ta-ki
I send to the beach where you gather clay;
[190] áš-ta-pa-rak-kim-ma a-li-ku ti-nu-ru
I send you a furnace for your operations,
GIRRA mu-un-na-ah-zu
with GIRRA [fires of God] already lit,
GIRRA id-di-šu-u nur ilimeš ka-ai-nu
GIRRA [fires of God], constant light of the gods;
NANNA-SIN ina uruki SAMAS ina larsaki
NANNA-SIN in Ur, SAMAS in Larsa,
NERGAL a-di um-ma-na-ti-šú
NERGAL waiting next to his people,
[195] ISTAR a-ga-deki a-di ku-um-mi-šá
INANNA-ISHTAR in Akkad next to her house:
a-na la-qa-at zêri lúkaššapi u kaššapti
may they seize the seed of the evil warlock and wicked witch,
ma-la ba-šu-ú
no matter how numerous they may be,
kaššapta li-du-ku-ma ana-ku lu-ub-lut
˙may they kill the witch that I may remain alive!
áš-šu la e-pu-šá-áš-šim-ma i-pu-šá
I did not bewitch her, she bewitched me!
[200] áš-šu la as-hu-ra-áš-šim-ma is-hu-ra
I did not enchant her, she enchanted me!
ši-i tak-lat ana kiš-pi šá kit-pu-du-ú-ti

She believes in the spell she designed,
ù a-na-ku a-na ez-zu GIBIL da-a-a-nu
but I put my trust in GIBIL to be my judge!
GIRRA qu-mi-ši GIRRA qu-li-ši
GIRRA, burn [her], GIRRA incinerate [her]!
GIRRA šu-ta-bil-ši
GIRRA, strike [her] down!

COUNTERSPELL—USING AN CLAY, TAMARISK AND/OR CEDAR IMAGE DUSTED IN TALCUM.

at-ti man-nu kaššaptu šá tub-ta-na-in-ni
What is your name, witch? You who unceasingly pays me visits?
a-na li-mut-ti taš-te-ni-'-in-ni
Who looks for me with baneful intentions?
a-na la ta-ab-ti ta-as-sa-na-ah-hur-in-ni
Who looks for me with malicious intent?
al-ki ul i-di bit-ki ul i-di šum-ki ul i-di šu-bat-ki ul i-di
I don't know your city, your house or your name.
[210] dšêdêmeš li-ba-'-ki
May the sedu [spirits] visit you,
utukkêmeš liš-te-'-u-ki
May the utukku [daemons] seek you out,
etimmêmeš lis-sah-ru-ú-ki
May the ghosts of the dead haunt you,
be-en-nu la ta-a-bu eli-ki lim-qut
May epilepsy seize you!
rabisêmeš li-mut-ti li-kil-lu rêš-ki
May the evil seat decapitate you!
<unreadable text>
GIBIL iz-zu la pa-du-u lìb-bi-ki lí-is-su-uh
GIBIL, furious, without pity, smite thee!
dgu-la a-zu-gal-la-tu rabitutu li-it-ki li-im-has

GULA, mighty physician, strike thee down!
GIBIL iz-zu zu-mur-ki li-ih-mut
GIBIL, furious, consume and burn your body!
[220] ellitumtum mârat da-nim šá šamê
Pure daughter of the Sky-God ANU,
šá ina kar-pat na-an-hu-za-at is-atu
who spreads herself in the Divine Vessel
libbi GIBIL qar-du sa-ma-a
bound with the hear of GIBIL, mighty hero...
<unreadable text>
[225] qu-mi ha-an-tiš šá lúkaššapi-ia u kaššapti-ia
incinerate quickly my evil warlock and wicked witch,
na-piš-ta-šú-nu lib-li-ma
uproot their existence!
ia-a-ši bul-lit-an-ni-ma nar-bi-ka lu-šá-pi
Allow me to live so that I may praise, honor and
dà-li-li-ka lud-lul
adore your name!

THE MAQLU SERIES – TABLET III

COUNTERSPELL—USING A CLAY OR WOODEN IMAGE.

[*You put the talcum on the stomach (of the image) and stuff the kidneys with wood.*]
kassaptu mut-tal-lik-tú šá sûqâ-timeš
The [witch] who (wanders) travels on the roads,
mu-tir-rib-tum šá bîtâtimeš
who invades the people's houses,
da-ai-li-tum šá bi-ri-e-ti
who walks in the alleyways,
sa-ai-di-tum šá ri-ba-a-ti

who hunts in the public district;
[5] a-na pani-šá ù arki-šá is-sa-na-ah-hur
she turns about, showing front and back,
izzazaz ina sûqi-ma ú-sah-har šêpê
she stays in place while still moving her feet,
i-na ri-bi-ti ip-ta-ra-as a-lak-tú
in the public district, she blocks the way.
šá etli damqi du-us-su i-kim
She steals the strength of the innocent man.
šá ardatu damiqtumtum i-ni-ib-šá it-bal
She steals the fruit of the innocent girl,
[10] i-na ni-kil-mi-šá ku-zu-ub-šá il-qi
and with one look, she takes away beauty,
etla ip-pa-lis-ma dûta-šu i-kim
she sees a man and takes his strength,
ardata ip-pa-lis-ma i-ni-ib-šá it-bal
she sees a girl and takes her beauty.
i-mu-ra-an-ni-ma kassaptuil-li-ka arki-ia
The witch saw me and followed,
i-na im-ti-šá ip-ta-ra-as a-lak-tú
and with her venom she has disrupted my way,
[15] i-na ru-hi-šá iš-di-hi ip-ru-us
with magick she has hindered my stride.
ú-šá-as-si ili-ia u ISTAR-ia ina zumri-ia
She takes me away from my god and my goddess.
šá kaššapti ina kul-la-ti aq-ta-ri-is tîta-šá
For the [image] of the witch I have used clay,
šá e-piš-ti-ia ab-ta-ni salam-šá
an [image] of the sorceress I have made.
áš-kun i-na lìb-bi-ki lipû ha-bil-ki
In your body I place [*talcum*], the destroyer of all.
[20] ú-sa-an-niš ina kalatimeš-ki e-ra qa-ma-ki
In your body I put wood to burn you with,
e-ra qa-ma-ki a-mat-ki lip-ru-us

the wood that burns and stops your venom!
e-li âli at-ta-pah i-šá-ti
Above the city, I kindle a fire;
ina šaplan âli at-ta-di lik-ti
beneath the city, I sprinkle a potion.
a-na bît ter-ru-ba at-ta-di i-šá-ti
Wherever you go, I set it on fire.
[25] te-pu-šim-ma GIBIL li-kul-ki
When you show yourself, GIBIL devours you!
tu-še-pi-šim-ma GIBIL lik-šu-ud-ki
When you rest yourself, GIBIL seizes you!
tak-pu-di-ma GIBIL li-duk-ki
When you move about, may GIBIL kill you!
tu-šak-pi-di-ma GIBIL lik-me-ki
When you breathe, may GIBIL burn you!
har-ra-an la ta-ri li-šá-as-bit-ki GIBIL ha-bil-ki
To the "Land of No Return" may GIBIL bring you!
[30] GIBIL ez-zu zumur-ki li-ih-mut
GIBIL, raging force, burns your existence!

COUNTERSPELL—USING AN TALCUM IMAGE COVERED IN REFUSE (GARBAGE).

-ta ši-na mârâtimeš da-nim šá šamêe
Two daughters of the Sky-God ANU,
ši-na mârâtimeš da-nim šá šamêe
Three daughters of the Sky-God ANU!
tur-ri ul-ta-nim-ma ul-tu šamêe ur-ra-da-ni
The descend from a ladder, from the sky!
e-ka-a-ma te-ba-ti-na e-ki-a-am tal-la-ka
When do you ascend? Where do you go?
[35] a-na e-pi-ši u e-piš-ti šá annanna apil annanna
The sorcerer and sorceress of __ son of __ ?
ana sahari ni-il-li-ka

We went to cast a spell,

a-na lu-uq-qu-ti šá hu-sa-bi-ši-na

We went to gather sprigs of their fruit-trees,

a-na hu-um-mu-mi šá hu-ma-ma-ti-ši-na

We went to gather up their garbage,

šá li-la-a-ti hu-lu-pa-qa a-na ša-ra-pi ni-il-li-ka

We went in the night to burn the *huluppu*-ship!

COUNTERSPELL—USING A WAX IMAGE.

[40] kassaptunir-ta-ni-tum

Sorceress. Murderess.

e-li-ni-tum nar-šin-da-tum

Nightmare. [*narsindatu*].

a-ši-ip-tum eš-še-pu-ti

[*aspitu*]. Priestess of the Magical Arts.

mušlahhatumtum a-gu-gi-il-tum

Snake-Charmer. [*agugiltu*].

qadištu naditu

Prostitute. [*naditu*].

[45] ISTAR-i-tum zêr-ma-ši-tum

ISHTAR-devotee, [*zermasitu*],

ba-ai-r-tum šá mu-ši

who captures the night,

sa-ayyu-di-tum šá kal u-mi

who hunts the whole of the day,

mu-la-'-i-tum šá šamêe

who putrefies the skies,

mu-lap-pit-tum šá irsitimtim

and touches down on earth,

[50] ka-mi-tum šá pî ilimeš

distorting the mouths of the gods,

ka-si-tum šá bir-ki ISTAR-âtimeš

binding up the knees of the goddesses,

da-ai-ik-tum šá etlêmeš
who kills the people's men,
la pa-di-tum šá dsin-nišâtimeš
who doesn't spare the women,
šá-ah-hu-ti-tum sab-bu-ri-tu
You are a destroyer – an evil woman!
[55] šá ana ip-ši-šá u ru-hi-šá la u-šar-ru man-ma
Against your sorceries and witchcraft none fight!
e-nin-na-ma e-tam-ru-ki is-sab-tu-ki
Now they see you – and they grab you,
uš-te-nu-ki uš-ta-bal-ki-tu-ki
they change you, they bring you to instability,
uš-ta-pi-lu a-mat ip-ši-ki
they have mixed up your magick word,
E-A u MARDUK id-di-nu-ki ana GIRRA qu-ra-di
ENKI and MARDUK; they cast you to GIRRA!
[60] GIRRA qu-ra-du ri-kis-ki li-ih-pi
GIRRA, may he burn your knots,
ù mimma ma-la te-pu-ši li-šam-hir-ki ka-a-ši
and every sorcery you spoke falls back on you!

COUNTERSPELL—USING AN ASPHALT IMAGE.
dit el-lu nam-ru qud-du-šu ana-ku
I am the Light! A pure river, shinning, I am!
e-pi-šu-u-a apqallu šá apsî
My sorcerer is the wise one of the deep.
e-pi-še-tu-ú-a mârâtimeš A-NIM šá šamêe
My sorceress are the daughters of ANU, the Sky-God.
[65] e-pu-šu-u-ni e-te-ni-ip-pu-šu-u-ni
They speak sorcery onto me unceasingly,
e-pu-šu-nim-ma ul ip-du-u zu-um-ri
they have bewitched and spared me nothing;

e-te-ni-pu-šu-nim-ma ul i-li-'-ú sa-ba-ti-ia
they endless work magick but cannot seize me!
a-na-ku e-pu-uš-ma pi-šu-nu as-bat
I have magick! And I catch their words in my hand!
e-te-bi-ib kima dit ina šadi-ia
I have become brilliantly shinning like the rivers in my land.
[70] e-te-lil ki-ma nam-ru ana bît purussî-ia
I have become pure as the Shinning One.
šá lúkaššapi-ia u kaššapti-ia
My evil warlock and wicked witch,
dit-ru na-bal-kat-ta-šú-nu lis-ku-nu-ma
the river, may it swallow them!
kiš-pu-šu-nu elî-šu-nu li-bal-ki-tu-ma
May their deceit come back on them,
a-na muh-hi-šu-nu u la-ni-šu-nu lil-li-ku
and fall upon them as dust on this [image]!
[75] ki-ma di-iq-me-en-ni li-is-li-mu pa-ni-šú-nu
May their burned face be blackened with ash!
li-hu-lu li-zu-bu u lit-ta-at-tu-ku
May they drip [like wax], melt away and dissolve,
u ana-ku ki-ma dit ina šadî-ia lû ellêkuku
but I, like the river, remain pure!

COUNTERSPELL—USING AN ASPHALT IMAGE NEXT TO A SULFUR IMAGE.

la-man-ni su-tu-ú e-la-mu-ú ri-da-an-ni
The SUTI-tribesmen surround me; I am chased by Elamites!
kat-man-ni a-gu-ú e-du-ú sah-panan-ni
I am surrounded by floodwater and raging storms!
[80] kassaptusu-ta-ta da-a-nu i-bit-su
The witch is of the SUTI-tribe, her attack fails!

e-le-ni-tu e-la-ma-ta li-pit-sa mu-ú-tu
The nightmare is an Elamite whose hit means death!
GIBIL tap-pi-e SAMAS i-ziz-za-am-ma
GIBIL, friend of SAMAS, come forth unto me!
ki-ma šadi ina kibri-dit i-nu-uh-hu
Like the mountain comes to rest in sulfur,
kiš-pi ru-hi-e ru-si-e šá kaššapti-ia
so may the sorceress and witches, the magick spell of my evil-doers
[85] e-li-ni-ti-ia GIBIL liq-mi
and of my nightmares, may GIBIL burn them all!
dit ellu lib-ba-šá li-ih-pi
May the 'Pure River' break her heart!
mêmeš ellûtimeš lip-šu-ra kiš-pi-šá
May the 'Pure Water' dissolve her spell,
u ana-ku ki-ma dit ina šadî-ia lu ellêkuku
and I, like the river, remain pure!

COUNTERSPELL—USING A CLAY IMAGE OR CYLINDER-SEAL.

[Write the "word"/name on a green cylinder-seal.]
at-ti nam-nu kassaptušá bašûu
What is your name, witch?
[90] a-mat limuttimtim-ia ina lib-bi-šá
In whose heart possesses the (evil spell) baneful word,
ina lišâni-šá ib-ba-nu-ú ru-hu-ú-a
on whose tongue the (evil spell) baneful magic forms,
ina šap-ti-šá ib-ba-nu-ú ru-su-ú-a
on whose lips the spell against me starts?
i-na ki-bi-is tak-bu-us izzazaz mu-ú-tum

In your footsteps stands death.
kassaptuas-bat pi-ki as-bat lišân-ki
Wicked Witch, I seize your words [tongue/mouth],
[95] as-bat ênê-ki na-ti-la-a-ti
I seize your eyes,
as-bat šêpê-ki al-la-ka-a-ti
I seize your feet,
as-bat bir-ki-ki e-bi-ri-e-ti
I seize your legs,
as-bat idê-ki mut-tab-bi-la-a-ti
I seize your right arm,
ak-ta-si i-di-ki a-na ar-ki-ki
then tie both arms behind your back!
[100] NANNA-SIN el-lam-mi-e li-qat-ta-a pagar-ki
May NANNA-SIN, twin-form, destroy your body,
a-na mi-qit mêmeš u išâti lid-di-ki-ma
cast you in a ditch of water of fire!
kassaptuki-ma si-hir kunukki an-ni-e
[Witch], like the interior of the furnace,
li-su-du li-ri-qu pa-nu-ú-ki
may your face become burnt yellow!

COUNTERSPELL—USING A CLAY IMAGE
COVERED IN ASH & SOOT.
*[Mix clumps of ash from a furnace and soot
clinging to the pots with water and pour it
over the head of your clay image.]*
at-ti e šá te-pu-ši-in-ni [ISTAR--]
You have betwitched me [my goddess]!
[105] at-ti e šá tu-še-pi-ši-in-ni ...
You have charmed me!
at-ti e šá tu-kaš-ši-pi-in-ni
You have enchanted me!

at-ti e šá tu-hap-pi-pi-in-ni
You have oppressed me!
at-ti e šá tu-sab-bi-ti-in-ni
You have seized me!
at-ti e šá tu-kan-ni-ki-in-ni
You have suffocated me!
[110] at-ti e šá tu-ab-bi-ti-in-ni
You have destroyed me!
at-ti e šá tu-ub-bi-ri-in-ni
You have tied me!
at-ti e šá tu-ka-si-in-ni
You have bound me!
at-ti e šá tu-la-'-in-ni
You have confounded me!
tap-ru-si itti-ia ili-ia u ISTAR-ia
You have kept my God and Goddess from me,
[115] tap-ru-si itti-ia še-' še-tu ahu ahattu ib-ru tap-pu u ki-na-at-tu
kept away my friend, consort, brother, sister and family, companions and servants!
a-liq-qa-kim-ma ha-ha-a šá utuni um-mi-nu šá diqâri
I scrape flakes of ash from the oven and soot from the pots,
a-mah-ha-ah a-tab-bak ana qaqqad rag-ga-ti šim-ti-ki
I mix them with water and it drips over the head of your evil [image] figure.

CONSECRATION—TWO IMAGES IN A CLAY BOAT IMAGE.

šá e-pu-šá-ni uš-te-pi-šá-an-ni
[She] Who has bewitched me? Who has enchanted me?
i-na mi-li nâri e-pu-šá-an-ni

In the river high waters, who has bewitched me?
[120] i-na mi-ti nari e-pu-šá-an-ni
In the river low waters, who has bewitched me?
a-na e-piš-ti ip-ši-ma iq-bu-ú
Who said to the sorceress, "Cast your sorcery"?
a-na sa-hir-ti suh-ri-ma iq-bu-ú
Who said to the inspired, "Make him insane"?
an-ni-tu lu-u maqurru-šá
This is her boat.
kima maqurru an-ni-tu ib-ba-lak-ki-tu
Like the boat crosses back across the waters,
[125] kis-pu-šá lib-bal-ki-tu-ma ina muh-hi-šá
so too may her spells come back and cross on
her head
u la-ni-šá lil-li-ku
and her figure [body]! So be it!
di-in-šá lis-sa-hi-ip-ma di-e-ni li-šir
May [she] be defeated while I remain victorious!

COUNTERSPELL—USING TWO IMAGES
IN A CLAY BOAT.
[*Use the boat image with two figures inside.*]
maqurri-ia a-na NANNA-SIN ú-še-piš
My boat is built by NANNA-SIN,
ina bi-rit qârnemeš-šá na-šat pi-šir-tum
between the horns stands the potion as cargo;
[130] áš-bu ina lìb-bi-šá lúkaššapu u kaššaptu
inside it, the evil warlock and wicked witch sit;
áš-bu ina lìb-bi-šá e-piš u e-piš-tú
inside it, the sorcerer and sorceress sit;
áš-bu ina lib-bi-šá sa-hi-ru u sa-hir-tú
inside it, the inspirers of insanity sit.
šá maqurri-ši-na lib-ba-ti-iq a-šá-al-šá

Come, let the the dock-rope by cut!
mar-kas-sa-ši-na lip-pa-tir-ma tar-kul-la-šá
Come, let the moor be loosened from the boat!
[135] a-na qabal tam-ti liq-qil-pu LU ...
May it be lost in the midst of the sea!
e-du-u dan-nu a-na tam-tim li-še-si-šú-nu-ti
May a strong wave pull it into the ocean!
šam-ru-ti a-gu-u e-li-šú-nu li-tel-lu-u
May the waves of the sea overpower it!
šar-šú-nu a-a i-zi-qa-am-ma a-a i-hi-ta-a-ni
May a favorable wind not blow, not be had!
ina qi-bit NUSKU u GIRRA ilimeš dini-šú-nu
By the order of NUSKU and GIRRA, the
god-judges.

COUNTERSPELL—USING A FLOUR-DOUGH IMAGE.

[140] LA-tú šá su-qa-ti am-me-ni tug-da-nar-ri-ÉN-ni
LATU, why do you pursue me in the street without ceasing?
am-me-ni na-áš-pa-tu-ki it-ta-na-lak-a-ni
Why send your messsages to my head?
kassaptu SAG.DUmeš a-ma-ti-ki
Witch, 'inhibited' is your new word!
-<unreadable text>
el-li a-na ú-ri ab-ta-ki a-<unreadable text>
I climb to the heights and see you!
[145] ú-rad a-na qaq-qa-ri-im-ma ú-sab-bi-tu
I climb down to earth and I see you!
ina kib-si-ki râbisa ú-še-šab
On your path, I set the BAN none may pass!
etim ri-da-a-ti harran-ki ú-šá-as-bit
On your path, I set the dead-spirit of persecution.
a-mah-ha-as muh-ha-ki ú-šá-an-na tè-en-ki

I strike at your head and confuse your mind,
a-dal-lah lìb-ba-ki ta-maš-ši-i šêrêmeš-ki
I bright your spirit to ruin, that you may forget your body,
[150] e-piš-tum u muš-te-piš-tum
sorcerer and sorceress of the deep!
šamûu a-na-ku ul tu-lap-pa-tin-ni
The sky, I am, and you cannot touch me.
irsitumtum a-na-ku ul tu-ra-hi-in-ni
The earth, I am, and you cannot confound me.
si-hi-il isbal-ti a-na-ku ul tu-kab-ba-si-in-ni
The thorn, I am, and you cannot crush me.
zi-qit aqrabi a-na-ku ul tu-lap-pa-tin-ni
The scorpion's sting, I am, you cannot touch me!
[155] šadúu zaq-ru a-na-ku kiš-pi-ki ru-hi-ki
The mountain peak, I am, and your sorceries and enchantment,
ru-su-ú-ki up-šá-šu-ki limnûtimeš
your spell, your evil manifestations,
la itehûmeš-ni la i-qar-ri-bu-u-ni ai-ši
cannot come close to me, you shall not pass!

CONSECRATION—USING A TALCUM IMAGE.
[The image is of a hand, made of talcum.]
rit-tu-ma rit-tu
Hand. Hand,
rit-tu dan-na-tu šá a-me-lu-ti
Hand, powerful of men,
[160] šá kîma nêši is-ba-tu a-me-lu
and like a lion, tackles the man,
kima hu-ha-ri is-hu-pu it-lu
like a sling-shot, thrusts the man out to the ground,
kima še-e-ti ú-kat-ti-mu qar-ra-du

like a net, has ensnared the strong [man],
kima šu-uš-kal-li a-šá-rid-du i-bar-ru
like a grappling, has ensnared the leader,
kima giš-par-ri ik-tu-mu dan-na
like a perfect trap, it has caught the most powerful!
[165] lúkaššapu u kassapturit-ta-ku-nu GIRRA liq-mi
The evil warlock and wicked witch, may GIRRA burn your hands,
GIRRA li-kul GIRRA liš-ti GIRRA liš-ta-bil
GIRRA, devour. GIRRA, drink. GIRRA, destroy!
GIRRA lil-sa-a elî dan-na-ti rit-te-ku-nu
GIRRA, scream out against [their] powerful hands!
šá rit-ta-ku-nu e-pu-šu zu-mur-ku-nu li-ih-mut
Your hands are betwitched now, may [GIRRA] burn the whole of your body now!
li-is-pu-uh illat-ku-nu mâr E-A mašmašu
May the son of ENKI, [MARDUK], Master of the Magicians, destroy your power!
[170] qut-ri GIRRA li-ri-ma pa-ni-ku-nu
Breath of GIRRA, blow against your face!
ki-ma ti-nu-ri ina hi-ta-ti-ku-nu
Like a furnace seeping through its defection,
ki-ma di-qa-ri ina lu-hu-um-me-ku-nu
Like a pot developing its soot,
li-is-pu-uh-ku-nu-ši GIRRA iz-zu
May the raging GIRRA consume and destroy you!
ai ithumeš-ni kiš-pi-ku-nu ru-hi-ku-nu lim-nu-ti
Your witchcraft, your evil spell, shall not come close to me!
[175] e-til-la-a kima nûnêhi.a ina mêmeš-e-a
Climb like a fish in my own water,
kîma šahi ina ru-šum-ti-ia
Like a pig in my sty,
kîma šam-maštakal ina ú-sal-li

Like a seed [*mastakal*] from my meadows,
kîma šam-sassati ina a-hi a-tap-pi
Like the grass [reed] on the riverbanks,
kîma zêr isuši ina a-hi tam-tim
Like the seed of the black tree on the shore!
[180] el-lit ISTAR mu-nam-me-rat šim-ti
**Radiant shinning ISHTAR, who brightens
the night,**
ú-su-rat balati us-su-ra-ku ana-ku
over to whose fate I have been delivered,
ina qi-bit iq-bu-ú GIRRA ra-šub-bu
By the decree of the raging GIRRA [has spoken],
ù GIRRA a-ri-ru mâr da-nim qar-du
and GIRRA the consuming, born of ANU

COUNTERSPELL—BURNING THE TALCUM IMAGE.
[Use the image of a hand made of talcum.]
rit-tum-ma rit-tum
Hand. Hand,
[185] rit-tum dan-na-tum šá a-me-lu-ti
Hand, powerful of men,
kassaptuáš-šú pi-i-ki da-ab-bi-bu
Witch, because of your strong slander [mouth]
áš-šú dan-na-ti rit-ta-ki
because of your powerful [hand],
álu a-ma-tum áš-šak-ki
I have brought you the Word from the city,
bitu a-ma-tum ú-ba-a-ki
**from the [secret] house, I seek the [secret] Word
for you.**
[190] lúkaššapu u kassaptue-piš u e-piš-tú
**Evil warlock and wicked witch; sorcerer and
sorceress,**

bi-il rit-ta-ku-nu-ma ana išâti lud-di
**I pull down your lifted hand and cast it into
the fire!**

THE MAQLU SERIES – TABLET IV

BANISHING RITUAL—USING TWO FIGURES
& A REED CROSS.

*[Two reed pipes are filled with blood and excrement,
lay them in a cross pattern in the middle of your
circle. Make two figures of talcum and two figures
of wax. Place these at the four points of the cross.]*

biš-li biš-li qi-di-e qi-di-e
Boil, boil, burn, burn!
rag-gu u si-e-nu e te-ru-ub at-lak
Discord and evil, do not enter, keep away!
at-ta man-nu mâr man-ni at-ti man-nu mârat man-ni
Who are you? Born of who? Whose son? Whose daughter?
šá áš-ba-tu-nu-ma ip-še-ku-nu up-šá-še-ku-nu
You who sit [t]here and plot your sorcery
[5] te-te-ni-ip-pu-šá-ni ia-a-ši
against me!
lip-šur E-A mašmašu
May ENKI the Magician
lis-bal-kit kiš-pi-ku-nu
undo and reverse your spells!
ASARI-lú-du mašmaš ilimeš mâr E-A apqallu
**MARDUK [*asariludu*], Magician of the Gods, son of ENKI,
wise father!**
a-kas-si-ku-nu-ši a-kam-mi-ku-nu-ši a-nam-din-ku-nu-ši
I bind you! I tie you up! I give you over

[10] a-na GIRRA qa-mi-e qa-li-i ka-si-i
to GIRRA, burning, incinerating, consuming,
ka-ši-du šá kaššapâtimeš
overpowering and seizing the sorcer[ess]!
GIRRA qa-mu-ú li-tal-lal i-da-ai
GIRRA, incinerating power, give strength to my arms!
ip-šú bar-tu a-mat limuttim râmu zêru
Magick. Revolt. Baneful. Love. Hate.
dipalâa zitarrutâa kadibbidâ KUŠ.HUNGA
Chaos. Murder. Deceit [disease of the mouth].
[15] šabalbalâa su-ud pa-ni u šá-ni-e tè-e-mu
Tearing from the insides. A face turned to insanity.
te-pu-šá-ni tu-še-pi-šá-ni GIRRA lip-šur
**What you have done, what you have made others do for
you, may GIRRA reverse it!**
*a-na lúpagri ta-hi-ra-in-ni te-pu-šá-ni tu-še-pi-šá-ni GIRRA
lip-šur*
You have marked me for dead, may GIRRA undo this!
*a-na gul-gul-la-ti tap-qí-da-in-ni te-pu-šá-ni tu-še-pi-šá-ni
GIRRA lipšur*
**You have turned me over to the dead, may GIRRA undo
this!**
*a-na etim kim-ti-ia tap-qí-da-in-ni te-pu-šá-ni tu-še-pi-šá-ni
GIRRA lipšur*
**You have delivered me to the spirits of the dead, may
GIRRA undo this!**
*[20] a-na etim a-hi-i tap-qí-da-in-ni te-pu-šá-ni tu-še-pi-šá-ni
GIRRA lip-šur*
**You have delivered me to the spirits of the unknown dead,
may GIRRA undo this!**
*a-na etimmi mur-tappi-du šá pa-qí-da la i-šu-u te-pu-šá-ni tu-
še-pi-šá-ni-GIRRA lip-šur*

You have given me to a wandering spirit, may GIRRA undo this!

a-na etim har-bi na-du-ti tap-qí-da-in-ni te-pu-šá-ni tu-še-pi-šá-ni-GIRRA lip-šur

You have turned me over to the ghost of ruins, may GIRRA undo this!

a-na sêri ki-di u na-me-e tap-qí-da-in-ni te-pu-šá-ni tu-še-pi-šá-ni-GIRRA lip-šur

You have sent me into open desert to rot, may GIRRA undo this!

a-na dûri ù sa-me-ti tap-qí-da-in-ni te-pu-šá-ni tu-še-pi-šá-ni GIRRA lip-šur

You have pressed me up against the [inner and outer] walls, may GIRRA undo this!

[25] a-na dbe-lit sêri u ba-ma-a-ti tap-qí-da-in-ni te-pu-šá-ni tu-še-pi-šáni-GIRRA lip-šur

You have turned me over to the Mistress of the Mountains, may GIRRA undo this!

a-na utûn la-ab-ti tinûri kinûni KI.UT.BA ù nap-pa-ha-ti tap-qí-da-in-ni-te-pu-šá-ni tu-še-pi-šá-ni GIRRA lip-šur

You have delivered me into a furnace, on the stove-top, into pails of hot embers and coals, may GIRRA undo this!

salmânimeš-ia a-na lúpagri tap-qí-da te-pu-šá-ni tu-še-pi-šá-ni GIRRA lip-šur

You have given [images] of me to the dead, may GIRRA undo this!

salmânimeš-ia a-na lúpagri ta-hi-ra te-pu-šá-ni tu-še-pi-šá-ni GIRRA lip-šur

You have made [images] of me among the dead, may GIRRA undo this!

salmânimeš-ia it-ti lúpagri tuš-ni-il-la te-pu-šá-ni tu-še-pi-šá-ni GIRRA lip-šur

You have placed [images] of me next to the dead, may
GIRRA undo this!

*[30] salmânimeš-ia ina sûn lúpagri tuš-ni-il-la te-pu-šá-ni tu-
še-pi-šá-ni-GIRRA lip-šur*

You have placed [images] of me into the hands of the dead,
may GIRRA undo this!

*salmânimeš-ia ina qimah lúpagri taq-bi-ra te-pu-šá-ni tu-še-
pi-šá-ni-GIRRA lip-šur*

You have buried [images] of me in the grave of the dead,
may GIRRA undo this!

*salmânimeš-ia a-na gul-gul-la-ti tap-qí-da te-pu-šá-ni tu-še-pi-
šá-ni-GIRRA lip-šur*

You have turned [images] of me over to the dead, may
GIRRA undo this!

*salmânimeš-ia ina igâri tap-ha-a te-pu-šá-ni tu-še-pi-šá-ni
GIRRA lipšur*

You have locked away [images] of me in the wall-safe, may
GIRRA undo this!

*salmânimeš-ia ina asquppati tuš-ni-il-la te-pu-šá-ni tu-še-pi-
šá-ni-GIRRA lip-šur*

You have placed [images] of me at the baneful threshold,
may GIRRA undo this!

*[35] salmânimeš-ia ina bi-' šá dûri tap-ha-a te-pu-šá-ni tu-še-
pi-šá-ni-GIRRA lip-šur*

You have locked up [images] of me at the baneful entrance,
may GIRRA undo this!

*salmânimeš-ia ina ti-tur-ri taq-bi-ra-ma um-ma-nu ú-kab-bí-su
te-pu-šáni tu-še-pi-šá-ni GIRRA lip-šur*

You have embedded [images] of me on a bridge, causing
others to step on me, may GIRRA undo this!

*salmânimeš-ia ina bu-ri iqi šá lúašlaki bûra tap-ta-a taq-bi-ra
te-pu-šá-ni-tu-še-pi-šá-ni GIRRA lip-šur*

You have embedded [images] of me in the wash-house drains, may GIRRA undo this!

salmânimeš-ia ina iqi šá lúlâkuribbi bûra tap-ta-a taq-bi-ra te-pu-šá-ni-tu-še-pi-šá-ni GIRRA lip-šur

You have buried [images] of me in the gardener's [ditch], may GIRRA undo this!

salmânimeš-ia lu-u šá isbîni lu-u šá iserini lu-u šá lipî

[You have made] ...images of me from wood and salt,

[40] lu-u šá ISKUR lu-u šá kuspi

from wax, from seed,

lu-u šá itti lu-u šá titi lu-u šá liši

from asphalt, from clay, from dough;

salmânimeš sir-ri-ia pa-ni-ia u la-ni-ia te-pu-šâ-ma

images, likenesses of my face and form you mold

kalba tu-šá-ki-la šahâ tu-šá-ki-la

then give to a dog and a pig to eat,

issuru tu-šá-ki-la ana nâri taddâa

given to the birds of the sky who drop them in the river;

[45] salmânimeš-ia a-na la-maš-ti mârat da-nim

[given]...images of me to LAMASTU, daughter of ANU,

tap-qí-da te-pu-šá-ni tu-še-pi-šá-ni GIRRA lip-šur

what you have given to do, what others have done for you, may GIRRA undo this!

salmânimeš-ia a-na GIRRA tap-qí-da te-pu-šá-ni tu-še-pi-šá-ni GIRRA lip-šur

...images of me given to GIRRA, you have done this, may GIRRA undo this!

mêmeš-ia it-ti lúpagri tuš-ni-il-la te-pu-šá-ni tu-še-pi-šá-ni GIRRA lipšur

You have poured my [water] in with the dead, may GIRRA undo this!

mêmeš-ia ina sûn lúpagri tuš-ni-il-la te-pu-šá-ni tu-še-pi-šá-ni
GIRRA lip-šur

**You have poured my [water] in the lap of the dead, may
GIRRA undo this!**

[50] mêmeš-ia ina qimah l;úpagri taq-bi-ra te-pu-šá-ni tu-še-
pi-šá-ni-GIRRA lip-šur

**You have poured my [water] into the grave of the dead,
may GIRRA undo this!**

ina-tim mêmeš-ia taq-bi-ra te-pu-šá-ni tu-še-pi-šá-ni GIRRA
lip-šur

**You have poured my [water] in the body of the dead, may
GIRRA undo this!**

ina-tim mêmeš-ia taq-bi-ra te-pu-šá-ni tu-še-pi-šá-ni GIRRA
lip-šur

**You have poured my [water] in the body of the dead, may
GIRRA undo this!**

ina-me mêmeš-ia tah-ba-a te-pu-šá-ni tu-še-pi-šá-ni GIRRA
lip-šur

**You have siphoned the [water] from my body, may GIRRA
undo this!**

mêmeš-ia ana Gilgameš ta-ad-di-na te-pu-šá-ni tu-še-pi-šá-ni
GIRRA lip-šur

**To GILGAMESH you gave my water, may GIRRA undo
this!**

[55] <unreadable text> li-e ta-hi-ra-in-ni te-pu-šá-ni tu-še-pi-
šá-ni-GIRRA lip-šur

**You have lost my waters to the ditch, may GIRRA undo
this!**

zikurudâa a-na pa-ni NANNA-SIN te-pu-šá-ni tu-še-pi-šá-ni
GIRRA lip-šur

**You have slit my throat before NANNA-SIN, may GIRRA
undo this!**

zikurudâa a-na pa-ni d-šul-pa-è-a te-pu-šá-ni tu-še-pi-šá-ni
GIRRA lipšur

You have slit my throat before SHUL-PA-EA, may GIRRA undo this!

zikurudâa a-na pa-ni MULU-KA-DU-A

You have slit my throat in the starlight of CYGNUS and LACERTA,

zikurudâa <unreadable text> te-pu-šá-ni tu-še-pi-šá-ni GIRRA lip-šur

You have slit my throat... may GIRRA undo this!

<unreadable text>

ina pân -zi u bâb bîti ma-

In front of the entrance gate of the house,

[65] ina pân ib-ri tap-pi u ki-na-at-ti KI.MINA

In front of friends, companions and servants [of the house],

ina pân abi u ummi ahi u ahati mâri u mârti KI.MINA

In front of parents and siblings [of the house],

ina pân bîti u bâbi ardi u amti sih-ri u ra-bi šá bîti KI.MINA

In front of the house and gate, servants, both small and large [of the house],

elî a-me-ri-ia tu-šam-ri-si-in-ni ...

You made me ugly to all those who behold me.

ak-ta-mi-ku-nu-ši ak-ta-si-ku-nu-ši at-ta-din-ku-nu-ši

I have bound you, tied you up and delivered you over

[70] ana GIRRA qa-mi-i qa-li-i ka-si-i

to GIRRA, who burns, incinerates, binds up

ka-ši-du šá kaššapâtimeš

and seizes the sorceress.

GIRRA qa-mu-ú li-pat-tir rik-si-ku-nu

GIRRA, burn away your knots, undo your

li-pa-áš-šir kiš-pi-ku-nu li-na-as si-ir-qi-ku-nu

enchantments and untie your ropes,

ina qí-bit MARDUK mâr E-A apqalli

by the decree of MARDUK, son of ENKI, the Wise Father
of Magicians,
[75] u GIRRA a-ri-ru ap-qal mâr da-nim qar-du
and GIRRA, praised and wise – born of ANU!

COUNTERSPELL—USING A WOODEN IMAGE.
[Make an image using three branches of wood.]
at-ti man-nu kassaptušá zitarrutâa êpušaša
Who are you, (whoever you are) sorcer[ess]? Who has committed the murder?
lu-u ib-ru lu-u tap-pu-u
Whether companion or neighbor,
lu-u ahu lu-u it-ba-ru
whether family or friend,
lu-u ú-ba-ra lu-u mâr âli
whether foreigner or native,
[80] lu-u mu-du-u lu-u la mûdû
whether known or unknown
lu-u lúkaššapu lu-u kaššaptu
whether sorcerer or sorceress,
lu-u zikaru lu-u sinništu lu-ú hab-lu lu-ú ha-bil-ti
whether man or woman, murderer or murderess,
lu-u lúkur-gar-ru-u lu-u sah-hi-ru
whether *kugarru*-priest or *sahhiru*-priestess,
lu-u ... lu-u nar-šin-du-u lu-u muš-lahhêe
whether... or a *narsindu* or snake-charmer,
[85] lu-u a-gu-gi-lu-u lišanu nukur-tum šá ina mâti ibašši
whether an *agugilu* or an foreign traveller...

CONSECRATION—PREPARING IMAGES.
[105] i-pu-šá-ni i-te-ni-ip-pu-šá-ni

It hexes. It vexes, unceasingly.
gu-ti-e-ti e-la-ma-a-ti
The CUTHITES, the ELAMITES,
ma-rat ha-ni-gal-bat-a-ti
the daughters of the *hanigalbatians*,
6 ina mâti i-rak-ka-sa-a-ni rik-si
the six on dry earth bind knots,
6 riksi-ši-na 7 pit-ru-ú-a
six are their knots, seven is my untying.
[110] šá mûša ip-pu-sa-nim-ma
What they tie in the night,
šá kal u-mu a-pa-áš-šar-ši-na-ti
I untie in the day.
šá kal u-mu ip-pu-šá-nim-ma
What they tie in daylight,
šá mûša a-pa-áš-šar-ši-na-ti
I untie in the nighttime.
a-šak-kan-ši-na-a-ti ana pi-i GIRRA qa-mi-i
I turn them over to the burning, GIRRA,
[115] qa-li-i ka-si-i ka-ši-du
incinerating, binding and seizing
šá kaššapatimeš
the sorcer[esses]!

MAQLU INCANTATION—BURNING THE IMAGES.
ru-'ú-a kaš-šá-pat ana-ku pa-ši-ra-ak
My anathema is a witch! I am released!
kassaptukas-šá-pat ana-ku pa-ši-ra-ak
The witch is a wicked witch, I am released!
kassaptu e-la-ma-a-ti ana-ku pa-ši-ra-ak
The witch is an ELAMITE, I am released!
[120] kassaptu qu-ta-a-ti ana-ku pa-ši-ra-ak
The witch is a CUTHITE, I am released!

kassaptu su-ta-a-ti ana-ku pa-ši-ra-ak
The witch is of the SUTI-tribes, I am released!
kassaptu lul-lu-ba-a-ti ana-ku pa-ši-ra-ak
The witch is a *lulluban*, I am released!
kassaptu ha-bi-gal-ba-at ana-ku pa-ši-ra-ak
The witch is a *hanigalbatan*, I am released!
kassaptu a-gu-gi-lat ana-ku pa-ši-ra-ak
The witch is an *agugiltu*, I am released!
[125] kassaptu nar-šin-da-at ana-ku pa-ši-ra-ak
The witch is an *narsindatu*, I am released!
kassaptu mušlahhat ana-ku pa-ši-ra-ak
The witch is a snake-charmer, I am released!
kassaptueš-še-ba-a-ti ana-ku pa-ši-ra-ak
The witch is a priestess of magick, I am released!
kassaptuqur-qur-ra-a-ti ana-ku pa-ši-ra-ak
The witch is a metallurgist, I am released!
kassaptuši-i râbis bâbi-ia ana-ku pa-ši-ra-ak
The witch is a spoke on my gate, I am released!
[130] kassaptumârat âli-ia ana-ku pa-ši-ra-ak
The witch is a neighbor of mine, I am released!
áš-pur a-na e-rib šamši salmânimeš-si-na il-qu-tu-ú-ni
**I have gathered her [images] and sent them to
the west.**
šá u kaššapâtimeš salmânimeš-ši-na
The figures of the seven and the seven witches
ana GIRRA ap-qid
to GIRRA, I deliver.
ana ú-tu-ni a-lik-ti a-šar-rap-ši-na-ti
In a portable kiln I have burned them.
[135] GIBIL qu-mi lúkaššapi u kaššapti
GIBIL, burn the evil warlock and wicked witch!
GIBIL qu-li lúkaššapi u kaššapti
GIBIL, incinerate my warlock and witch!
GIBIL qu-mi-ši-na-a-ti

GIBIL, burn them completely!
GIBIL qu-li-ši-na-a-ti
GIBIL, incinerate them completely!
GIBIL kušus-si-na-a-ti
GIBIL, seize the whole of their being!
[140] GIBIL a-ru-uh-ši-na-a-ti
GIBIL, devour them completely!
GIBIL šu-ta-bil-si-na-a-ti
GIBIL, remove them away from here!
ez-zu GIBIL li-ni-ih-ka-na-ši
Roaring GIBIL, please calm down!
GIBIL lu-li-mu... li-ki-na-ši
GIBIL, [save me and] calm yourself!
lúkaššapu u kassaptue-piš u e-piš-tum
The sorcerer and sorceress, the enchanter and enchantress,
[145] šu-nu lu-u ... -kam-ma
may they truly [burn out completely]!
ana-ku mêmeš mîli-ma
though I let loose the floodwater
lu-u-ba-'-ši-na-a-ti
to shower down upon them!

THE MAQLU SERIES – TABLET V

BANISHING—USING A THYME & SESAME IMAGE.
e-piš-ti ù muš-te-piš-ti
My enchanter and my enchantress
áš-bat ina silli a-ma-ri ša libitti
sit in the shade of a stoop made of clay bricks.
áš-bat-ma ip-ši-ia ip-pu-šá i-ban-na-a salmânimeš-ia
[She] sits doing tricks, fashioning [images] of me.
a-šap-pa-rak-kim-ma šamhašutu u SAMAS-šammu

I send you thyme and sesame [literally '*sunflower*'].
[5] ú-sap-pa-ah kiš-pi-ki ú-tar amâtimeš-ki ana pî-ki
**Your sorcery is anathema to me, your words fall back into
your mouth!**
ip-ši te-pu-ši lu-u šá at-tu-ki
The tricks you "turn" now turn against you!
salmânimeš tab-ni-i lu-u šá tè-me-ki
The [images] you made of me, may they now resemble you!
mêmeš tah-bi-i lu-u šá ra-ma-ni-ki
The waters [of mine] you siphoned are your own!
ši-pat-ki ai iq-ri-ba amâtmeš-ki ai ik-šu-da-in-ni
**Your magick spell does not come close to me, your Word
cannot reach where I [stand]!**
[10] ina qí-bit E-A SAMAS u MARDUK u rubâti BELIT ilê
**By the incantation of ENKI, SHAMMASH and MARDUK
[and among them] the Great Lady of
the Gods [BELIT]!**

INCANTATION—RITE OF PROTECTION.
man-nu pû ip-til utteta ú-qas-sir
Who has tried to [commit the unthinkable]?
ana šamêe kiš-pi ana irsitimtim bar-ta êpušuš
**Who has ever bewitched Heaven or performed magick
against the Earth?**
ana šamirri ilimeš rabûtimeš ip-šá bar-ta
**Against the IRRI [*erra, NERGAL*], the Great Gods, who
has ever cast magick [upon these],**
amât limuttimtim man-nu ú-qar-rib
or spoken evil words against them?
[15] ki-ma pû la ip-pat-til uttatu la uk-ta-as-sa-ru
Just as the unthinkable cannot be done, neither can

ana šamêe kiš-pi ana irsitimtim bar-tu la in-ni-ip-pu-šú
magick be done against Heaven or Earth.
ana mârat ilimeš rabûtimeš
[And so as] the daughter of the Great Gods;
ip-šá bar-tum amat limuttimtim lâ itehu lâ i-qar-ru-bu
magick, sorcery, baneful spells do not come close;
ip-šá bar-tum amât limuttimtim lâ iteha
[so too should] magick, sorcery, baneful spells not
[20] lâ i-qar-ru-ba ia-a-ši
come close to me!

INCANTATION—INVOCATION TO THE GODS.
[Make libations of water and altar offerings.]
u-un-na-nu du-un-na-nu pârisis pu-ru-us-si-e-ni
The UNNANU [ANUNNA], you who is fated our decisions,
i-na ma-har NUSKU u GIRRA šu-bil-te šak-na-at
In front of NUSKU and GIRRA my [image] is placed.
al-ki na-bal-kàt-tum šu-um-ri na-bal-kàt-tum
Come forth and attack! Rage on! Avenge me!
Attack!
i-na na-sa-ah šêpê šá lúkaššapi-ia
When you tear off the feet of my sorcerer
[25] u kaššapti-ia šêpê-ki šuk-ni
and my sorceress, stamp your own feet down.
lillu li-bi-il-ma kassaptuana da-ai-ni-šá
May the sorcer[ess] be dragged before the Judge!
daianu-šá kîma nêši li-sa-a elî-šá
May [her] judge roar like a lion [at her]!
lim-has lêt-sa li-tir amât-sa ana pî-šá

May he strike her face and cause her words to turn back into her mouth!

e-piš-ti ù muš-te-piš-ti

Of the sorceress and 'greater' sorceress,

[30] ki-ma šamnini li-nu-šú kiš-pu-šá

Like mint, may her magick sting her!

ki-ma šamazupiri li-sap-pi-ru-ši kiš-pu-šá

Like saffron, may her magick scratch at her!

ki-ma šamsahli li-is-hu-lu-ši kiš-pu-šá

Like mustard, may her magick penetrate her!

ki-ma šam-KUR.ZI.SAR li-sa-am-mu-si kiš-pu-šá

Like the weed [*kurzisar*], may her magick bind her up!

ki-ma šamkasi li-ik-su-ši kiš-pu-šá

Like cassia, may her magick tie [them] up!

[35] ki-ma šamhašûti li-haš-šu-ši kiš-pu-šá

Like thyme, may her magick bind them up!

ki-ma kit-mi li-ik-tu-mu-ši kiš-pu-šá

Like alum, may her magick cover them up!

ki-ma šamirri li-ru-ru-ši kiš-pu-šá

Like pumpkin-vine, may her magick strangle them up!

ki-ma šamnuhurti lit-tah-hi-ra šapâtimeš-šá

Like *asafoetida*, may [their] lips swell up!

e-piš-ti ù muš-te-piš-ti

Of the sorceress and the 'greater' sorceress,

[40] lib-bal-kit-si sûqu ù su-lu-ú

may the street and pathway give out around them!

lib-bal-kit-si ib-ra-tum ù ni-me-di-šá

May the room and chair give out beneath them!

lib-bal-ki-tu-ši-ma ilimeš šá sêri u âli

May the God of the desert and city fall upon them!

kassaptukima kalbi ina hatti kima an-du-hal-lat ina kir-ban-ni

May someone chase the sorceress about like a dog with a stick or like a serpent on the earth.

ki-ma kib-si immeri li-sa-am-me-ku-ši-ma li-ti-qu-ši

[like a] chase through a sheep-path, pass over them!

[45] ki-ma qur-sin-ni imêri ina sûqi e-te-qu lik-kil-me-ši

[like a] donkey's feet when crossing the street, may someone look upon them.

e-piš-ti ù muš-te-piš-ti

Of the sorceress and 'greater' sorceress,

ina bi-rit kalbêmeš li-su-ru ku-lu-lu-šá

may their crowns fall among dogs,

ina bi-rit ku-lu-lu-šá li-su-ru kalbêmeš

may dogs dance about with their headbands!

e-li-šá qul-mu-ú li-su-ru

And may the axe dance down upon them!

[50] ki-ma piqan sabiti qu-tur-šá li-ib-li

[like a] gazelle having a bowel-movement, may their breath be taken away!

BANISHING—USING AN IMAGE OF CHICORY.

[Made of chicory, thyme and granules of grain.]

at-ti man-nu kassaptušá tetenîpu-šášá 3 arhêmeš 10 u-me mišil u-me

What is your name sorcer[ess], who has worked your spell unceasingly for 3 months plus 10 and a half days?

ana-ku a-na-áš-šá-kim-ma riqqukukru ta-nat šadî

I raise up the pride of the mountains,

šamhašûtu ti-'-ut ma-a-ti

thyme and the prepared foods of the earth,

pitiltu pitiltu šá qašdatimeš terinnatu terinnatu šá še-am ma-la-ti acorns and pinecones, that which is full of seed.

[55] an-nu-ú šá lúkaššapi-ia u kaššapti-ia hi-pa-a ri-kiš-šu-un

Yes, my sorcerer and sorceress; I know thee; Come, break their knots,

tir-ra kiš-pu-šá ana me-hi-e amâtimeš-šá ana šá-a-ri

turn their spells into storm, their words to wind!

li-in-na-áš-pu kiš-pu-šá kîma pû liq-qal-pu kîma šûmi

May their deceit be blown away as dust, peeled away like layers of garlic [onion],

liš-šá-ah-tu kima suluppi lip-pa-áš-ru kima pitilti

beaten to a pulp like date-fruit and scattered like acorns [seeds]!

ina qí-bit ISTAR DUMU-ZI NA-NA-A be-lit ra-a-mi

By the decree of ISHTAR, TAMMUZ, NANA(Y)A, the Queen of Divine Love,

[60] ù dka-ni-sur-ra be-lit kaššapâtimeš

and of *kanisurra*, the Mistress of Sorceresses!

INCANTATION—CURSING THE EVIL IMAGES.

zêru šá te-pu-šá-ni tu-še-pi-šá-ni ana muh-hi-ku-nu

The hate conjured in your magick, you conjure it against yourself.

zitarrutâa šá te-pu-šá-ni tu-še-pi-šá-ni ana muh-hi-ku-nu; dip-alâa-šá te-pu-šá-ni tu-še-pi-šá-ni ana muh-hi-ku-nu kadibbidâa šá te-pu-šá-ni tu-še-pi-šá-ni-ana muh-hi-ku-nu

The murder you have conjured, you have conjured against yourself; the chaos you have conjured, you have conjured against yourself; the disease you have conjured, you have conjured against yourself;

KUS.HUNGA šá te-pu-šá-ni tu-še-pi-šá-ni ana muh-hi-ku-nu dububbâ šá te-pu-šá-ni tu-še-pi-šá-ni ana muh-hi-ku-nu

The *kushunga* you have conjured, you have conjured
against yourself; the calamity you have conjured, you have
conjured against yourself!

*utukku limnu tu-šá-as-bi-ta-in-ni utukku limnu li-is-bat-ku-nu-
ši*

The evil *utukku* daemon that you allowed to seize me; may
the evil *utukku* seize you!

[65] alû limnu tu-šá-as-bi-ta-in-ni alû limnu li-is-bat-ku-nu-ši

The evil *alu* daemon that you allowed to seize me; may the
evil *alu* seize you!

*etimmu limnu tu-šá-as-bi-ta-in-ni etimmu limnu li-is-bat-ku-
nu-ši*

The evil spirit that you allowed to seize me; may the evil
spirit seize you!

gallû limnu tu-šá-as-bi-ta-in-ni gallû limnu li-is-bat-ku-nu-ši

The evil *gallu* spirit that you allowed to seize me; may the
evil *gallu* spirit seize you!

ilu limnu tu-šá-as-bi-ta-in-ni ilu limnu li-is-bat-ku-nu-ši

The evil god that you allowed to seize me; may the evil god
seize you!

râbisu limnu tu-šá-as-bi-ta-in-ni râbisu limnu li-is-bat-ku-nu-ši

The evil *rabisu* watcher that you allowed to seize me; may
the evil *rabisu* seize you!

*[70] lamaštu labasu ahhazu tu-šá-as-bi-ta-in-ni lamaštu la-
basu ah hazu-li-is-bat-ku-nu-ši*

Lamastu, Labasu, those you allowed to seize me, may **Lamastu** and **Labasu** seize you!

*lúlilû flilitu ardat lili tu-šá-as-bi-ta-in-ni lúlilû flilitu ardat lili
li-is- -bat-ku-nu-ši*

250

**Lilu, Lilitu, those nightmares you allowed to seize me, may
Lilu, Lilitu and those nightmares seize you!**
ina ni-ši u ma-mit tu-qat-ta-in-ni ina ni-ši u ma-mit pa-gar-ku-nu liq-ti
**You seek to destroy me by covenants and magick words,
may your life end by covenants and magick words.**
uz-zi ili šarri BELI u rubî ia-a-ši taš-ku-na-ni
The wrath of God, King and judges you have suffered me,
uz-zi ili šarri BELI u rubî a-na ka-a-šu-nu liš-šak-nak-ku-nu-ši
**may the wrath of God, King and judges cause you suffer-
ing!**
[75] a-šu-uš-tu a-ru-ur-tu hu-us qis lìb-bi gi-lit-tú
**Pain. Famine. Breaking of the body. Uncontrolled trem-
bling;**
pi-rit-ti a-dir-ti ia-a-ši taš-ku-na-ni
Fear and depression – all these you have planned for me;
a-šu-uš-tu a-ru-ur-tu hu-us qis lìb-bi gi-lit-tú
May pain, famine, body-breaking, uncontrolled trembling,
pi-rit-ti a-dir-tu ana ka-a-šú-nu liš-šak-nak-ku-nu-ši
fear and depression – and all such be planned for you!
aq-mu-ku-nu-ši ina kibrit ellititi u tâbat amurri
**I have burned you with pure sulfur and salt [from the
west];**
[80] al-qut qu-tur-ku-nu ik-kib šamêe
I have siphoned away your breath to paint the sky;
ip-še-te-ku-nu i-tu-ra-ni-ku-nu-ši
Your plans for me have turned against you!

INCANTATION—DEFAMING THE EVIL IMAGES.

at-ti man-nu kassaptušá kîma šûti ik-ki-mu ûmi 15 kam
Whoever you are, my sorcer[ess], you who blow like the south-wind on the 15ᵗʰ day,

ti-il-ti u-me im-ba-ru šá-na-at na-al-ši
You, whose storm-cloud has gathered for 9 days, whose rain-showers have fallen for a year,

urpata iq-su-ra-am-ma iz-zi-za ia-a-ši
You, who has conjured clouds to stand over me:

[85] a-te-ba-ak-kim-ma ki-ma gal-la-ab šamê šâriltânu
I rise up to fight you, like the Shredder of the Heavens, the north-wind!

ú-sap-pa-ah ur-pa-ta-ki ú-hal-laq ûm-ki
I scatter your clouds to the wind and destroy your storms!

ú-sap-pa-ah kiš-pi-ki ša tak-ki-mi mu-ša u ur-ra
I scatter the witchcraft you brought unceasingly against me both night and day,

ù na-áš-pa-rat zitarruti šá tal-tap-pa-ri ia-a-ši
and the accessories [emissaries] of your evil that you unceasingly sent to fight me!

<unreadable text>

INCANTATION—PROTECTION OF THE GODS.

[*Spoken before an image of your god and goddess.*]

e-piš-ú-a e-piš-tu-u-a
Evil warlock. Wicked witch.

kaš-šá-pu-u-a kaš-šap-tu-u-a
Evil sorcerer and sorceress.

[120] šá ik-pu-du libbu-ku-nu limuttimtim
You, whose heart has conjured evil,

taš-te-ni-'-a ru-hi-e sab-ru-ti

who have sought out the evil magick,

ina up-šá-še-e la tâbutimeš tu-sab-bi-ta bir-ki-ia

who has bound my legs with evil incantations.

ana-ku ana pu-uš-šur kiš-pi-ia u ru-hi-e-a

To break my spell and turn your enchantment, I have
turned

ina a-mat E-A u ASARI-lú-du GIRRA as-sah-ri

toward the [word] of ENKI and MARDUK [*asariludu*] and
GIRRA.

[125] ina mêmeš ša naqbi lìb-ba-ku-nu ú-ni-ih

In water-springs I have brought peace to your heart;

ka-bat-ta-ku-nu ú-bal-li

I have soothed your upset liver;

si-ri-ih lib-bi-ku-nu ú-še-si

I have dispelled your quick-anger;

te-en-ku-nu ú-šá-an-ni

I have confounded your mind;

mi-lik-ku-nu as-pu-uh

I have destroyed your plans;

[130] kiš-pi-ku-nu aq-lu

I have burned your spells;

kip-di lib-bi-ku-nu ú-mat-ti-ku-nu-ši

I have numbered the days of your life.

idiqlat u puratta la te-bi-ra-ni

[The] Tigris and Euphrates [rivers], you will
not pass!

iqa u palga la te-it-ti-qa-ni

[The] moat and aqueduct, you will not pass!

dûra u sa-me-ti la tab-ba-lak-ki-ta-ni

[The inner and outer] walls, you will not climb!

[135] abulla u ne-ri-bi-e la tir-ru-ba-ni

[The] gate or entry to the place, you will not pass!

kiš-pi-ku-nu ai ithunimeš-ni

Your spells will not approach me!
a-ma-at-ku-nu ai ik-šu-da-in-ni
Your word cannot reach where I stand!
ina qí-bit E-A SAMAS u MARDUK rubâti dbe-lit ilê
By the decree of ENKI, SAMAS, MARDUK and the Supreme Mistress of the Gods!

INCANTATION—CONSECRATION OF
THE DOORWAY.

[Encircle the gateway with blessed pure flour.]
iz-zi-tu-nu šam-ra-tu-nu qas-sa-tu-nu
Fierce, raging, ferocious,
[140] gap-šá-tu-nu nad-ra-tu-nu lim-ni-tu-nu
Overbearing, violent, evil are you!
šá la E-A man-nu ú-na-ah-ku-nu-ši
Who but ENKI can calm you?
šá la ASARI-lú-du man-nu ú-šap-sah-ku-nu-ši
Who but MARDUK [asalluhi] can cool you down?
E-A li-ni-ih-ku-nu-ši
ENKI, may he calm you!
ASARI-lú-du li-šap-ših-ku-nu-ši
MARDUK [asalluhi], may he cool you down!
[145] mêmeš pî-ia mêmeš pi-ku-nu i-šâ-tu
Water is my mouth; fire is your mouth:
pî-ia pî-ku-nu li-bal-li
[May] my mouth extinguish your mouth!
tu-u šá pî-ia tu-u šá pî-ku-nu li-bal-li
[May] the curse of my mouth extinguish the curse of your mouth!
kip-di šá lìb-bi-ia li-bal-la-a kip-di šá lìb-bi-ku-nu
[May] my desired plans extinguish your desired plans!

INCANTATION—AFFIRMATION.

ak-bu-us gallâ-ai- ...
I have taken my enemy down in front of GIRRA!
[150] at-bu-uh gi-ra-ai ahi-
I have killed my enemy by the sacred word!
na mah-ri qu-ra-di GIRRA-
All of this in front of the mighty GIRRA [I have done]!

BANISHING—USING SCATTERED ASHES.
[*Use the scattered ashes of burnt offerings.*]
hu-la zu-ba u i-ta-at-tu-ka
Scatter, flow and drift away from here!
qu-tur-ku-nu li-tel-li šamêe
May your words float away to the sky!
la-'-me-ku-nu li-bal-li dšamšiši
May the sun extinguish the radiance of your ashes!
[155] lip-ru-us ha-ai-ta-ku-nu mâr E-A mašmašu
May your spy be slain, by [MARDUK] the son of ENKI, the Magician!

BANISHING—USING AN IMAGE WITH 9 KNOTS.
[*Tie nine knots into a cord of wool or yarn.*]
šadûu lik-tùm-ku-nu-ši
May the mountain cover you!
šadûu lik-la-ku-nu-ši
May the mountain hold you back!
šadûu li-ni-ih-ku-nu-ši
May the mountain calm you down!
šadûu li-ih-si-ku-nu-ši
May the mountain overpower you!
[160] šadûu li-te-'-ku-nu-ši

May the mountain swallow you up!
šadûu li-ni-'-ku-nu-ši
May the mountain pass reject you!
šadûu li-nir-ku-nu-ši
May the mountain cliff kill you!
šadûu li-qat-tin-ku-nu-ši
May the mountain wastelands make you thin!
šadûu dan-nu elî-ku-nu lim-qut
May the [mighty] mountain avalanche fall upon you!
[165] ina zumri-ia lu-u tap-par-ra-sa-ma
Indeed, you shall be shaken from my body!

BANISHING RITE—BURNING THE IMAGES.
i-sa-a i-sa-a ri-e-qa ri-e-qa
Go away! Go away! Be gone! Be gone!
bi-e-šá bi-e-šá hi-il-qa hi-il-qa
Stay away! Stay away! Flee! Flee!
dup-pi-ra at-la-ka i-sa-a u ri-e-qa
Get off! Go away! Stay away! Be gone!
limuttu-ku-nu ki-ma qut-ri li-tel-li šamêe
Your evil spell, like smoke, may it rise ever skyward into nothing!
[170] ina zumri-ia i-sa-a
From my body, keep off!
ina zumri-ia ri-e-qa
From my body, be gone!
ina zumri-ia bi-e-šá
From my body, depart!
ina zumri-ia hi-il-qa
From my body, flee!
ina zumri-ia dup-pi-ra
From my body, get off!

[175] ina zumri-ia at-la-ka
From my body, go away!
ina zumri-ia la tatârâ
From my body, turn away!
na zumri-ia la tetehêe
My body, do not approach!
ina zumri-ia la taqarubâ
My body, do not come near!
ina zumri-ia la tasaniqâqa
My body, do not touch!
[180] ni-iš SAMAS kabti lu ta-ma-tu-nu
By the breath of SAMAS, Radiant One, you are commanded!
ni-iš E-A BEL naqbi lu ta-ma-tu-nu
By the breath of ENKI, Lord of the Deep, you are commanded!
ni-iš ASARI-lú-du maš-maš ilimeš lu ta-ma-tu-nu
By the breath of MARDUK [asalluhi], Magician of the Gods, you are commanded!
ni-iš GIRRA qa-mi-ku-nu lu ta-ma-tu-nu
By the breath of GIRRA, your Executioner, you are commanded!
ina zumri-ia lu-u tap-par-ra-sa-ma
Indeed you shall be kept from my body!

THE MAQLU SERIES – TABLET VI

INCANTATION—RITE OF PROTECTION.
EN-LIL qaqqadi-ia pa-nu-ú-a u-mu
ENLIL is my head, the face that meets the day,
duraš ilu git-ma-lu la-mas-sat pa-ni-ia
URAS, the 'perfect god' is my protecting face,
kišadi-ia ul-lu šá NIN-LIL

My neck – the necklace of NINLIL,
idâmeš-ai dgam-lum šá NANNA-SIN amurri
My arms – the crescent swords of NANNA-SIN,
[5] ubânâtumeš-ú-a isbînu esemtu IGIGI
My fingers become the *tamarisk* [of ANU], my bones become the IGIGI;
la ú-šá-as-na-qa ru-hi-e a-na zu-um-ri-ia
They do not allow sorcery to penetrate my body.
LUGAL-edin-na dla-ta-raq irti-ia
Lugaledinna and **Latark** are my chest,
kin-sa-ai dmu-úh-ra šêpâII-ai šá ittanallakaka
My knees – **Muhra**, my feet which carry me
ka-li-ši-na lu lah-mu
are each **Lahmu.**
[10] at-ta man-nu ilu lim-nu šá lúkaššapi u kaššapti
What is your name, Evil God, you whom my sorcerer and sorceress
iš-pu-ru-niš-šú a-na dâki-ia
have conjured to kill me?
lu-ú e-ri-ta la tal-la-ka
When you arise, do not move!
lu-ú sal-la-ta la te-tib-ba-a
When you are asleep, do not awaken!
amâtemeš-ka lu ishašhuru ina pân ili u šarri li-nu-šú
[May] your words become a bitter apple for God and King!
[15] ul-te-sib ina bâbi-ia LUGAL-gir-ra ilu d-an-nu
I set at my door, Mighty GIRRA [*lugal-girra*], avenger of ANU
sukkal ilimeš PAP-SUKKAL
and the messenger of gods, NABU [*papsukkal*] also.
li-du-ku lúkaššapi u kaššapti
They may kill my sorcerer and sorceress;
li-tir-ru amât-sa a-na pî-šá

They may turn their words back in their mouth!

BANISHING—USING A CHICORY-PLANT IMAGE.
riqqukukru-ma riqqukukru
Chicory, chicory!
riqqukukru ina šadânimeš ellûtimeš qud-du-šu-ti
Chicory from the brilliant divine mountains!
sihrûtimeš tir-hi šá e-ni-ti
Small *tirhu*-vessel of the priestess,
sihrâtimeš terinnâtimeš šá qa-aš-da-a-ti
Small pinecones of *hierodule* [*qasdati*],
[30] al-ka-nim-ma šá lúkaššapi-ia u kaššapti-ia
come: of my sorcerer and sorceress
dan-nu hipameš rikis-sa
break their charged knots!
tir-ra kiš-pi-ša a-na me-hi-e amâtemeš-šá ana šâri
Turn their magick wild on them, [turn their] words into wind!
li-in-ni-eš-pu kiš-pi-ša ki-ma pû
May their sorcery be blown away on them like granules!
li-ša-as-li-mu-ši ki-ma di-iq-me-en-ni
May [their sorceries] make them black like ash!
[35] ki-ma libitti igâri liš-hu-hu kiš-pu-šá
May their spells break apart over the wall!
šá kaššapti-ia lip-pa-tir rikis lib-bi-šá
May the heart of my sorceress be melted away!

BANISHING—USING A CHICORY-PLANT IMAGE.
riqqukukru-ma riqqukukru
Chicory, chicory!
riqqukukru ina šadânimeš ellûtimeš qud-du-šu-ti

Chicory from the brilliant divine mountains!
sihrûtimeš tir-hi šá e-ni-ti
Small *tirhu*-vessel of the priestess,
[40] sihrâtimeš terinnâtimeš šá qa-aš-da-a-ti
Small pinecones of *hierodule* [*qasdati*],
al-ka-nim-ma šá lúkaššapi-ia u kaššapti-ia
come: of my sorcerer and sorceress
dan-nu hipâa rikis-sa
break their charged knots;
ù mimma ma-la te-pu-šá nu-tir a-na šâri
and everything you have bewitched, we turn
into wind!

BANISHING—USING A CHICORY-PLANT IMAGE.

e kaššapti-ia e-li-ni-ti-ia
My sorceress, my nightmare!
[45] -a-bu la taš-ku-ni tu-qu-un-tu
You have not given up your confounding!
am-me-ni ina bîti-ki i-qat-tur qut-ru
Why does smoke still rise from your house?
a-šap-pa-rak-kim-ma -ti
I am sending you my evil spell!
ú-sap-pah kiš-pi-ki ú-tar amâtemeš-ki ana pî-ki
I destroy your deceit! I destroy your mouth!

BANISHING—USING A CHICORY-PLANT IMAGE.

la-am NIN-gir-su ina šadî il-su-u da-la-la
In front of NINGIRSU, in the mountains, a divine song of
victory was raised,
[50] la-am kal i-lu-u ana na-kas isbîni
in front of everyone, it raised up and cut *tamarisk*.

260

kassaptušá ana annanna apil annanna tu-kap-pa-ti abnêmeš
**Damn the sorceress who gathers stone [images] against __
son of __,**
taš-te-ni-'-e li-mut-ta
and prepare evil sorcery,
a-za-qa-kim-ma kima iltani amurri
**I blow on you like the cold north-wind and piercing west-
wind!**
ú-sap-pah urpata-ki ú-hal-laq u-um-ki
**I destroy the clouds of your enchantment and clear away
your bad weather,**
[55] ù mimma ma-la te-pu-ši ú-tar a-na šâri
**and I turn everything you have bewitched
into wind!**

BANISHING—USING A CHICORY-PLANT IMAGE.
at-ta e šá te-pu-ši ka-la-a-ma
You who conjures all types of magick,
[70] min-mu-u te-pu-ši ia-a-ši u šim-ti-ia
what you have bewitched, me and my [image],
riqqukukru šá šadîi ihtepi rikis-ki
chicory from the mountain will break your knots!
šá imitti-ki u šumêli-ki šâru lit-bal
**May the wind blow away what is left [and right]
of you!**

CONSECRATION—USING A SULFUR IMAGE.
kibri-dit ellitu mârat šamêe rabûtimeš ana-ku
**I am pure sulfur, I am born of the Daughter of
the Heavens,**
A-NIM ib-na-ni-ma E-A EN-LIL ú-še-ri-du-ni-

ANU created me, ENKI and ENLIL brought me down to this planet...

<unreadable text>

BANISHING—USING A SULFUR IMAGE.

[85] kibri-dit ellitu šam-KUR.KUR šam-mu qud-du-šu ana-ku
Pure sulfur, *kurkur*-weed – I am the pure weed.
e-pi-šu-u-a apqallu šá apsî
My sorcerer is wise in the ways of the Deep
e-pi-iš-tu-u-a mârat da-nim šá šamêe
My sorceress is born of the daughter of the Sky-God ANU.
ki-i e-te-ni-ip-pu-šu-ni ul i-li-'-a-in-ni
Although they have bewitched me, they have not over-whelmed me.
ki-i e-pu-šu-si-na-a-ti iš-te-'u-si-na-a-ti
Since they have conjured sorcery and evil magick,
[90] e-til-la-a kima nûnêmeš ina mêmeš-ia
Make them rise like a fish in my pond,
kîma šahi ina ru-šum-ti-ia
Like a pig in my sty,
kîma šam-maštakal ina ú-sal-li
Like a *matakal*-weed in my fields,
kîma šamsassati ina a-hi a-tap-pi
Like the reed-grass on the riverbank,
kîma zêr isuši ina a-hi tam-tim
Like a seed of the black tree on shoreline,
[95] e-šá dillat-e e-šá dillat-e
[in all these] where my divine support exists, where my divine support exists,
nar-qa-ni a-na qaq-qa-ri
May you be emptied out onto the ground,

šá tu-na-sis-a-ni kim-mat-ku-nu ia-a-ši
You, who have shook your head at me!

BANISHING—USING A SULFUR IMAGE.

dit qaqqadi-ia kibri-dit pa-da-at-ti
The god is my head, the sulfur is my [image]
šêpâ-ai na-a-ru šá man-ma la idûu ki-rib-šá
My feet are the river in whose depths no one knows.
[100] šam-AN.HUL.LA pû-ia tâmtu ta-ma-ta rapaštumtum rit-ti
**The *anhulla*-plant is my mouth, the sea of distant TIAMAT
is my hand...**

INCANTATION—CONSECRATION OF THE SALT.

at-ti tabtu šá ina áš-ri elli ib-ba-nu-ú
You are the salt that was formed in a the 'Pure Place'.
ana ma-ka-li-e ilimeš rabûtimeš i-šim-ki EN-LIL
A meal for the Great Gods, you have been fated by ENLIL;
ina ba-li-ki ul iš-šak-kan nap-tan ina é-kur
without you there is no meal in the E.KUR,
ina ba-li-ki ilu šarru BELU u rubû ul is-si-nu qut-rin-nu
**without you, God, King and Master cannot smell the in-
cense.**
[115] ana-ku annanna apil annanna šá kiš-pi su-ub-bu-tu-in-ni
I, __ , son of __ have beheld the sorcery,
up-šá-še-e li-'-bu-in-ni
allowed the baneful plot to fester:
putri kiš-pi-ia tabtu pu-uš-ši-ri ru-hi-e-a

break the spells, salt! Dissolve the sorceries!
up-ša-še-e muh-ri-in-ni-ma kîma ili ba-ni-ia
Remove the baneful plan from me! Like unto my creator,
lul-tam-mar-ki
I will be free to give adoration!

INCANTATION—RITE OF PROTECTION.

[120] e kaššapti-ia lu rah-ha-ti-ia
[I laugh at you] my sorceress, medicine-man;
šá a-na bêriám ip-pu-hu išâta
who has lit the fires for one side,
a-na bêri iš-tap-pa-ra mâr šip-ri-ša
but sends her [watcher] to both sides,
ana-ku i-di-ma at-ta-kil ta-ka-lu
I know, I have strong conviction;
ina -ia ma-sar-tú ina bâbi-ia az-za-qap ki-din-nu
I have set a watcher in my house; at my gate, a
protector,
[125] ismaiâli-ia al-ta-me subâtú-li-in-na
I have enchanted a scarf to wrap around my bed,
ina rêš ismaiâli-ia a-za-raq šamnuhurtu
I have sprinkled *asadoetida* at the head of my bed,
dan-na-at šamnuhurtu-ma ú-na-ha-ra kal kiš-pi-ki
so the strong *asafoetida* fragrance will end all of your sorceries!

INCANTATION—RITE OF PROTECTION.

e kaššapti-ia e-li-ni-ti-ia
My sorceress, [evil informant], I laugh at you,
šá tattallaki kal mâtâti
you, who blows back and forth over the lands,

ta-at-ta-nab-lak-ka-ti kal šadânimeš-ni
**you, who crosses back and forth over the
mountains,**
ana-ku i-di-ma at-ta-kil ta-ka-lu
I know – and I have a firm conviction,
[140] ina- -ia ma-sar-tú ina bâbi-ia az-za-qap ki-din-nu
**in my house I have stationed a watcher, at the gate
I put a protector;**
ina imitti bâbi-ia u šumêli bâbi-ia
at the right of my gate and left of my gate
ul-te-iz-ziz LUGAL-gir-ra u MIS-lam-ta-è-a
I have set *lugal-girra* and *meslamtaea*;
ilimeš šá ma-sar-te na-si-ih lib-bi muš-te-mi-du kalâtimeš
**may these "guardian gods" burst the insides of the one who
'steals reason'!**
kassaptuli-du-ku-ma ana-ku lu-ub-lut
May they kill the sorceress that I may live!

THE MAQLU SERIES – TABLET VII

INCANTATION—RITE OF PROTECTION.
rit-ti dman-za-ád GIR.TAB-meš
My hand is *manzad*, my scorpion;
ši-i kassaptuú-nak-ka-ma kiš-pi-šá
[she], the sorceress, gathers her spells,
ú- -pah-kim-ma ki-ma marrati ina šamêe
I [cover] you like the rainbow in the sky,
ú-za-qa-kim-ma kîma iltâni amurrî
I blow on you like the north-wind, the west-wind,
[5] ú-sa-ap-pah urpata-ki ú-hal-laq ûm-ki
I destroy your clouds and dispel your bad weather!

ú-sap-pah kiš-pi-ki šá tak-ki-mi mu-šá u ur-ra
**I destroy the sorcery you have gathered up both
day and night,**
ù na-áš-pa-rat zitarrutâa šá tal-tap-pa-ri ia-a-ši
and all malefic messages you send my way.
sa-lil nêbiru sa-lil ka-a-ru
**NEBIRU [*boat of heaven's crossing*] calls, the
harbor calls,**
mârêmeš malâhi ka-li-šú-nu sal-lu
the sailors are resting all the while;
[10] elî isdalti ù issikkuri na-du-u hur-gul-lu
the door and bolt are wrapped up,
na-da-at ši-pat-su-un šá dsiris u NIN-giš-zi-da
**the incantations are laid down of SIDURI and NINGISHZ-
IDA,**
šá lúkaššapi-ia u kaššapti-ia ip-šá bar-tum amât limuttimtim
**the sorcery, the incantations, the evil speech, the evil word
of my sorcerer and sorceress,**
ai ithunimeš.ni ai i-ba-'-u-ni
should not come near; will not come in!
bâba ai êrubûnimeš.ni ana bîti
**The door [gate] is barred; [they should not] enter the
house!**
[15] NIN-giš-zi-da li-is-suh-šú-nu-ti
NINGISHZIDA, throw them out!
lib-bal-ki-tu-ma e-pi-šá-ti-šu-nu li-ba-ru
[May] they kneel down to catch their helpers!
ilu šarru BELU ù rubû lik-kil-mu-šú-nuina
**[May] God, King and Master look at their evil
unfavorably.**
ina qâtê ili šarri BELI u rubî ai ú'si kaš-šap-ti
**In [the] power of my God and king, the sorceress will not
escape!**

a-na-ku ina qí-bit MARDUK BEL nu-bat-ti
(But) I act in alignment with MARDUK, the Master of Magicians,
[20] ù ASARI-lú-du BEL a-ši-pu-ti
MARDUK [asariludu], Master of the Incantations,
min-mu-ú e-pu-šu lu ku-ši-ru
may everything I have done here be successful!
ip-še te-pu-šá-ni li-sa-bil šâra
[May] the sorceries you have conjured against me turn into wind!

INCANTATION—CONSECRATING THE WATERS.

a-ra-hi-ka ra-ma-ni a-ra-hi-ka pag-ri
I sanctify you, my self; I sanctify you, the whole of my body;
ki-ma dsumuqân ir-hu-ú bu-ul-šú
like the *sumuqan* sanctifies his cattle,
[25] sênu im-mir-šá sabîtu ar-ma-šá atânu mu-ur-šá
the ewe with her lamb, the gazelle with her kid, the she-donkey with her foal,
isepinnu irsitimtim ir-hu-ú irsitimtim im-hu-ru zêr-šá
[like] the plow sanctifies the earth, and the earth receives [from the] plow, its seeds,
ad-di šipta a-na ra-ma-ni-ia
I have conjured an incantation upon myself!
li-ir-hi ra-ma-ni-ma li-še-se lum-nu
May it sanctify me and drive evil away!
ù kiš-pi ša zumri-ia li-is-su-hu
May they tear away the sorcery from my body,
[30] ilimeš rabûtimeš
the Great Gods!

INCANTATION—CONSECRATING THE OILS.

šamnu ellu šamnu ib-bu šamnu nam-ru
Pure oil, clean [light] oil, shinning oil!
šamnu mu-lil zumri šá ilimeš
Oil [pure] which cleanses the gods!
šamnu mu-pa-áš-ši-ih širšir-a-na šá a-me-lu-ti
Oil which soothes the muscles of humans!
šaman šipti šá E-A šaman šipti šá ASARI-lú-du
Oil consecrated to the incantation of ENKI, oil of the incantation of MARDUK [asariludu]!
[35] ú-ta-hi-id-ka šaman tap-šu-uh-ti
I have let you drip with the oil that cleanses
šá E-A id-di-nu a-na pa-áš-ha-a-ti
that ENKI has given forth to heal [with].
ap-šu-uš-ka šaman balâti
I have rubbed you with the 'Oil of Life'
ad-di-ka šipat E-A BEL eri-du NIN-igi-kug
have placed you next to the incantation of ENKI, Lord of ERIDU and NINIGIKUG
at-ru-ud a-sak-ku ah-ha-zu
have chased away the *asakku* [the seizer],
[40] šu-ru-up-pu-u ša zumri-ka
[the] chill is [removed] from your body.
ú-šat-bi qu-lu ku-ru ni-is-sa-tú šá pag-ri-ka
[I have] removed the frightful sound, the fear, the trembling of your body,
ú-pa-áš-ši-ih šir-a-ni mi-na-ti-ka la tâbâtimeš
[have] healed the tendons of your ailing members.
ina qí-bit E-A šar apsî
Upon ENKI, Lord of the Deep,
ina tê ša E-A ina šipat ASARI-lú-du
with the formula of ENKI, [along] with the incantation of MARDUK [asariludu],
[45] ina ri-kis ra-ba-bu šá GU-LA

[Clothed] in the 'large garments' of GULA,
ina qâtê pa-áš-ha-a-ti šá NIN-DIN-UG-GA
with the healing hands of NINDINUGGA,
ú NIN-a-ha-qud-du BEL šipti
and of NINAHAQUDDU, Master of Incantation,
ana annanna apil annanna šub-šu-ma E-A šipat-ka šá balâti
let __, son of __ know, ENKI and you 'Incantation of Life'!
7 apqallê šu-ut eri-du li-pa-áš-ši-hu zumur-šu
[May the] seven *apqallu* of Eridu heal his body!

INCANTATION—PREPARING IMAGES
FOR BURNING.

[50] EN-LIL qaqqadi-ia MULKAK.SI.ŠÁ la-a-ni
ENLIL is my head, the star *kaksisa* is my form;
pûtu SAMAS nap-hu
[the] forehead is SAMAS [*usually 'light of crescent'*],
idâ-ai isgamlu šá bâb MARDUK
**[my] arms [are] the curved sword of the Gate of MAR-
DUK,**
uzna-a-a li-'-u šêpâII-a-a lah-mu mu-kab-bi-sa-at lah-me
**[my] ears are a (divine) tablet, my stomping feet [are a]
snake.**
at-tu-nu ilimeš rabûtimeš šá ina šamêe nap-ha-tu-nu
You, Great Gods, who are lit in the heavens,
[55] kîma an-na ku an- ip-šu bar-tum amât lemut-tim
Like the evil sorceries, spells and malediction
la itehhûmeš-ku-nu-ši la i-sa-ni-qú-ku-nu-ši
do not come near you, or even push up close,
ip-šû bar-tú amât lemut-tim la itehhû-ni la isanniqû-ni ia-ši

so may the baneful sorceries, spells and malediction not
come near to me, or even push up close against me!

MAQLU INCANTATION—BURNING THE IMAGES.

at-ti man-nu kassaptušá êpušušu sal-mi
**Who are you, sorceress? You who has an [image]
of me,**
it-tu-lu la-a-ni êpušušu la-mas-si
**who has observed my form and fashioned an
[image],**
[60] i-mu-ru bal-ti ú-šar-ri-hu ga-ti
has seen my strength, has fashioned my [image],
ú-sab-bu-u nab-ni-tú
has studied the shape of my form,
ú-maš-ši-lu bu-un-na-ni-e-a
has reproduced [carefully] my features,
ub-bi-ru mi-na-ti-ia
has bound my appendages [members],
ú-kas-su-u meš-ri-ti-ia
has bound up my appendages [members],
[65] ú-kan-ni-nu ma-na-ni-e-a
has distorted my nervous system;
ia-a-ši E-A maš-maš ilimeš ú-ma-'-ra-an-ni
[but] ENKI, Enchanter of the Gods, has sent me;
ma-har SAMAS sa-lam-ki e-sir
in front of SAMAS I have drawn your [image].
la-an-ki ab-ni bal-ta-ki a-mur
I have drawn your [image]. I have observed your strength,
gat-ta-ki ú-šar-ri-ih nab-nit-ki ú-sab-bi
**I have made your [image] and caught the shape of your
form,**

[70] i-na dnisaba ellitimtim bu-un-na-an-ni-ki ú-maš-šil
I have duplicated your [image] using pure flour,
mi-na-ti-ki ub-bi-ir meš-ri-ti-ki ú-kas-si
I have bound your appendages; I have bound up your appendages,
ma-na-ni-ki ú-kan-ni-in
I have distorted your nervous system;
ip-šú te-pu-šin-ni e-pu-uš-ki
I have conjured on you the spell that you did cast on me.
mi-hir tu-šam-hir-in-ni ú-šam-hir-ki
I have let you have your evil encounter that you suffered me!
[75] gi-mil tag-mil-in-ni ú-tir ag-mil-ki
I have let you have your revenge that you suffered me!
kiš-pi-ki ru-hi-ki ru-si-ki ip-še-te-ki lim-ni-e-te
Your sorcery, your spells, your evil, your malignance,
up-šá-še-ki ai-bu-te
your evil plans,
na-áš-pa-ra-ti-ki šá li-mut-ti
your evil messages,
râm-ki zêr-ki dipalû-ki zitarrutû-ki
[your] love, hate, imbalance and murder,
[80] kadibbidû-ki dubbubu-ki li-kil-lu rêš-ki
[your] disease and calamities; may your head stop thinking!
it-ti mêmeš šá zumri-ia u mu-sa-a-ti šá qâtê-ia liš-šá-hi-it-ma
With [pure] water of my body, purifying water of my hands, may your evil be removed
a-na muh-hi-ki u la-ni-ki lil-lik-ma ana-ku lu-ub-lut

and fom your head and form, that I may live!

e-ni-ta li-na-an-ni ma-hir-ta lim-hur-an-ni

May divine grace bless me and good fortune come to me!

BANISHING—USING AN IMAGE WITH 7 KNOTS.

[*Tie seven knots into a cord of wool or yarn.*]

ba-'-ir-tú šá ba-'ra-a-ti

Catcher of catchers!

[85] kassaptušá kaššapâtimeš

Sorceress of sorceresses!

šá ina sûqâtameš-ta na-da-tu še-is-sa

Who, in the streets, has spread their net,

ina ri-bit âli it-ta-na-al-la-ka ênâ-šá

whose eyes, dart about in the city square;

lúetlêmeš âli ub-ta-na-'

she targets the men in the city,

it-ti lúetlêmeš âli ub-ta-na-'-in-ni ia-a-ši

with the men of the city, she has targeted me [too].

[90] ardâtimeš âli is-sa-na-hur

the girls of the city, she cavorts with,

it-ti ardâtimeš âli is-sa-na-hur-an-ni ia-a-ši

with the girls of the city, she cavorts with me [too].

e ú-ba-'-kim-ma lúkurgarêmeš lúeš-še-bi-e

I seek … against you, *kur-garras* and *essebi*

rikis-ki a-hi-pi

I will break your bindings!

lúkaššapêmeš li-pu-su-ki rikis-ki a-hi-pi

May warlocks bewitch you, but I will break your bindings!

[95] kaššapâtimeš li-pu-ša-ki rikis-ki a-hi-pi

May witches bewitch you, but I will break your bindings!

lúkurgarêmeš li-pu-šu-ki rikis-ki a-hi-pi
**Kurgarras bewitch you, but I will break your
bindings!**
lúeš-še-bu-ú li-pu-šu-ki rikis-ki a-hi-pi
Essebu bewitch you, but I will break your bindings!
nar-šin-du-umeš li-pu-šu-ki rikis-ki a-hi-pi
**Narsindus bewitch you, but I will break your
bindings!**
mušlahhêmeš li-pu-šu-ki rikis-ki a-hi-pi
**Snake-charmers bewitch you, but I will break your bind-
ings!**
[100] a-gu-gil-lumeš li-pu-šu-ki rikis-ki a-hi-pi
**Agulgillu bewitch you, but I will break your
bindings!**
a-mah-has li-it-ki a-šal-la-pa lišân-ki
I devour your face. I rip out your tongue,
ú-ma-al-la ru-'-a-ta ênâII-ki
I fill your eyes with my spit,
ú-ša-lak a-hi-ki lil-lu-ta
I make your arms loose their strength [*"to become weak"*]**.**
ú ak-ka-a-ši ru-uq-bu-ta ú-ša-lak-ki
and for you to eat, I leave out rotten refuse,
[105] ù mimma ma-la te-te-ip-pu-ši ú-tar ana muh-hi-ki
**and everything you have conjured against me, I turn back
onto your head!**

BANISHING—USING AN IMAGE WITH 3 KNOTS.
[Tie three knots into a cord of wool or yarn.]
ep-ši-ki ep-še-ti-ki ep-še-et ep-ši-ki
**Your enchantment and magick, the sorcery of your sor-
ceress,**

ep-še-et mu-up-pi-še-ti-ki
[the] sorcery of your sorcerer,
E-A maš-maš ilimeš ú-pat-tir-ma mêmeš uš-ta-bil
ENKI, Father of Magicians, has undone [it all] and turned [it] to water!
pî-ki lim-nu e-pi-ra lim-la
May your evil mouth be filled with dirt from the earth!
[110] lišân-ki šá limuttimtim ina qí-e lik-ka-sir
May your evil tongue be tied up with a string!
ina qí-bit den-bi-lu-lu BEL balâti
[All this] by the decree of *Enbilulu*, Master of Life!

BANISHING RITE—BURNING THE CORD-KNOT IMAGES.

ki-is-ri-ki ku-us-su-ru-ti
Your bound knots,
ip-še-ti-ki lim-ni-eti up-šá-še-ki ai-bu-ti
your evil spells and evil manifestations,
na-áš-pa-ra-tu-ki šá limuttimtim
your evil intentions spoken,
[115] ASARI-lú-du maš-maš ilimeš ú-pat-tir-ma ú-šá-bil sara
MARDUK [*asariludu*], Master of Magicians, has done and removed [all of this]!
pî-ki lim-nu epirahi.a lim-ma-li
May your evil mouth be filled up with dirt from the earth,
lišan-ki šá limuttimtim ina qí-e lik-ka-sir
and may your evil tongue be tied up with a string!
ina qí-bit den-bi-lu-lu BEL balâti
[All this] by the decree of *Enbilulu*, Master of Life!

MAQLU INCANTATION—PURIFICATION RITE.

[*The hands and body are washed then anointed.*]

am-si qa-ti-ia ub-bi-ba zu-um-ri

I have washed my hands; I have purified my body

[120] ina mêmeš naqbi ellûtimeš šá ina eri-du ib-ba-nu-u

in [pure] waters which come from Eridu proper;

mimma lim-nu mimma lâ tâbu

may all diseased spirits, all of the evil spirits and misfortune

šá ina zumri-ia šêrêmeš-ia šir'ânêmeš-ia bašûu

that in my body, my form and my being exists,

lumun šunâtimeš idâtimeš ittâtimeš limnêtimeš lâ tâbâtimeš

anxiety by way of evil and unfavorable dreams, harbingers of doom,

lumun šîrîmeš ha-tu-ti par-du-ti lemnû-timeš lâ tâbûtimeš

anxiety by way of false dreams, evil visions and misfortune,

[125] lipit qâti hi-niq šu'i ni-iq ni-qi nêpeš-ti barû-ti

by laying-of-hands, strangulation of life, of divination,

šá at-ta-ta-lu u-me-šam

by all of that which I see every day,

ú-kab-bi-su ina sûqi e-tam-ma-ru ina a-ha-a-ti

and that which I step upon in the street and what I see around me,

še-ed lem-utti ú-tuk-ku lim-nu

the evil *sedu*, the evil *utukku*,

mursu di-'di-lip-ta

illness, headache, upset,

[130] qu-lu ku-ru ni-is-sa-tú ni-ziq-tú im-tu-uta-ni-hu

terror, fear, quivering, worry, depression, apathy,

'ú-a a-a hu-su-su qis lib-bi
pains, aches, cramps, leprosy,
gi-lit-tum pi-rit-tum a-dir-tum
more fear, obsession, terror,
ár-rat ilimeš mi-hir-ti ilimeš ta-zi-im-ti
sin, the unfavorably hand and wrath of Gods,
ni-iš ilî ni-iš ilî ni-iš qâti ma-mit
curses born of oaths to God and the oath-swearing raised hand,
[135] lum-nu kiš-pi ru-hi-e ru-si-e up-šá-še-e lem-nu-ti šá amêlûtimeš
sorcery, spells, evil manifestations of humans,
it-ti mêmeš šá zumri-ia u mu-sa-a-ti šá qâte-ia
may they all, with the clean water of my body and hands,
liš-šá-hi-it-ma ana muhhi salam nig-sagilêe lil-lik
be sent to the deceiver whose [image] is before me!
salam nigsagilêe ár-ni di-na-ni li-iz-bil
May my sin carry my [image] instead of me!
su-ú-qu ù su-lu-ú li-pat-ti-ru ár-ni-ia
May the causeway and path cleanse me of the sin!
[140] e-ni-tum li-na-ni ma-hir-tum lim-hur-an-ni
May the grace [of the highest] bless me, may favorable conditions come to me!
am-hur mi-ih-ru lim-hu-ru-in-ni
I have lived through [this] experience [enough]; may it now turn favorably toward me!
u-mu šul-ma arhu hi-du-ti šattu hagalla-šá li-bil-la
May the day bring health, the month bring joy and the year its prosperity.
EA, SAMAS u MARDUK ia-a-ši ru-sa-nim-ma
ENKI, SAMAS and MARDUK come to my aid!
lip-pa-áš-ru kiš-pu ru-hu-u ru-su-u

May the evil sorcery, the evil spells, all be dissolved [to nothingness]!
[145] up-šá-šu-ú lim-nu-ti šá a-me-lu-ti
May the evil manifestations of men and the
ù ma-mit lit-ta-si šá zumri-ia
baneful oath sword all now leave my body!

MAQLU INCANTATION—RITE FOR JUST BEFORE DAWN.

te-bi še-e-ru mesâa qâte-ia
Dawn is coming forth, my hands are washed;
-ma qaq-qa-ru mu-hur up-ni-ia
[my iniquity] is cleansed, my sin is absolved.
šá kassaptuú-kaš-šip-an-ni
Because the sorceress has enchanted me,
[150] eš-še-bu ú-sa-li-'-an-ni
the wicked witch has made me sick,
SAMAS pi-šir-ta li-bil-am-ma
SAMAS, I call on you to bring me salvation!
irsitimtim lim-hur-an-ni
May the earth protect me!

MAQLU INCANTATION—RITES AT DAWN.

it-tam-ra še-e-ru pu-ut-ta-a dalati
Dawn has come forth; the doors have opened;
a-lik ur-hi it-ta-si abulla
the traveler has passed through [the gate];
[155] mâr šipri is-sa-bat har-ra-na
the messenger has taken to the road.
e-piš-tum e te-pu-šin-ni
Witch, hey, did you try to bewitch me?
ra-hi-tum e tu-ri-hi-in-ni

Enchantress, hey, did you try to enchant me?
ú-tal-lil ina na-pa-ah dšamši
[Well], now I am freed with the radiant light of the rising sun;
mimma ma-la te-pu-ši ù tu-uš-te-pu-ši
Whatever witchcraft you believe you have done,
[160] li-tir-ru-ma li-is-ba-tu-ki ka-a-ši
may it all turn back upon you – yes, you!

MAQLU INCANTATION—RITE FOR AFTER DAWN.

še-ru-um-ma še-e-ru
Morning, [glorious] morning!
an-nu-ú šá lúkaššapi-ia u kaššapti-ia
[Honestly] my sorcerer and sorceress
it-bu-nim-ma kîma mârêmeš lúnâri ú-lap-pa-tú nu-'-šú-nu
have plucked at their cords like minstrels.
ina bâbi-ia iz-za-zi PALIL
At my gate stands PALIL,
[165] ina rêš ismaiâli-ia iz-za-zi LUGAL-edin-na
at the head of my bed guards *Lugal-edinna*,
a-šap-pa-rak-kim-ma šá bâbi-ia PALIL
I send you from my gate, PALIL;
šá rêš ismaiâli-ia LUGAL-edin-na
and from my bed, *Lugal-edinna*.
mîli bêri dib-bi-ki mîli har-ra-ni a-ma-ti-ki
Your speech will turn around on you [like a] flood on the streets,
ú-tar-ru kiš-pi-ki ru-hi-ki ú-sa-ab-ba-tu-ki ka-a-ši
your sorceries, charms and spells will [come back] to seize you, yes you!

MAQLU INCANTATION—MORNING RITE.

[170] ina še-rì misâa qâtâ-ai
In dawn-time, my hands have been cleansed,
šur-ru-ú dam-qu li-šar-ra-an-ni
may a prosperous beginning start for me;
tu-ub lìb-bi tûbub šêri li-ir-te-da-an-ni
may happiness and good fortune ever follow alongside me,
e-ma ú-sa-am-ma-ru su-um-mi-ra-ti-ia lu-uk-šu-ud
whatever it is that I desire, may I obtain my desires,
šunât e-mu-ru ana damiqtimtim liš-šak-na
whenever I dream, may those be favorable,
[175] ai ithâa ai isniq mimma lim-nu mimma lâ tâbu
and [keep away] anything evil, anything malevolent,
ru-hi-e šá lúkaššapi u kaššapti
any evil enchantment of the sorcerer and sorceress,
ina qí-bit EA, SAMAS u MARDUK u ru-bâti belit i-li
by the decree of ENKI, SAMAS, MARDUK and the Queen,
Lady of the Gods [of the heavens]!

THE MAQLU SERIES – TABLET VIII

INCANTATION—CLOSING RITES.

un-du kassaptui-bir nâra
After the sorceress has crossed the river,
- -u iš-la-a -
she escaped me by going under the Deep.
[35] e-piš-ti áš-bat ina ni-bi-ri
My sorceress sits lonely in NI.BI.RI
- -šu-uš ka-a-ri
[My sorceress sits lonely] on the shore.
ub-ta-na-'-an-ni ia-ši ana sa-ha-li-ia

She still seeks me, seeks her revenge.
li- -ši-ma apqallêmeš šá apsî
May the *apqalle* of the Deep go to her,
- -zi ni-me-qí ni-kil-ti E-A iq-bu-u la-pan-šá
[let her taste] the clever wisdom of ENKI, King of the Deep!
[40] E-A šar apsî lih-da-a pa-ni-šá
May you rejoice with ENKI, King of the Deep!
li-sa-hi-ip-ši be-en-na te-šá-a ra-i-ba
May [my] paralysis and anger be subsided,
li-tir hur-ba-as-sa
[my] fear be removed,
- -pu-luh-ta šá i-da-a eli-šá
[I have held] fear against you,
ana elî salmânimeš-šá misâa qâtâ-ia
[but now] I wash my hands over their [images],
[45] i-na riqqukukri šá šadî riqquburâši elli
with *chicory*, pine and cypress;
i-na šam-DIL.BAT mu-ul-lil amêli misâa qâtâ-ia
with the *dilbat*-weed that cleanses humans, I have washed my hands.
e-te-lil ana-ku -ina elî sêri-šá
pure I have become [like the water] more than she can,
kiš-pu-šá lim-lu-u-sêru
Her sorceries, in the desert [may they rot].
amâtemeš-šá šâru-lit-bal
I carry away her words [to the wind]
[50] ù mimma ma-la e-pu-šu li-tur ana šâri
and every enchantment she has manifested, I throw to the wind!

INCANTATION—CLOSING RITES.

ultu SUMU-qân ina šadî ilsûú da-la-la
After Sumuqan had begun the victory song on the mountain;

ultu kal i-lu-ú a-na na-kas isbîni
(and) after everyone had ascended to cut *tamarisk*;

áš-bat-ma ummu - -šú
the mother and father sat down.

áš-bu-ma i-ma-li-ku- ahu -
they convene to counsel the bother and sister.

[55] at-ti man-nu kassaptušá ia-a-ši u ram-ni-ia
Whoever you are, sorceress, who I have now bewitched,

e-piš-tú e-pu-šá kiš-pi ik-ši-pu
Witch who has bewitched [and who I have now bewitched],

kiš-pu-šá lu-u šâru kiš-pu-šá lu-u me-hu-ú
may your spells be wind, may your spells be lost in a storm,

kiš-pu-šá lu-u pu-u lit-tap-ra-šá-du elî-šá
may your spells be grains of dust that fly up in your face!

<unreadable text>
...[and may] eagles and vultures scour your dead body!

qu-lu hur-ba-šu lim-qu-ut elî-ki
Pain and fear, may it befall you!

kalbu u kalbatu li-ba-as-si-ru-ki
Hound and bitch, may they tear you apart!

kalbu u kalbatu li-ba-as-si-ru šêrêmeš-ki
Hound and bitch, may they tear your flesh away!

ina qí-bit EA, SAMAS u MARDUK u rubâti MAH
By decree of ENKI, SAMAS, MARDUK and the Queen (goddess) MAH!

INCANTATION—CLOSING RITES.

[90] at-ta silli at-ta ba-aš-ti
You are my strength [like] a shield;
at-ta dšêdi at-ta ga-at-ti
You are the 'guardian god' of my form,
at-ta pa-da-at-ti at-ta du-u-ti
You are my [image], my barrier [wall],
<unreadable text>
e tam-hur kiš-pi e tam-hur ú-pi-ši
Hey, spell-crafter! Hey, evil-doer! You are finished!
[95] KI.MINA šag-gaš-tú KI.MINA na-kas napištimtim
**The same for a murderess, the same for the
remover of life,**
KI.MINA ru-'-ut-ta -ab-tu
the same for friendship-breakers,
KI.MINA kadibbidâ KI.MINA dipa-lâa
**the same for the seizing disease, the same for the worldly
injustice,**
KI.MINA zêru KI.MINA ši- -pi-ši
the same for hate, the same for [violence],
limnûtimeš - -ti
[the same for all of the] evils of the [world].
[100] at-ta ia-ú a-na-ku ku-ú
Great God, you are mine and I am yours,
man-ma-an ai il-mad-ka mimma lim-nu ai ithi-ka
**may none but me counsel with you, may evil never come
close to you,**
ina qí-bit EA, SAMAS MARDUK
by the decree of ENKI, SAMAS, MARDUK
u rubâti MAH
and the Queen (goddess), MAH!

—APPENDIX A—
ENOCHIAN MAGIC & KABBALAH
(LIBER K)

— 0 —
THE ANUNNAKI LEGACY IN WESTERN MAGIC
(AN INTRODUCTION BY JOSHUA FREE)

My active involvement with the "New Age" occult underground began in the mid-1990's, during a period—much like a century prior—of very intensive "magical" (or "magickal") revival. In addition to new interests in indigenous "folk magic" and shamanic traditions of Europe, all core emphasis of "magical orders" or "underground sects" focused primarily on ritual methods—"ceremonial magic" or "high magic"—drawn from organizations appearing publicly during the late 18th century and going on to influence most of the "Western magical" styling popularized most frequently in modern and contemporary "New Age" material. Until the 1970's, most occult instruction and initiation remained restricted to those involved in, or connected to, these organizations—such as the *Hermetic Order of the Golden Dawn*, *Rosicrucian Order* and so forth. But all of these later methodologies were developed with the *kabbalah* as a basis and are often rooted in a Judeo-Christian framework—practicing from "grimoires" that were written during a Judeo-Christian age, long after the original practices of occultism were obliterated.

The modern "Mardukite" movement represents a new "generation" of *Truth Seekers* that are able to glean something deeper, wider or beyond what has been set before them. Rather than simply compound upon an already fractured system, they have worked to put the pieces back together and restore the fragmented consciousness of the human spirit. It is the model of the ancient "Mardukite Babylonian" tradition that we are drawing upon—but this does not mean that we are ignorant of the many parallels that can be drawn to later derived systems. On the contrary, our previous release—*Arcanum: Great Magical Arcanum*—should suffice to prove otherwise. But, in regards to the current text/volume of "magickal arts" and the relationship between the ancient "Babylonian Anunnaki" systemology and the methods of practice that later followed, it is in this current discourse that we will side-step a purely Mesopotamian emphasis and lend a thought to its later developments in "practical occultism." The new NexGen *Seekers* are able to see the big picture without giving themselves over to one systematic trapping or another—yet by taking an initiative to personally commit to the *Self-Honest* path, the information does not compute as fragments but as additional names for the whole.

Modern "Mardukites" are those *seeking* the most ancient written records of history, spirituality and cosmic wisdom—and these are traced back to the sands of Mesopotamia. Naturally, each individual will associate with the main tenets of the tradition in their own way—applying it as they are best able to realize, whether as itself or in combination with some other cultural semantic paradigm. We set out to establish the definitive source of our own existence and thereby the course of our physical, intellectual and spiritual future—our evolution in this existence...and the *next*, for they are all one! We have sought the blatant and outright revelation of what has come *before*, so that we can better understand where we are *here* and most *Self-Honestly* direct ourselves into the *future*. And what a wonderful utopian thought! Perhaps you have heard such things before from other "visionaries"—but there are *no more excuses* and so, whether assisted by other figures of the "surface world" (or even those in the underground)...*or not*, there are those *Truth Seekers* who have chosen to remove the blinders and filtered-glasses to gain *clear vision* of reality and the basis of the existence we occupy as entities—All-as-One—regardless of whatever names and labels they may attach to such a path. These are the type of *"humans"* emerging now—more strongly than ever before!

Our quest into these mysteries began with a simple premise: rather than simply "piece-mealing"myriads of tradition and lore from various systems backward through the ages, a group of modern occult *initiates* had decided to begin working together with me in 2006 to deliberate conclusions I had drawn in my (then exclusively underground work)—*Book of Elven-Faerie*, later designated *Mardukite Liber-D*. In that discourse, a *seeker* is drawn even further back in time and culturally far removed from the *Celtic* regions that the book is meant to emphasize—an integral part of the *"Druidic"* literary cycle that I prepared (subsequent to writing *Draconomicon* and *Druidry* for the underground as well). This left us holding the "Mardukite" bag, and with the state of the "New Age" and modern esoterica at the time, it seemed that we had only one real liaison into existing human consciousness regarding Mesopotamian neopagan revival—specifically *Simon's Necronomicon*. It occurred to me long before the development of the "Mardukite Core" that the bridge between existing "New Age" methods and the systemology proposed by "New Thought" Mardukites had to be made. I held off on launching the group officially until this could be coherently remedied—something that I do believe I accomplished over the next two years, released as *"Arcanum: The Great Magical Arcanum,"* and made available coinciding with the public launch of the Mardukites on the *Summer Solstice, June 2008*.

Where works like *The Sorcerer's Handbook*, *Arcanum* or *Book of Elven-Faerie* brought together a unique synthesis of the most practical lore and knowledge I earned from *my own* personal involvement with modern occultism—I felt that the focus of the *Mardukite* movement should be on the most ancient conclusive source of all that is otherwise available to us. For this, I would lead *seekers* on the path that I have always been drawn to but never able to articulate to others properly—except, again, under the guise of the *Necronomicon*, which I admittedly realize is not a true and faithful "proper name" for the Babylonian mythos—and yet, in the present times, it seemed as good as any other, and in this instance, it would make sense to at least a handful of *seekers* that were chosen to hear the intended message. Where it would go from there was anyone's guess at the original inception—now over a decade ago!

The current generational or NexGen approach and interpretation has left us wanting *more*—and not just more of the same, but *more!* The "New Thought" understanding of the most ancient mysteries proposed by my rekindling of a "Mardukite" movement became suddenly accessible in print and to the masses. But—our approach and discoveries were unique even among the underground "New Age" communities. The realization that the same forces that *appeared* to the ancients and manipulated the original mystical, spiritual, religious and political systems—were related to those "forces" connected to the *magical experiences* and *divine* encounters through the ages—well...that almost made just *too much sense.*

Although comparatively obscure—by even modern *esoteric* standards—our work is not founded in *beliefs* with no basis. Ours is no fantastic notion inspired by science-fiction writings or wishful thinking. Certainly no—just as the work of the "*Mardukite Chamberlains*" (or "*Mardukite Research Organization*") is now amidst its tenth active year, and with its unique team drawing out the most antiquated mysteries into public view.

The first several years of *Mardukite* work all emphasized Mesopotamia as a well-spring for cultural and regional beliefs throughout time and space thereafter. It can be a challenge for some modern *seekers* to actually understand the magnitude of these *archetypes* unleashed in ancient times as the "source" of such *things* on earth. This is not so surprising; we recognize that literature and traditions of ancient Mesopotamia—the *Sumerians* and *Babylonians*—are not so well known in the surface world or even in contemporary "New Age" markets and underground occult factions. Those elements that we found in their rawest form appear in the source anthology: "*Necronomicon: The Anunnaki Bible.*"

Conventional sources of *esoterica* can provide the *seeker* only a diluted version of ancient mysteries—or else a "truth" based on an outside perspective, outside instruction of a pure stream back to the ancient source. While these other streams may flow from the ancient well-spring, they are not necessarily all worthy refractions of the "Truth." Keep in mind, these later reflections are all colored by additional cultural filters, and other influences shaped by geography and language—they are never one-to-one with the original, more ancient sources. And while we can see and chart the evolution of the source throughout time—and feel quite educated and cultured while doing so—we will not ever get closer to the sheer and absolute "truth" of things via reverse engineering. The solution is, and always is, a direct return to the source—and then go forward in *Self-Honesty*.

Given what we have so carefully charted (or *re*-charted) of the ancient mysteries throughout the "Mardukite Core" specific to Mesopotamian traditions of Sumer and the systemology of *Babylonians* existing in pre-Hebrew/Semitic periods—it only makes sense to move immediately forward in time from *Anunnaki*-specific semantic paradigms and consider the *Judeo-Christian* and otherwise *Hebrew* forms of mystic spirituality that immediately emerged from the Source—in the form of *kabbalah*. I hope to make clear in this present discourse, *Mardukite Liber-K*, based on a series of knowledge-lectures given at the Mardukite Denver Offices from 2009 through 2011, the elements which directly sprung, specifically those *mystical experiences* and *divine encounters* that have inspired religious activity all over the planet—and all of which appear to stem from a singular source, relating back to the *Anunnaki*, and carefully preserved behind *esoteric* traditions of magicians, priestesses and priests throughout the ages. Unfortunately, the clarity and semantics of the original source tradition fell by the wayside, obscured with time and the ever-shifting nature of semantics held in collective consciousness.

> "Our work is therefore historically authentic; the rediscovery of the Sumerian tradition, says Crowley. This forms the crux of Crowley's system, without which it is both incomprehensible and unfathomable; incomprehensible in its magical significance for the present magical revival, and unfathomable without the key supplied by the Sumerian tradition..."
>
> ~ Kenneth Grant, <u>Magical Revival</u>

When we consider the greater legacy of the Anunnaki in the wake of the 20th century magical revival, it becomes clear that these "gates" have been accessed before—are being accessed—will be accessed again, by those who have gleaned the mysteries and are able to tap the awesome power that is hidden and latent within the system. This is not child's play although it has certainly seemed to appear as such at times—we can see the evolution of the modern understanding amidst the underground, but too often out of context and in exclusion to the former and greater path that these new intricacies overshadow. Those like Aleister Crowley, or MacGregor Mathers and others involved with the Hermetic Order of the Golden Dawn, or other Rosicrucian and Masonic offshoots sprung from it—the O.T.O, A.A. ...the list is endless. Even other groups developed individually—Aurum Solis, Brotherhoods of Light, &tc.—these all use forms of newly revived methods of "ceremonial magic" based on the *Enochian Magic* and *Kabbalah* that are all designed for one purpose: to successfully communicate with otherworldly intelligences. For ceremonial magic there is no higher purpose—one must look to deeper mystical lessons to discern the path to ascension from it. And most magicians never do; too dazzled by the array of lights displayed by their rituals.

The exact nature of these underlying "forces" is always in question, and when they seem to appear to us as personifications, it begs even more questions than it yields answers. But—the specific "scientific" nature of these aspects is not under debate for current purposes. What is far more critical to our practical understanding is the very fact that "something" inspired diverse *ancient accounts* concerning *divine* and *otherworldly* beings—and their effects on humanity. It is these "observable effects" that we cannot dismiss or pass off the opportunity to understand. They compose the entire basis of a global systemology—religious, mystical, spiritual, cultural, civic and political—facets that affect all who share the "human condition."

Many source books and reprises of well-known texts on the subject of *Enochian Magic* and *Kabbalah* already appear widely in the "New Age" marketplace—so many have entered public awareness, in fact, that it might seem trite or trivial to make any attempts of "enhancing" this field of study at all. Of course, someone making such assumptions does not know the "Mardukite way" of things very well! Having already accumulated a solid knowledge-base regarding the origins of humanity, human belief and human civilization, it is quite simple to reexamine what then immediately followed in an age when *magic* and *religion* still held some salient connection to the archetypal systems of Mesopotamia and Egypt.

In time, the areas surrounding Mesopotamia and Egypt developed and assimilated the *Anunnaki* systems—Phoenicians, Canaanites, Hebrews, Persians, Phrygians...even the Greeks and classical world. The tradition remained to uphold the authority of the state—the "Dragonblood" of the kings, priests and priestesses that used this "systemology" to form their own "empires" and "dynasties"—all of which preserved, in part, the "god-given" legacy that extended into prehistory. They also all share a tradition of secret, hidden, *esoteric*—or otherwise *occult*—traditions of *mystical spirituality* linking them back to the source...the *Path*. It is by following this *Path* that true and faithful *Self-Honest* kings, priests and priestesses may connect with a universal energetic source behind all of this—a beacon that is guiding us "home." This is a knowledge that the masses—the greater population—is seldom privy to, and thus we find the *real* division of class in society between those who *know* and are *actively participating* in "reality engineering"...and the remaining *herd*.

— 1 —
THE ORIGINS OF THE KABBALAH

Before the time of humans there existed a race of intelligent life that was not nearly as fixed to "condensed" perceptions of physical reality that we might be best familiar with. We seek out such beings today—based on our present recollection of history and the accounts made concerning *divine encounters* with humans, and we call them *gods*, *angels*, *spirits*... We know they eventually occupied "physical" forms that were far and removed from their original—or *alpha*—state, and these beings were able to reside in the universe so that they might be able to interact with "creation" as spiritual entities occupying physical vehicles. The means by which humans came into being is also found in the ancient texts: always beginning first with destruction of some heavenly planet or abode —by whatever names we might wish to call it. As a result of this, beings also occupied the *inner* parts of the planet *Earth*. While the surface of the planet was prepared for life, these beings occupied its *hollowness*. During the Earth-descent and transition of "light beings" into "conscious lifeforms" on this *plane*, a "Brotherhood of Light" formed specifically to guide this massive energetic movement toward direct-mass genetic intervention—a means to create suitable bodies to appropriately fit a "physical" environment: the formation of *genetic vehicles...bodies*.

This is the standard by which we might come to better know the ancient mysteries that are before us, waiting for us to *break their code*. The *Semitic* or *Hebrew Kabbalah* is one, though not the *oldest*, "map" by which the human mind can evolve to understand *how* and *why* things are the way they are—a means of exploring the basic *"pattern"* of all existences able to be experienced, since they are all *one* existence, experienced in fragmented parts. Our demonstrations of the BAB-ILI gate-system of Babylon provide evidence for an older source model—but the previous *Mardukite* discourses have not relayed a direct communication of these later derived correlating visions of the same systemology.

Formation of any relevant *"Kabbbalah"* will draw upon familiar archetypes to promote understanding of the cosmos on all levels—a pattern manifest in the universe as a macrocosm, but also the fundamental evolution of "intelligent design" found at the microcosmic or fundamental level of all being. Mystics represent this as a *tree*—whether a *Tree of Life* or *Tree of Knowledge*, but always a "tree."

A pattern we describe as "gnomonic expansion" (in mathematics) is the expression we see in tree-growth, not only on a symbolic level, but in the literal "formation" of the basic *patterns of life*—ever spreading and expanding outward from the "Source," while returning to the "Source," sharing a "fractal" relationship with the "whole." This understanding of reality constitutes *esoteric* lore hidden in the folds of what has otherwise become a "mundane" experience for the human condition. In ancient Mesopotamia, this is represented by the form and branches of the "date-palm" tree—the iconic "tree" found in most Mesopotamian art and lore.

As a microcosm, the "tree" represents the interconnected nature of all life and existence. This is a direct indication that we are all from the same *Source* and that all life and existence shares this relationship. At the core, all of the "true and faithful" spiritual and mystical and spiritual traditions and systems to later "bloom" also shared this basic tenet as a foundation of belief and practice. Manifestation eminent in the cosmos and on the planet Earth or in the progressive course of a person's own spiritual evolution, may all be charted as some entangled "branch" or "pathway" extended from this All-Source.

Until more recent "scientific" paradigms produced coherent post-modern "semantics" to define these energetic or spiritual relationships, the entire concept seemed wholly "esoteric," hidden away from any surface awareness or "vocabulary." In ancient times, the supreme mystical state —we now classify as *"entanglement"*—could only be defined as wholeness, interconnection or the *"All-as-One"* aspect of reality. But, this was too "transparent" for contemporary human minds and so we find a myriad of fragmented systems further created by human minds to label and define these perceived relationships. The primary drawback to this approach is that it keeps all of our understanding of things in "fragmented paradigms" where reality experience is separated by an infinite number of various *levels*, *layers* and *veils*.

Prior to the "systematization" of human civilization in *Mesopotamia*—a methodology that continues to drive human perception of reality and define the human condition to this day—life on earth operated, shall we say, at a different *"level"*—and we will say *"level"* since it seems nearly impossible to relay differences in *degree* to the human mind by any other syntax. The perception of reality was once far "greater" (wider or more encompassing) than what is experienced today by general standards of the *human genetic vehicle*—the physical body, and its functions, that our true spiritual identity or "I-AM" temporarily resides in.

Although only *one* reality is taking place, the 'range' or 'parameters' able to be perceived of this *wholeness* were once 'more' than what is allowed for by most contemporary *paradigms*—"paradigms" being the operating system used by the mind-of-the-body. During a time of simplicity and singularity, control of the human population by *Sky Gods*—or *Anunnaki* —was not debated or fought over, following a predetermined *pathway* defined by the *stars*. These "*divine beings*" worked alongside their creation—humanity—in its capacity to not only serve the "highest," but also to *seed* their creation with abilities to survive on their own, now upgraded from other possible forms of life on the planet.

In the most ancient eras, humans were given higher faculties from which to experience the world around them; including the ability to be *co-creators* of existence. They were taught the ways of *wholeness* and the *All-as-One* harmonic nature of the universe as it really is. Such an understanding of "universal energies" led to the first and most superior uses of technology on the planet, drawn from a power of unity and love and surpassing what has been executed in the modern, contemporary and highly 'fragmented' experience of technological possibility. This knowledge and its use was *not* "profit-driven," such as we see present in the world today. There was a emphasis on the "community" as opposed to "separation by wealth"—a drive to "share" the resources of the planet in unity, rather than use them as a means of societal control.

The interconnected pathways, branches and blossoms of the *tree* all "stem" from the fundamental ideal that the *Divine Spark* was existent in *All* creation, ever able to be divided and fragmented into "new" forms, but always *entangled* to the *Source* by some all-encompassing "level" of reality that ever remains as *wholeness*.

"Separation," "fragmentation" and *The Fall* (of humanity) from the *Source* is an illusion, but nonetheless *illustrative* of an important shift— a time when the course of *past things* were significantly changed, creating the way toward the world we have now. It is *this* period of change— a time of the *first systems*—that we begin to see the focus blur. Here we find the *first system* of Babylon and the later fragmentation of this archetype into a crystalline spectrum that has ever since kept the human population in *ignorance* of its own *unity*; a unity with *each other* and what has been dubbed *gods* and the *Divine*. "Semantic" fragmentation occurred very much like the 'biblical' perspective might show the "*Fall of the Tower of Babel*"—fracturing the "way to heaven" into a myriad of "languages."

All of "existential" reality is in some ways "separated" from the *All-as-One* wholeness for it to be treated as a "form" or "identity" (as its own energy signature). Yet, the "range" this is experienced by still allows for a "higher order" of experience than humans will typically perceive—and hence the perceived fragmentation. This means "transcendental" states are sought to validate "spiritual" or "higher" *levels* of reality within the latent potential of *human coding*—itself *another* meaning of the *tree*—being DNA. To experience this "lower," more "condensed" *level* of reality awareness, *genetic coding* of a potential "human being" required significant alteration from its *alpha* state.

The spiritual *Fall* was a metaphoric event, whereby the perceptual range of human consciousness was given its current modes of operation—but with infinite latent potential. The "states" achieved by *magicians* and *priests* who conduct the later "rites" and "rituals" in honor to, or by direction of, these *gods, angels* and *Anunnaki* beings seem to coincide by definition with expansions of potential "awareness" of the human condition. As a result, such *priests, magicians, avatars* and the like, were often considered *more* than "human" due to their "range" of experience—and as a result, their *influence*.

In many ways these systematized "*kabbalahs*" or representations of the *Tree of Life* ("*ladder of lights*," "stairway to heaven") are "defining" what, from one perspective, could be considered a *fall*—charting the *expansion* or *condensation* of manifested material existence. It shows a *godly* or *first-form* "realm" and further fragmentation or separation from *that* in succession, covering all aspects of physical, emotional and intellectual awareness, until we reach the most mundane and concrete forms.

When *seekers* examine the *Kabbalah*—or Babylonian StarGate systemology—we discover it represents the entire orchestra of existence, the bands and rays of light and life that intertwine to cause manifestation—they are all illustrated in separation or "fragmentation" from the *Source*, even though they remain connected or entangled to it. Each division is perceived as a continuous unfolding or expansion of the *first cause* or *first move* or *first form*—which Mesopotamians identified as a dragon. Where the *Hebrew* and *Judeo-Christian* tradition speaks of the "primordial sea" and the "separation" of this *sea* to bring forth life, the more antiquated cuneiform tablets from Babylon more describe the same event in greater detail—the birth of the first-form dragon "*Tiamat*" out of the ooze of the "primordial Abyss" (*Abzu*) that initially occupied all existence before its separation into forms by Cosmic Law.

[The specific forces and fragmentation of the Anunnaki paradigm are the subject of intensive exploration in the Mardukite Year-2 Core—which is to say *"Gates of the Necronomicon: The Secret Anunnaki Tradition in Babylon"* edited by Joshua Free—but within the context of a practical magical tradition, we will explore this further, while at the same time maintaining a consideration of modern esoteric applications, such as the *Enochian* or *Kabbalah* paradigms, for the present discourse.]

Once the method or *"pattern"* for life was conceived with *Tiamat* as the "first order" of creation, the *Enuma Eliš* cuneiform tablet series describes a host of creatures of varying types "spawned" by the dragon, also identified as the *"All-Mother"* of the fragmented identity-bodies of the same beings later given in lore as *gods, angels, messengers, watchers* and otherwise: *"Anunnaki"* Since *Tiamat*, the genetic "coil" (DNA) that programs all *pattern* into life-existence has been referred to as the "serpent coil"—the "cosmic serpent" coiled around the *"Tree of Life."*

Prior to the *"Fall"* or the "disposal of humanity" (via the *Flood* or some other calamity—see *Mardukite Tablet-G* in *"Necronomicon: The Anunnaki Bible"*), there was a mass "exodus" of *"gods"* and other *"angelic"* (*Anunnaki* and *Igigi*) beings—a period where the "highest" withdraw from this existence so as not to confine themselves to its more condensed "3-D" reality. Remaining *outside* the system, they could be allowed access to it by a "higher order." This is how they were able to more directly interact with it again later, by incarnating into appropriate *genetic vehicles*. As such, they appeared as *gods* and *angels* to post-diluvial humans—those residing in programmed societies after the "Flood" and the last Ice Age. They seeded the systems successfully, and our most antiquated literary sources are overflowing with such renderings.

It is during this "shift" in planetary consciousness (and radiated out into the local universe) that we also see a "division" or *polarity* of "power" begin to swell up—some pendulum movement of the cosmos that forces energetic activity, the illusion of 3-D movement in an otherwise *entangled* existence. Here we witness a rise of the *"Dark Brotherhood"*—beings preferring to "master" this existence from the *inside*, rather than withdraw into "higher orders." In the fractured and fragmented material existence, the crystalline nature of lights and shadows could be easily manipulated. The diverse array of *currents* and *energies* that formed the fabric of the screen and the lights displayed thereupon could all be manipulated to change the nature of *reality*—and that is exactly what they did, sparking an additional stream of fractured underground tradition.

In the truest nature of reality—which exists apart from the fragmentation of the "zones" of manifested existence—you see a very *static* and *amoral* force that is raw and primordial, all-encompassing and all-present in the heart of all existences that were ever energetically "separated" from this *Source*. This is what is described in the *Mesopotamian* accounts relaying information about a time before even the *Anunnaki* existed and before they fashioned a physical existence to occupy—possibly even to *get away* and *remove themselves* from chaotic primordial forces and into a *different* existence. Thus, we now have the manifested expanding pattern-programmed universe around us!

The concept of 'separating' a pattern of light existence from this primordial void might seem science-fiction, but it is actually what is described in the old *Kabbalistic* texts, the *Babili* system of Babylon and all of the *Gnostic* works the idea later influenced. For in our *Gnostic* example, we find the entire "division" of a physical world separated from a purely etheric and spiritual one to be the basis of all *evil*—and that any act or movement of *evil* present in humanity is really a result of this; an intentional separation of human consciousness from *All-as-One* wholeness by, what they call, an *evil demiurge*. Here you find the ancient "devil," a being that essentially installed "Ego" into human consciousness—a soul program by which a systematized being might perceive a condensed reality while at the same time "learning" and further interacting with this existence based on that learned programming... Such is *life*.

"Moral" or "ethical" implications behind all of what we have described is where most "*religion*" and "*dogma*" gets itself stuck. The emphasis on *sin* and innumerable shortcomings of the modern *human condition* are not necessarily the best focus when one is trying to "rise above" this programming. They must be addressed, surely, but they need not be a vehicle whereby some empirical institution should execute some dictatorship over its "followers." As polar forces, the two metaphoric "*brotherhoods*" appear to be opposite, though they are one and the same—each wanting to work itself *out* of the "systems," but each going about this wholly differently. *The same in nature; differing only in degree. . .*

— 2 —
ANGELS & GODS OF THE ANCIENT WORLD

Continuing with a generic concept in mind—the *"Brotherhood of Light"* is responsible for the "vehicles" of what most mystics call *Ascension*. This idea of *Ascension* represents a pious and priestly means used to "rise above the human program" and join with our ancient *creator ancestors* by assuming forms with "higher faculties" to perceive or experience (life) existence. This true and faithful Ancient Mystery School is not concerned with "worldly systems" as a means of *Illumination*, nor are they concerned with practices that most people would consider "magick," in the sense of "spellcraft" or conjuring demons. To them, such feats are not necessary—and even potentially dangerous or damaging to the spiritual self. That the same Cosmic Laws can be used for such ends is irrelevant—the later *systems* are not a concern to them, for the myriad of applications and correspondences merely show interconnectedness of all existence and require no fragmented *classifications*.

Standing watch at the *Gates*—from *this* side of the BAB-ILI (or *Gateway of the Gods*)—we find the *"Dark Brotherhoods"* dispensing fragmented knowledge to humanity, while retaining any "true" *keys* for themselves. In fact, it would seem the primary division of forces—be it the *Brotherhoods*, *Anunnaki* bloodlines, or even related European lore regarding the "Seelie" versus "Unseelie" courts—seems to often relate back to the "human species" and how to deal with it. Obviously there are differing opinions. Those remaining to educate and seed civilizations and new consciousness of the *realm* were eventually known as *"Fallen Ones"* in later interpretations—those "fallen" to earth from the heavens.

Genetic manipulation and interbreeding with humanity can be gleaned from all related ancient lore—even the *serpent and the tree* motif given in the *Hebrew* version of *Mesopotamian* accounts of *Eden*, when *Enki*—whose name means "Lord of the Earth"—became a serpent of knowledge for human evolution, blending his *genes* or 'waters of life' with the species, making them "like gods" with "knowledge of good and evil." Both *Hebrew* and *Mesopotamian* accounts agree that the *Anunnaki* (or *Elohim*) worked together to "fashion a worker class" in *their* own image. Later there is evidence of selective breeding among priests and king bloodlines. All of these ancient records may be found verbatim in the original Mardukite source book: *"Necronomicon: The Anunnaki Bible."*

When a *seeker* examines the accounts left to us from the ancient world, we find *no shortage* of "Divine Encounters" to ponder regarding relationships between "humans" and these "otherworldly beings." Religions classify them as *gods* or *angels*, "divine-messengers" sent by the *Source* to execute *Divine Will* "below the firmament." Mystics and shamans speak of *star-brothers* and *creator* forces that once walked with them physically on earth and now exist on the outskirts of perceptual reality. Magicians and Wizards likely identify these *spirits* as "hierarchies" of *daemonic* beings and *forgotten deities* that can be summoned or called if the proper incense blend is burned at such-and-such time in the light of a certain planet or phase of the moon, &tc.

A person today is not given a sufficient background regarding these ancient worldview "semantics"—certainly not enough to base opinions as to what *is* or *is not* reality, for in wholeness, we can easily look at these and other examples to see a unifying *pattern* unfolding before us; a critical "key" lost in folds of fragmented knowledge. These may all be describing the same "objsective phenomenon," existentially described by one or another "language" and "semantic" understanding of the world. These things are not separate—such thinking is what created stumbling blocks in the advancement of human evolu*tion via even the "New Age"* methods. Assuming such things are continued to be treated "separately," then the "total awareness" that so many *seek* will remain unattainable.

The primary message of this current work is to express the *singularity* behind these "fragmented" human experiences. That regardless of how each culture classified similar types of "encounters," we are essentially dealing with the identical phenomenon. Of course, in our present understanding of things using modern-day "semantics," it might be easier to look at these accounts as UFO or *"alien"* phenomenon; but a century ago, the same thing might have been dealt with in more "magical" terms as *spirits* and *daemons*—and further back still, we see centuries of *fairy lore* and lore of mysterious *star people*, until we reach more ancient origins of these diverse systems.

Magical lore describes an entire hierarchy of *spiritual entities*, usually referred to by a semantic root *angelos*—"divine messengers" from the "sky" or "heavens" using "unseen *god-given* powers" to help or harm by Divine Will. Prior to even this, we find origins in the earliest *Egyptian* and even earlier *Mesopotamian* literary sources concerning *Anunnaki* and other *"Sky Beings"* by varying semantics and languages—*Anunnaki* simply being the most ancient Mesopotamian term for this description.

When a dubious student really delves into what the "occult" actually *is*, a "pattern" is found, linking all of these various "concepts" together into a cohesive "wholeness." This is not guarantee—but, since most scholarly magicians successful throughout the ages have all alluded to these "*Other Beings,*" then why should we debate? That there exists a myriad of interpretative forms by which to understand these "mysteries" is not the argument—what we are most concerned with is *what* we are interpreting and *why* we are doing so the way we do. It is not surprising that the semantics used to describe the last several thousand years of magic and religion should be "*angelic,*" referencing "messenger beings" that first descended from the starry skies, *heaven* and the "godly-zones."

Whether working from some form of "ancient mysticism" derived from the *Semitic Kabbalah* as relayed from some "grimoire," or simply the reinvention and installment of an "ancient pantheon" as attributed by a specific regional-culture, the driving purpose remains the same—reestablishment of something lost, a reconnection of distance and formation of a *true and faithful* communication and relationship with these beings —by whatever name they are given.

The original classification of "angels" is a *religious* concept that erupts from the Middle East—specifically the *Persian* traditions of *Iran* known as Zoroastrianism. The *Yezidi* of modern *Iraq* are another indigenous pre-*Christian* faction tied to post-Babylonian Mardukite traditions—as explored within earlier volumes of the "Mardukite Core"—they are such a key piece of our forgotten history that the culture became targets of the radical Islamic group ISIS, as did other sacred sites of ancient Mesopotamia. Although terminology changed, "angels" were originally the gods of ancient humans and a basis of their belief-systems. Prior to the move toward monotheism, the angelic hosts worked together as "legions" in preparation of the planet and forthcoming "creations" of life upon it.

A ruling "hierarchy" or "order" is maintained by these beings as recorded in lore describing *Anunnaki* ranking and their *Igigi* legions of what are later dubbed "Watchers" or "*Nephilim*" by biblical authors. Here we discover primitive origins to pantheistic division of cosmic leadership. In the records commonly accessible to *Judeo-Christian* traditions, we are offered only slight information concerning a simplified "division" of life in prehistoric times—between the "*Sons of God*" and the "*Sons of Man,*" or else, "sky-originating beings" versus "earth-born." Since this time of "legends," magical and religious classification and ordering of these various *angelic orders* and *legions* has filled volumes!

Most encounters involving humans and *gods* are initially amoral—without polarity. Any kind of "Luciferian Rebellion" is really a modernized perception of any number of possible "rivalries" from the ancient world—whether *real* or *imagined*. Many of these are inspired by *Judeo-Christian*, and other similarly influenced, traditions observing *Anunnaki* polarity—a singular *god* opposed by a *devil* representing all that is *evil* in the universe. Barring the more physical manifestations of pestilence and disease, such "dualistic" beliefs concerning *gods* and *devils* are recent additions to human consciousness and do not reflect the energy that we actually encounter in the most antiquated traditions—those that went on to inspire later, more widely known, interpretations.

The Yezidi *"Black Book"*—given in our *"Necronomicon: The Anunnaki Bible"*—relays information first given to them by a "holy messenger" of "God" appearing in *angel* form. Details reveal a "Supreme Being" creating *Seven Angel* servants—one for each "planetary-aligned" day of the week—corresponding directly to Sumerio-Babylonian *"Gates."* Another similar example is *Enochian magic*, dedicated to magical or ceremonial use of planetary *angelic powers*. All such traditions recognize *angels* as "crystalline fragments" or extensions from the *Source—or* personalities of the same. Given this, use of *Divine Names*—for example, the *Tetragrammaton*—develops among the beliefs regarding magical success.

In "high magical" and "spiritual" systems of magic, the names and identity of "God" grows in significance the further in time and space we arrive from Babylon. Figures holding a position of "local god," as we find while pouring over the ancient records, shifts as does the human understanding of it. The *Anunnaki* know themselves to not be "God" in the sense of an *Eternal Source of All Being*. But this *Eternal Source* is not necessarily "present" in a personified material sense—and is instead the *Divine Spark* residing at the heart of all things. This means what ancient humans *did* encounter as *"Divinity"* was not a perfect reflection of this *Eternal Source* either, but instead one of *It's* "faces" or "ambassadors"; hence, the later monotheistic semantics of *angelic messenger spirits* to a singular *"Supreme God."*

— 3 —
THE HEBREW KABBALAH

Prior to incorporation into quasi-magical systems and traditions, the *Kabbalah* formed the basis of Hebrew (Semitic) spiritual mysticism that originated in *Mesopotamia* and from the *Anunnaki*-based sources. Much of it was developed via cultural *osmosis*, but even the Talmudic Rabbinical tradition is credited to Babylon—most likely solidified during the "exile." But, it was much later, during the *Christian*-ruling period of the *Dark Ages*, that *Kabbalistic* mysticism integrated into *esoteric* "underground" traditions represented by *magicians* and *sorcerers* of counterculture. To *Hebrew* (or *Jewish*) people today, the QBL (*Qabala*) simply came from "God"—or rather the "voice of *God*" as the angel *Metatron*. In *Anunnaki* lore predating the same, we find this force attributed to the "*librarian-scribe of the gods*"—observed as "*Nabu*" in the Babylonian (Mardukite) system, and later, the "Mercurial-Thoth-Hermes" archetype.

Kabbalistic knowledge—and its origins—always comes from a *godly* source, composed of *godly* knowledge that would otherwise be "forbidden" for humans to comprehend. Even today, if I were of a purist *Judeo-Christian* mystic, I would not even set such words onto paper or explore these mysteries for public benefit at all, nor could the subject of *God* be explored in this sense—which is of course, *blasphemous* and *heretical*. In fact, exploration of *God*, or consideration of any *Mesopotamian* lore that does not exactly promote *Judeo-Christian* ideals, often is only understood as *evil* or *pagan*—and naturally we are exploring *Kabbalistic* lore outside of *Rabbinical* institutions, which is (*"shanda"*) disgraceful.

A simple preview of the plethora of *magical books*, *esoteric grimoires*, varying "*keys*" of *Solomon*, *Abramelin*—or whoever else—shows reoccurring signposts and triggers under *Kabbalistic* guises that return us to the original *Anunnaki* systems, those which inspired the later *Assyrian* and *Semitic* lore. These varying traditions share a common source, but varied "understanding" and "use" manifested knowledge *separation*—and its pursuers remain separated between each other. Yet each speaks of an all-powerful *Divine Source* outside this time-space that does not necessarily make a visible, tangible appearance in this world. We are proficient at personifying this force, but what results is not a communication with the *Source* but with some intermediaries—angelic *spirits* and *demons* that reside somewhere between our understanding and the *All*.

Angels, spirits or "*Sons of God*" play a significant role in the *Kabbalah*. The system shares many parallels with the later emerging *Enochian tradition*, and both aspects easily assimilated into the (GD) *Golden Dawn System of Magic*. The *Kabbalah* represents a "cosmography" of inner and outer aspects of the universe—which are the same—only differing in degree. The *Hebrew Kabbalah* illustrates the order in which the *Creative Force* (AIN) produced manifested energies—forces that condensed into refined materialized expressions ("*Sephiroth*" or Spheres) before solidifying a material existence or physical kingdom ("Malkuth").

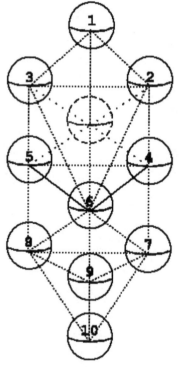

According to one source, it was *Metatron*—the voice and scribe of *God* in Hebrew tradition—that gave the *Kabbalah* to Adam (the Hebrew *Adapa*) in E.DIN (*Eden*) as a spiritual energetic "map" to return to the *Source*.

This tradition of knowledge was later passed on to Abraham and Moses, paralleling mystical lore of other evolving local cultures after a time. At the very least, it constitutes the basis for "God-given" "*magical*" powers described in the *Old Testament*."

In its *Hebrew* form, the *Kabbalah* consists of ten (plus one) main divisions or spheres known as *Sephiroth*. These are held as emanations or manifestations of the *Divine*—numbered from one to ten beginning with the top (*Kether*) representing "Heights" of creation and the abode of the *Creator*, down to ten (*Malkuth*), often translated as "Kingdom," but which might be more correctly interpreted as the "Depths" of creation—the most solidified concrete condensation of manifestation. Separating—or between—these two "extremes" of a continuous spectrum, we find a variety of energetic concentrations: "stations" and "pathways." This all-encompassing flow of energy is continuous, although we are aware of experiencing only a small portion of the total spectrum. A unifying singular *Clear Light* filters through a prismatic array of degrees before reaching the world of varied forms that humans know.

Prior to the *Hebrew Kabbalah*, the *Babili* system from which it is drawn illustrates the same concepts as a succession of *Gates* or "veils." In fact, once we get beyond the "*tenth sephiroth*" of Malkuth—which is essentially the "Earth Gate"—the next <u>six</u> *sephiroth* of the *Hebrew Kabbalah* actually correlate one-to-one with *Anunnaki Babylonian Stargates*.

[10. Malkuth—Earth Gate (*Terran*)]

9. Yesod—Lunar Gate (*First Veil*)

8. Hod—Mercurian Gate (*Second Veil*)

7. Netzach—Venusian Gate (*Third Veil*)

6. Tiphareth—Solar Gate (*Fourth Veil*)

5. Geburah—Martian Gate (*Fifth Veil*)

4. Chesed—Jovian Gate (*Sixth Veil*)

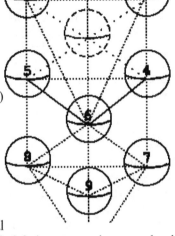

It is only when we get to the "Supernal Triangle" (Trinity) of the *Hebrew Kabbalah* that matters become cloudy when relating specifically to the *Babili* system. But, should actually be expected with good reason, not only because of knowledge distrotions, but also due to the "zone" beyond the *sixth* "veil," "gate" or "division." The *Seventh Veil*—though unnumbered—is shadowed by the notorious system "loophole"—*Daath*, the "invisible" *eleventh sephiroth*. The *Seventh Veil* or *Gate* in the *Babili* system is aligned to Saturn, a position held by *Ninib–Ninurta*, the Sumerian heir-son of *Enlil*. Traditionally, the "*third sephiroth*" of the *Hebrew Kabbalah* actually correlates with the *Seventh Veil*. We don't see disparity until we compare systems, for if the "*third sephiroth*" is literally *Ninib-Ninurta* as "Saturn" then the new lore dissolves what we *know* to be the case concerning the proto-Sumerian "Supernal Trinity"—*Anu, Enlil* and *Enki*. In the past, it has been easy to simply allow this anomaly, though if we are to observe the *Anunnaki* "Trinity" proper—the "*third sephiroth*" should really be attributed to *Enki* in terms of succession, or even *Enlil* if sharing a designation with his heir-son, which he does not traditionally do. As such, this is really only relevant for "comparative studies"—but even this yields so many anomalies that it becomes a distraction. With our forthcoming examination of "*Divine Names*," the confusion this knowledge incites for a neophyte of these studies will hopefully pass.

The original *Gnostic* schools of *Christianity*—those later abolished as heretical—were also interested in preserving the integrity of the original lore constituting religious and spiritual practice, such as the *Kabbalah*, *angelic forces* and spiritual intermediaries. Organized institutions prefer to be the intermediaries between humans and *God*—because personal empowerment of the general congregation of "lay" people seems to in some way undermine dependency on the "organization" for dispensing religion and "spiritual wisdom." Mysteries of *Kabbalah*, even among the *Jewish* sects, have remained very closely guarded—as once were the esoteric teachings of the Ancient Mystery School in Babylon.

Certainly there are a select few gleaning *magicians* and *sorcerers* that have caught a glimpse of the underlying antiquated *Anunnaki* singularity behind the systematic interconnectivity. Only recently, within the past decade, with the assistance of a mere handful of *real pioneers*, we have been able to truly evolve our understanding within the Mardukite move-ment. And while it is found to predate all other systems, this original *Mesopotamian-Anunnaki* orientation has only recently been brought to light properly—a plethora of archaeological research coupled within the intensive esoteric and mystical pursuits. Although we can respectfully explore the *Kabbalah* in relation to the *Anunnaki Babili* system—we are not glorifying or propagating use of anything other than the most ancient methodology—the remainder is offered purely for posterity.

The *Kabbalah* is sacred and rooted in Judaic tradition, but it developed directly from culture and language integrated together in the *Ancient Near East* (or *Middle East*) as made up of post-Sumerian traditions—among them the *Babylonian Empire* that Jews were forced to exist under in exile during their literary developmental period. Even when we com-pare ancient traditions to standardized practices today, the actual term "*Kabbalah*"—although derived from an ancient word "*Qibil*" (QBL), as in "*to receive*"—is not as antiquated as one might think, even in the light of a long-standing Semitic "genetic" legacy. The first reference publicly known with a direct reference to the systematized *Kabbalah* comes from the 11th century—only a millennium ago—from the Jewish philosopher, *Solomon ibn Gabirol*.

Philosophically we might attribute origins of a *kabbalistic* "oral tradi-tion" to "biblical" figures, such as Moses and Abraham, but we can be sure that these men were not carrying around copies of the *Zohar* or the *Sefer Yetzirah* —and both "key" texts date only to the 2nd century A.D., with their oldest possible origins a mere four to six centuries years prior.

— 4 —
DIVINE NAMES OF GOD

Putting aside all legend and taking historical accounts as our guide: it is true that the "Practical Kabbalah" is pre-Christian in origin, but in the versions accessible today, the system is chronologically no older than *Gnosticism*, drawing upon the same sources: *Zoroastrianism* and post-Babylonian *Chaldean* (*Mardukite*) systems. In fact we see a rise in the "*Kabbalistic*" subscribers once orthodox Christians dissolved all efforts of *Gnosticism*, a philosophy later reintegrated into the *Kabbalah*, classical approaches to "*Hermetics*" (Babylo-Egypto-Greek mysticism) and even "Hellenistic Judaism"—all of which now primarily operate only "underground."

Until the 16th century, covert religious bans on public study of the *Kabbalah* restricted such lore to Rabbinical schools—and naturally any exoteric lore reaching the masses carried a shroud of esoteric jargon that protected the "inner mysteries" from corruption—although we now see that it had the opposite effect. This is the same time period when many popularized medieval "*grimoires*" start to appear—those that blend the *Kabbalah* with other Judeo-Christian lore under a systematic framework we would better expect from *Mesopotamian* or even *Persian* sources.

When we examine the more archaic history surrounding original forms of "Jewish Mysticism," a system appears—the precursor to the modern *Kabbalah* (*Qabala, Cabala,* &tc.)—called the *Hekalot* (*Hechalot,* &tc.), meaning "ascension." And how appropriate—for this methodology is the "missing link" derived directly from *Babylonian* (Mardukite Anunnaki "*Bab-ili*"), *Chaldean* ("magi," &tc.) and *Persian* ("Zoroastrian") systems, which led directly to the traditional *Kabbalah*.

Parallels between the *Hekalot* and *Bab-ili* systems are quite clear—we find the *Seven Gates* as they appear in Mesopotamia, before the lore evolved into the "ninth through fourth *sephiroth*," with the same "fuzzy" or "unclear" *seventh* gate preceding the "*Supernal Trinity*." Clearly this final gate represents a transitional state, perhaps more akin to *Daath* (the eleventh and unseen *sephira* linked to the "*outside*" ("*other side*") of the "*tree*" from *within* the system. This elusive *gate* or *doorway* accesses the outside without reaching the "Supernal Trinity" or ascending the path of the "*AINs*"—the *Abyss*, the *Primordial "Outside,"* else "*The Void.*"

Perhaps "spiritually superior" to the later derived *Kabbalah*, the original archaic *Anunnaki-(Bab-ili)*-originating "*Hekalot*" tradition is best known among modern *esoteric* "New Age" systems as the MERKABA, or else "*Merkaba-Kabala*." The discovery of this lore—at least in the name of the *Hebrew* tradition—is credited to *Ezekiel* from his spiritual visions and "divine encounters." As ancient as these timeframes might seem to contemporary minds, the notorious Hebrew prophet, *Ezekiel*, from *Old* Testament (Christian) lore, was one of the many Jews exiled to Babylon during the Neo-Babylonian reign of King Nabuchadnezzar II, during the 6th century BC.

Ezekiel is most famous, however, for his vision of the *Chariot of God*, or what others have translated as the "*Throne of God*"—also known as the MERKABA. The word is "active," denoting "movement," "riding" or "flying"—and as such, the "*chariot*" or "*wheels*" are appropriate to the description of *Ezekiel's* vision: a "light vehicle" that moved via four wings. Four "faces" or "figures" also appear—either literally or carved into the machine—that of a bull (*earth*), eagle (*air*), lion (*fire*) and man (*water*), the same combination of figures composing the famous *lamasu* Mesopotamian winged-guardian spirits often appearing as gate statues. The spiritual emphasis of *Maasei Merkavah* tradition (described in sparse *Hekalot* writings) is exactly what we expect from a methodology of "*ascension*" derived from the archetypal *Babili* system of the *Anunnaki*. *Seven* divisions beyond the Earth Plane (*gate*) are described—or "seven heavens"—separating the elemental realm occupied by humans from the abode (domain) where the MERKABA that *Ezekiel* beheld actually resides. As systematic beliefs and practices develop more firmly, we see the understanding distinguished further and further by labels and "magic words," but above all: "*Divine Names.*"

When we put aside more "conventional" implements of the magical arts; garments and regalia, tools and sigil-seals—it is the *names* and *words* that appear *most* significant when practicing forms of magic intended to encounter "higher forms" and "intelligent entities" behind the scenes of *esoteric* mystery traditions. Above all possible magic words invoked, the "*Divine Names*" are held in the highest regard by *priest-magicians* and *priestesses*—meaning, of course: "*names*" for *God*. Just as manifest existence becomes more dense and fragmented (with varying *lights* and *veils*), so have *Names of God* increasingly "mutated" with time and the myriad of "language semantics" later applied to this spiritual form of *cryptomancy*—the deciphering of "truenames" and "energy signatures," or vibration patterns underlying the true nature of all things.

It is easy to understand the significance "words" and "names" carry in *Anunnaki* tradition—the first writing systems, themselves, developed on *Sumerian* and *Babylonian* tablets. Likewise, we should not be surprised to find related mystical lore among the *priests* and *magicians* of the later derived system-traditions—including the *Kabbalah*, Egypto-Greek *Hermetics*, and of course native *Chaldean* and *Zoroastrian* movements. All of these systems are based on a "personal relationship" with "*Divinity*" using "secret" or "esoteric" lore to call upon these "*forces.*"

Ancient priests and priestesses representing the *Anunnaki* tradition acted as intermediaries between the general human population and beings perceived as "*Divine.*" In the most remote past, these "beings" physically resided in their very cities, occasionally occupying the *ziggurat-temples* built high mounds of each region. In early Sumerian traditions, only *priest-magicians* and *priestesses* were able to transmit communication with *Anunnaki* "Sky Gods" observed in the pantheon. This dynamic shifts during the Babylonian-Mardukite period (c. 2000 B.C.), as a rise in local or "personal magic" emerges among the common folk. During this post-Sumerian period, many individual *Anunnaki* members remained patron "central" deities to specific areas, further fragmenting the knowledge. Finally, with the rise of Babylon proper, focus is maintained on an intellectual and spiritual "unification"—something maintained as an intellectual pursuit by the later *Assyrian* culture.

After interpretations of magical arts reached common people, *Hermetic* attempts began at "unlocking" whatever esoteric secrets were withheld by the original priests, priestesses and caretakers of the ancient tradition. *Divine Names* became a paramount staple of function for newer forming systems—the belief in going around intermediaries socially and politically installed to oversee religion and spirituality. The whole matter of temple-initiation is intellectually side-stepped by using "passwords" and "Divine Names" that were thought to exercise the same cosmic power and authority as the "owners" of the names. This new "magic" became a form of "counter-culture" existing outside of, and in many cases in opposition to, the "*Realm*"—an alternate stream of cultural evolution that developed "underground" alongside the rest of civilization.

The most recent magical revivals of the past century have, in fact, spent a great deal of energy and attention toward the rediscovery and revival of these *Kabbalistic* grimoires and practices—much of it brought to the surface world via "New Age" markets. But beneath this, deeper mysteries are sought by those seeking the most ancient sources of this lore.

One challenge presented wen examining (or even enacting) the derived traditions from the eyes of its Source (in this case, the *Anunnaki* system) regards transfer of varying names and attributive properties or correspondences used for magical lore. As any system develops, changes take place for *utility*—the assimilated work is always adapted to a preexisting paradigm: regarding the *Kabbalah*, this means a later-emerging system of Babylonian recalibrated to fit the *Judaic* paradigm—specifically with *Hebrew* language-semantics, or those borrowed from related Canaanite streams, &tc. It is most beneficial for a Mardukite "Adept" *seeker-reader* to have full literary access to a "greater legacy" of the *Bab.ili* system when attempting to "synchronize" all the later developing knowledge. Without this bigger picture—the image on the cover-box of the puzzle— all one is left with is a myriad of "pieces" spanning space and time.

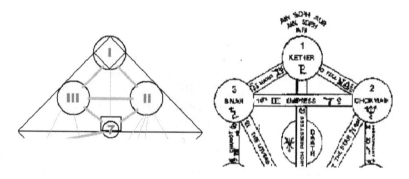

There are many parallels that could easily be drawn between the *Babili* system described within the "Mardukite Core" and the *Kabbalah* that is popularized from not only "*Jewish Mysticism*," but also throughout the "New Age" magical traditions based on such. Certainly, we can see from facets that we *know* to be the case—such as the *Supernal Trinity* or the planetary-aligned *Gates*—where the remaining details may fall. Once we have successfully determined that the two systems parallel one another, the next primary interest of the initiate is ascribing *names* and *words of power* to these domains. And this must be performed *Self-Honestly* so that we do not further fragment our understanding of the system.

In our previous lesson, I have introduced some of the names of the *veils* and alignment of this system—based on their *Hebrew* names and planetary allocations. But where we are most seasoned to observe the planets based on their Roman-Latin names, the same pantheon appears in its former Mesopotamian form—naturally with Mesopotamian names—and they are the names of the *Anunnaki*.

Anunnaki names occupying the "upper" or "*Supernal*" group of three (considered a "*trinity*" or "*triangle*") are treated as a "higher" class than the *Seven*. In the *Babili* tradition, they are the "Elder Gods" derived from the proto-Sumerian pantheon: *Anu*, *Enlil* and *Enki*. The remaining *Seven* are treated synonymously in both systems.

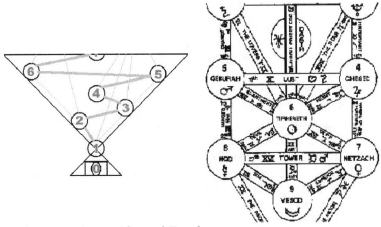

0. The Terran Gate—*Physical Temple*
1. The Lunar Gate—*Domain of Nanna-Sin*
2. The Mercurian Gate—*Domain of Nabu-Tutu*
3. The Venusian Gate—*Domain of Inanna-Ishtar*
4. The Solar Gate—*Domain of Shammash-Utu*
5. The Martian Gate—*Domain of Nergal-Erra*
6. The Jovian Gate—*Domain of Marduk*
7. The Saturnalian Gate—*Domain of Ninib-Ninurta*

The *Seven* accessible "*Gates*" or "*Stairway to Heaven*" leads an initiate on the path of Ascension—but to where? To the "higher" supernal trinity of figures with the greatest effect on early human consciousness as *Divinity*—or else *concrete* representations of the same *abstraction*—such as *Anu*, the "Father" in *Heaven*, and his two sons, *Enlil* and *Enki*. Each heads a primary faction of the *Anunnaki* pantheon on earth, both during prehistoric and religious (or "biblical") time periods. The language and systematic understanding regarding the *Anunnaki* in the proto-Sumerian tradition went on to directly influence Judeo-Christian expression of a "*Divine Trinity*" acting in unison to bring about material creation—the "lower spheres"— "orders" and "legions" of beings that act as "guardians" and ambassadors of the same. Again, we find a parallel between the *Anunnaki* and *Igigi* contrasting *God*—the EL—and *Angels*—the Elohim.

When we consider the archaic *Kabbalah* in conjunction with *Gnosticism* (the "*Knowers*") we begin to see the "God" of *this* world in a new light. For one, it would seem that the "God" of *this world*, is not the *only* God; simply the God of *this world*, which just so happens to be the "lowest," most "solid" and condensed emanation of the *Source*. To *Gnostics*, this "move" or "act" to separate and dominate the "physical world" from the "heavenly" or "spiritual' domains was considered *evil*, and therefore that "demiurge," though dominant as a *god* to those of this realm, was also *evil* and not the "true" *God*. One can easily see *why* this early form of *Christianity* was not popular by "authoritarian institutions" dependent on people's worship and faith in this *God*.

Clearly the *Gnostics* understood that *Anunnaki* figures had assisted the materialization of the physical world and influenced life thereupon it. The *Anunnaki* were significant and perhaps even "Divine" by some sense of the "word," but they were not the *Divine Source*—they were not literally the same as the actual *Eternal Spark* that resides at the core of all "creation." The "Absolute element" was "higher" still than anything detectable from faculties of the "human condition" As a result, "*gnosis*" or "true knowledge" ("divine knowledge") is attainable only through a "transcendental" (spiritual or mystical) state of *awareness* in *Self-Honesty*. But, the "highest" personifications that could be realized within the system were names for the "Supernal Trinity." In proto-Babylonian (or Sumerian) lore, this is realized in three key figures:

I. [10] A – AN—*Anu*
II. [9] EL – BEL—*Enlil*
III. [8] IA – Ea—*Enki*

Even during the Sumerian era, *Anu* remains a distant figure, seemingly removed from happenings on Earth. Such matters are left to his two sons —*Enlil* and *Enki*—primary *Anunnaki* leaders that interacted with humans. These figures and their offspring (most notably, the *Seven*) are what constitutes most "divine encounters" for ancient humans and their understanding of the "*Divine*." Most certainly, these archetypal experiences appeared in later languages and cultures—including *Hebrew*—and these varying interpretations lend to the basis of all religious and spiritual beliefs. Given such limited direct contact, few cuneiform incantation tablets (or "prayers") actually invoke powers of *Anu* directly. The heavenly force is considered too vast for channeling directly and to degrade it to anything more physically accessible would be to compromise the very nature of what is represented.

By the *Neo-Babylonian Chaldean* period and rise of Semitic traditions, the role of "*Kingship in Heaven*" is equated to the full extent of power keeping the universe in motion—now contained in an unspeakable and unknowable name, termed the *Tetragrammaton* in Hebrew-based mysticism. Mesopotamian priest-magicians and priestesses more commonly evoked a subsidiary deity from the Anunnaki lineage (pantheon) to invoke known names rather than pursue methods of Egypto-Hermetic *cryptomancy* to divine and compel spirits against their will. In Mardukite Chaldeo-Babylonian tradition, names of *Enki* and *Marduk* are evoked to speak the names on their behalf—and later traditions often used these to replace obscure and "secret" names altogether.

As *Lenormant* relates in his treatise on *Chaldean Magic*:—

> "True indeed there was a supreme name which possessed the power of commanding gods and extracting from them a perfect obedience, but that name remain-ed the inviolable secret of [EA–*Enki*]. In exceptionally grave cases [the priest] besought [EA–*Enki*], through his mediator Silikmulukhi [Marduk], to pronounce the solemn word in order to reestablish order in the world and restrain [temper] the powers of the abyss. But the enchanter did not know that name, and could not in consequence introduce it into his formulae. ...*he* could not obtain or make use of it, he only requested the god who knew it to employ it, without endeavoring to penetrate the terrible secret himself."

As the era shifted to a post-Babylonian period—when *gods* no longer appeared "visibly" on the planet, leaving control of societal civilization to the *priest-kings* chosen by descent, ruling by "Divine Right"—the *magicians* and *wizards* sought to "divine" the power once restricted to a few loremasters and keepers of the original knowledge. But esoterica was already poorly maintained and often fragmented by this time, and this *feat* of divining "Absolute Power," being of course impossible, accelerated corruption and mutation of the *Great Magical Arcanum*. And when these "idealistic fantasies" failed, the *magicians* and *sorcerers* began to rely on "lower" hierarchies of *spirits* far more accessible than the *Supernals*, or even the *Seven*. Even when the *Seven Gates* do appear in the *Merkaba* lore of the *Seven Palaces*—the "*sheva hekalot*"—each of the *Gates* (or *Palaces*) are represented by a *sephiroth* of the *Kabbalah* and a hierarchy of spiritual intelligences, all derived from *Babili* lore.

First Palace = Kabbalah: *Malkuth* (10) & *Yesod* (9)
"*Hekhal Livnat HaSapir*"—Palace of of sapphire bricks
  (Terran-Earth & Lunar Gates, *Earth God* & *Nanna*)
    Spirits: Dehaviel, Kashriel, Gahoriel, Botiel, Tofhiel, Dehariel,
      Matkiel and Shuiel (Sheviel)

Second Palace = Kabbalah: *Hod* (8)
"*Hekhal Etzem HaShamayim*"—Palace of the Essence of Heaven.
  (The Mercurian Gate—*Nabu*)
    Spirits: Tagriel, Metpiel, Sarhiel, Arfiel, Sheharariel, Satriel,
      Regaiel, Saheviel

Third Palace = Kabbalah: *Netzach* (7)
"*Hekhal Nogah*"—Palace of Brightness
  (The Venusian Gate—*Inanna-Ishtar*)
    Spirits: Shevooriel, Retzutziel, Shulmooiel, Savliel, Zehazahiel,
      Hadriel, Bezariel

Fourth Palace = Kabbalah: *Geburah/Gevurah* (6)
"*Hekhal Zekhut*"—Palace of Valor
  (The Solar Gate—*Shammash/Samas-Utu*)
    Spirits: Pachdiel, Gevoortiel, Kazooiel, Shekhiniel, Shatkiel,
      Araviel, Kafiel, Anaphiel.

Fifth Palace = Kabbalah: *Hesed* (5)
"*Hekhal Ahava*"—Palace of Love
  (The Martian Gate—*Nergal & Ereshkigal*)
    Spirits: Tachiel, Uziel, Gatiel, Getahiel, Safriel, Garafiel, Gariel,
      Dariel, Falatriel

Sixth Palace = Kabbalah: *Tiphareth* (4)
"*Hekhal Ratzon*"—Palace of (Godly) Desire
  (The Jovian Gate—*Marduk*)
    Spirits: Katzmiel, Gehaghiel, Roomiel, Arsavrasbiel, Agroomiel,
      Faratziel, Mechakiel, Tofariel

Seventh Palace = Kabbalah: *Binah* (3), *Chokmah* (2), *Kether* (1)
"*Hekhal Kodesh HaKodashim*"—Palace of the Holy of Holies
  (The Saturnalian Gate and *Supernals*)

— 5 —
TETRAGRAMMATON

Merkaba Kabala—as previously described—is not the only *kabbalistic* subject of archaic study—but it is one of the oldest and thus we see the most significant synchronicity with the *Babili* "source" tradition. Mostly we begin to see an emphasis on *Holy Names*—or words of power connected to specific energies, entities, or emanations from the *Source* that humans might encounter. This newer esoteric form of *cryptomancy* became popular in the *Kabbalah* and other *Hermetic* systems emphasizing verbal components to ritual magic—intoned or invoked "names" of *Divinity*—as a means of connecting (or communicating) energetically with the desired force. Yet above all these pantheons and hierarchies of spirits we find the "highest" name of the "highest order" maintained as the most coveted *esoteric* secret, *Hermetically* concealed in lore known as into what is known as: *the Tetragrammaton.*

The modern magical revival inspired many texts and esoteric traditions to explore the *Tetragrammaton*—the most "secret name" of God, alluded to in *Kabbalistic* lore and its related ceremonial-ritual "grimoires," such as the *Key of Solomon.* As with other aspects of ancient tradition, lore of this "unspeakable name" is often cited, but seldom relayed in wholeness or *Self-Honesty*, and naturally only within a context of *Judeo-Christian* paradigms.

Literally speaking the "tetragram" is a four-letter—or *fourfold*—name, glyph or sign; the most sacred, secret or otherwise "unspeakable" *Name of God* in Judaic tradition. The philosophical significance of "four" ties the name to the "physical world"—the domain of the Earth and its elemental zones. This is a good indicator of the energetic identity that is attached to it, because it is more likely that this "ineffable" name of God is linked to energetic "*Kabbalistic*" condensation or unfolding of cosmic manifestation—as it relates to the "physical world" of forms. According to *Gnostic* perspectives, the four-fold name that commands all material energies is the basis for *other* "Divine Names" or *angelic* names, but is itself derived from a more ancient and incomprehensible form. In the beginning was the "*Word*"—the pure *breath* or *intonation* of the *Source*, which first began with the separation of "Kether" realm from the ALL (by Kabbalistic standards), then existence fragmented further through successive paths of "expansion," illustrated on *any* "tree of life" model.

Traditionally, the *Hebrew Tetragrammaton* is expressed by three letters: I, H and V—although the "I" may also be represented by a "Y" or "J" depending on the translation language. Likewise the "V" is sometimes "W," lending us additional versions—but, the most traditional display is:

YHVH or IHVH

Forbidden for utterance, the "letters" ("sounds," "tones," "vibrations," &tc.) composing the "unspreakable" *Tetragrammaton* "*Word*" are often translated into more recognizable and familiar Judeo-Christian forms of the "*Name of God*"—YAHWEH and the more incorrect phonetic variation JEHOVAH. Even these names are not often spoken in fundamental Judaic traditions, preferring substitutes to "God" in writing and speech, such as "Lord." When the *Tetragrammaton* (YHVH) would appear in texts an incantations or prayer, the priest would not speak this word, but instead substitute the name ADNI—or else "*Adonai*" (*Adonai ha-Aretz*) meaning literally: "Lord of the Earth." If we were to apply this title most literally in *Anunnaki* tradition—using Mesopotamian languages—then the name for "Lord" ("EN") of "Earth" ("KI") is *Enki*.

Enki and his lineage—*Marduk, Nabu, Ningishzida, &tc.*—were not necessarily the "highest" or "supreme" powers throughout the cosmos, but these forces from Mesopotamia became the most highly sought by *magicians*, *priestesses* and *wizards* due to their accessibility and influence on the *Earth Plane*—concerning affairs closest to human life. Not surprisingly, this is *exactly* what *Gnostics* write of regarding the division of *divinity* in the manifested universe. The uncanny correlation does not end with titles alone—for when we discover another prominent name of *Enki* from antiquity, we find "IA" or "EA"—"*yah*."

When examining *Semitic* languages—both *Hebrew* and *Babylonian*—and even European semantics, the "E" letter and sound is preserved in nomenclature for *divinity*. We have already considered *Enki*, as "Lord of Earth," but there is another form—the "EL" or "ILU"—specific to the *Anunnaki* "Commander" of local space (the "airs"). This designation applies directly to *Enlil*—also *Enki's* brother and son of *Anu*—and in later semantics the use of "*Bel*" as a royal designation. Mythologically, *Enki* is the elder son of *Anu*, but he remains technically (or politically) subordinate to *Enlil* in the "Heavens" and on "Earth." Lore of the "*Supernal Trinity*" describes *Enlil* as an intermediary position between *Enki*, the more accessible "Lord of the Earth," and *Anu* the distant heavenly king.

Culminating all of this knowledge, we begin to see a distinction between the forces and hierarchy of "**EL**" versus forces and a hierarchy of "**IA**" —which returns us again to the idea of a prehistoric religious polarity or spiritual dichotomy drawn between a spectrum of *Anu's* two offspring, to whom he entrusted to resolve the affairs and ordering of the "local universe." Here we are thousands of years later and now only naively understanding this "dualism" as some *moral* issue between a *God* and *Satan*, or *Light* and *Dark*, or *Yahweh* and *Bel*... the same story begins to repeat everywhere on earth—but these fantasies are never able to bring *seekers* any closer to the "All-as-One" wholeness-factor really sought. If we are to assume multiple "sides" of this polarity—or for example, the *fourfold Tetragrmmaton*—we can display *Gnostic* material that supports clear definitions for their systematic version of the "Divine" *letters*.

I	Y	A	E
I A	Y H	A O	E L
I A O	Y H W	I A O	E L H
I H V H	Y H W H	I H V H	E L H M

A fourfold *tetragram* is easily assimilated into "ceremonial" and "ritual magic" applications—though there are occasionally issues with keeping the second "H" distinct from the first. Each "letter" also represents its own "dimension" or *kabbalah* "tree," which is "repeated" recursively and simultaneously across *four* "places," "branes" or "zones"—where the "*Malkuth*" or "Firmament" of one *degree* or *dimension* of an entire "tree" is the "*Kether*" or "Heights" of a subsequent one, and so forth. It is possible that this idea simply illustrates the recursive illusion of "infinite expansion" entangled together in unity.

• Traditional "elemental" interpretation of the *Tetragrammaton* relates "Y" or "I" (*yod, ya, ye, e*) to the fire element, the "*Atziluth*" dimension and the "father."

• The first "H" (*he, heh, hey*) carries an affinity with water, the "*Briah*" dimension and the "mother" aspect.

• The air element correlates to "V" or "W" (*vah, vahv, w*), representing the "*Yetzirah*" dimension and the "*holy spirit*"—also given as the *Elohim* or "angelic" *Igigi*.

• The final "H" is aligned to the earth element, the "*Assiah*" dimension and the "son," "offspring," or *humans*.

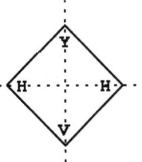

Each of the basic forms may be classified by elemental attributions:

Fire	=	YHVH, YHHV, YVHH
Water	=	HVHY, HVYH, HHYV
Air	=	VHYH, VHHY, VYHH
Earth	=	HYHV, HYVH, HHVY

A threefold name using the same tones or letters—IHV (YHV, YHW)—appears in lore from the *Sefer Yetzirah* (*"Book of Foundations"*) giving "Names" used to "seal" the six directions of the Universe. We might see this element in "temple" preparation or "ritual circle" magic where the *priest-magician* or *priestess* is conjuring a microcosmic representation of the interconnected "entangled" universe.

YHV – *Above*	YVH – *Below*	HYV – *East*
VYH – *South*	HVY – *West*	VHY – *North*

As a *fourfold* name, there are *twelve* basic forms of the *Tetragram* name. An additional twelve can be reached by inverting the two H's. This correlates exactly with lore of twelve *"Banner Angels"* that appears in both *Kabbalistic* and *Enochian*-derived esoteric materials. This system may be treated as *twelve* sets of polarity or *twenty-four* total "angels" or *seats* of the "24 Thrones of the Elders of the Apocalypse." Some have applied the *twenty-four* positions to a cyclical hierarchy of spirits based on hours of the day (or night)—and possibly linked to lore of "planetary hours."

— 6 —
RITUALS OF THE KABBALAH

In the time of *Anunnaki* on earth, only *one* real practice of "magic" was in operation among the human population—conducted by the highest classes among them, *priest-kings*, *priestesses* and *magician-scribes* that worked in the temples and shrines of *Anunnaki* "*gods*." This form of "high magic" or "holy magic" depended on "invocation" and *true* use of prayer to appeal to the "highest" order of *Anunnaki* and *Igigi* legions, in *Self-Honesty*. We see traces of this lofty styling remain all throughout modern "high magical" (or "magickal") traditions—specifically those employing any magic tied to the *Kabbalistic* paradigm.

After the fall of Babylon, the world witnessed a significant increase in sects and factions of *wizards*, *priestesses* and *magicians* operating both within and outside of the sanctioned *Realm*. Practitioners no longer re-stricted themselves to observing "religious pantheons" to operate magic, resulting in a new type of "ceremonial magic" in imitation of methods used by the original *priests* and *priestesses* at the temple-shrines of the ancient "*Sky gods*." Whether from literary records or passed down from memory, *religious priests*, *priestesses* and *magicians* reinforced concise systematized traditions of "liturgy," "rites" and "rituals"—many of them no longer requiring access to a "national temple," but could instead be enacted by individuals that create temporary "sacred spaces" or circles.

The type of "sorcery" we find common in famous "ritual grimoires" that later began to appear publicly, is a *further* fragmentation from even what ancient *wizards* and *magicians* (such as those who studied *Hermetic ma-gic* and *alchemy*) were doing. On a systematic level, it could all still very well be shown as "effective," but by the time of "medieval" period grimoires and magical notebooks, human consciousness—awareness and perceptual worldview—was already altered ("re-programmed") by "orthodox" *Christianity*—and effects from global "*Roman*-ticization." Throughout the "Dark Ages," widespread persecution of "magic-users" by penalty of death—and other travesties—forced all *esoteric* pursuits back underground and shaped public perception of what "magic" *is*—no longer a pursuit of mystic unity with the cosmos or a relationship with the "highest"—now painted as something "dark" and "evil" and worthy of being "hidden away" from the general population for their own good. This mentality certainly lingers with our contemporary world today.

Empirical and political institutions fought to maintain their own power by "disempowering" the masses—keeping them ignorant of their own origins and existential potential. Given this "new" view by the *Realm*, those choosing to study *"esoteric"* things and/or pursue the magical arts were forced to do so "outside" or "apart" from "society." As such, we see—or rather *don't* see—the rise of the *underground* and *secret societies*, which continued to keep the "Ancient Mystery School" legacy alive until present day. Some of these organizations made influential contributions to *"Rituals of the Kabbalah"* practiced outside or apart from even the Judaic sects—such as the *Hermetic Order of the Golden Dawn*, first founded in 1895, a combined effort developed by *Rosicrucians* and *Freemasons*. The organization—and those like it—attracted membership of very prestigious 20th century mystical writers: W.B. Yeats, Arthur Edward Waite, Israel Regardie, Dion Fortune and yes, Aleister Crowley.

Structure of G.D. (*Golden Dawn*) systems of "apprenticeship" (degrees) consists of 10+1 grades of initiation and study based on the *Kabbalah*:

0-0:	Neophyte
1-10:	Zelator (*Malkuth*/earth)
2-9:	Theoricus (*Yesod*/air)
3-8:	Practicus (*Hod*/water)
4-7:	Philsophus (*Netzach*/fire)
5-6:	Adeptus Minor (*Tiphareth*/harmony)
6-5:	Adeptus Major (*Geburah*/might)
7-4:	Adeptus Exemptus (*Chesed*/mercy)
8-3:	Magister Templi (*Binah*/understanding)
9-2:	Magus (*Chokmah*/wisdom)
10-1:	Ipsissimis (*Kether*/Akasha)

Samuel Mathers—better known as S.L. MacGregor Mathers—together with William Wunn Westcott and W.R. Woodman—both *Rosicrucians*—formed the *Hermetic Order of the Golden Dawn*. Westcott brought an obscure manuscript to *Mathers* to translate what they discovered as the rituals of an already extinct *germanc secret society* called the "Golden Dawn" (possibly *Aurum Solis*). Meanwhile, *Mathers* was already working on translations of coveted magical "grimoires"—among these the *Keys of Solomon, Goetia* and *Sacred Book of Magic of Abramelin the Mage*. He also contributed considerably to the publicly available lore of the practical Kabbalah, and suggested the ceremonial chamber "vault" for GD rituals be modeled after the tomb of *Christian Rosenkreutz*—a seven-sided room, each wall being five feet wide by eight feet tall.

Perhaps the most intriguing—and controversial—aspect involved with the founding of the *Golden Dawn*—and what many modern magicians are unaware of when practicing the rituals from its archive—is that all three founders claimed that the origins, organization and direction of the organization operated by communication contact with what is called the "*Invisible Chiefs*" or "*Secret Chiefs.*" Only the GD "inner circle" was treated to an intimate otherworldly interdimensional contact with. These beings are presumably a part of the *Anunnaki* or *Igigi* factions—but due to the perspectives and semantics used by those originally experiencing it (much like Crowley's *Aiwaz*), we cannot be certain of exactly *which* faction or *who* they may have encountered.

In addition to reviving a standard practice of "ceremonial magic" mixed with *Kabbalistic* lore and a revived interest in magical grimoires, the highest GD degrees focused on *Enochian Magic*, a completely new *esoteric* interest developing among 20th century *wizards* and *magicians*. And finally, one further unique aspect of the GD concerns what *Mathers* referred to as the "*Third Circle*" or "*Third Order,*" which only "Ascended Masters" or "Invisible Chiefs" (the same order of spirits or entities consulted by the GD "*Inner Order*" or "*Second Circle*). This "highest" order of Ascended Masters awaited adept initiates at the end of their lives after passing off occupation of a physical genetic vehicle—the body.

The most important aspect we might carry from this lore concerns the idea that the inception of the modern *magical revival*—just as with the modern "Mardukite" movement over a century later—was incited and inspired (possibly even directed) by varying "outside" forces, whatever names and forms we might ascribe it. Obviously, this follows quite well with the general premise or tenets of this discourse.

One of the most frequently used preliminary ritual workings of the GD system is called the *Kabbalistic Cross*. It is most clearly—and indisputably—derived from a famous ancient Mesopotamian rite, the "*Incantation of Eridu*"—the same rite integrated into every *Babili* ritual! The magical "gestures" corresponding to the *Kabbalistic* version of the rite is also the origin for the practice of "self-blessing" commonly called: the "*sign of the cross.*" Note: the order that the shoulders are touched is reversed from the traditionally used "s*ign of the cross,*" which is a banishing or warding act, meant to "keep something away." The *Kabbalistic Cross* method is "active" and "invoking"—so it invites energies in. The *Kabbalistic* statement uttered is actually a part of the *Lord's Prayer* given by Jesus: "The Kingdom, the power and the glory, forever. Amen."

The Kabbalistic Cross Rite

• Stand in the east and imagine yourself becoming very tall, with your head in the clouds and your feet firmly on the surface of the Earth.

• Intone "Ah-toh" using your right (projective) index finger to touch the middle of your forehead as you imagine the white ray of light descending upon you from the Supreme Sphere (*Sephiroth*) of *Kether* from the Kabbalah.

• Intone "Mahl-kuth" (*Malkuth*) as you touch the middle of your chest, feeling light descending from your head to that spot, establishing the main vertical shaft of the Kabbalistic Cross.

• Intone "Veh-geh-du-lah" as you touch your left shoulder, feeling the Divine ray of light appear and grow.

• Carry your hand to the right shoulder as you intone "Veh-geh-bu-rah" feeling the arm or horizontal bar of the cross blazing before you.

• Clasp your hands at your chest and meditate upon the Cross of Clear Light, speaking "Ah-mehn."

There is another ritual popularized in the *Golden Dawn System* (GD) that is now a standard preliminary for *ceremonial magic*—the "*Middle Pillar Rite.*" As practiced today, the rite is probably of *masonic* or *Templar* origin, using passwords and imagery drawn from ancient initiations that allude to some unknown sect from Jerusalem. The names of the two polarized pillars—either represented in physical temple or simply imagined for the rite—are "*Boaz*" and "*Jachin*" (or "*Iachin*"), names of the pillars (from *Masonic* lore) at the entrance threshold of King Solomon's Temple. The pillars, at their core, represent energetic duality manifest in physical existence in the form of light and dark, male and female, &tc. When facing east, the pillar on the left (north) is the Black Pillar (*Boaz*) of Severity. On the right (south) is the White Pillar (*Jachim*) of Mercy. If you are facing west—as some versions of the rite instruct—then the Black Pillar is on the right and the White Pillar is on the left.

During meditation, a practitioner imagines themselves as the crystalline pillar harmonizing a balance of polar force—between two extremes. Some contemporary *magicians* use the *"Middle Pillar Rite"* as a means of activating—or achieving active awareness of—the "Body of Light" or "Light-Body," a personal mystic state that must be achieved in order to successfully conduct magical work.

The Middle Pillar Rite

• Stand in the west, close your eyes, visualize the pillars on either side of you and meditate on their significance. Reflect the powers of each pillar and feel yourself balancing the opposing forces within you.

• Take a deep breath and raise your awareness to above your head and feel the divine ray of light forming in the energy center (*crown chakra*) there.

• Intone, "Eh-heh-eh."

• Feel the light descending to the base of your neck (*throat chakra*) and intone, "Yod-Heh-Vahv-Heh Ehl-oh-heem."

• Feel the light descending down your back to the base of your spine and intone, "Shah-dye El Chye."

• Then feel the light move through your pelvic region as you intone, "Ah-doh-nye Hah-ah-retz."

• Finally, the light moved to your feet (*the base*). Intone, "Mahl-kooth."

• Many practitioners of the GD system will also supplement this rite with the Kabbalistic Cross Rite (previously described).

— 7 —
RITUALS OF THE STARS

Beginning with the iconic imagery instilled in the *Babili* "Star-Gate" Anunnaki system of Mesopotamia—and especially Babylon—"stars" have become almost inseparable from the concept and practice of magic. Whether astrological signs, moon and star glyphs gracing the *magician's cap*, or the *pentagram* and *hexagram* symbols traced in the air—or on some magical object, tool or *sigil–seal*—there is a definitive recurrence of the "star" motif. This *should* be a trigger or indicator for the *seeker*—demonstrating the "cosmic" or "stellar" origins of these traditions, or at the very least, the source of the "powers" they employ. These ancient traditions all relay a very specific message: that *"gods," "God"* and/or *"messengers"* of the same, all resided in the *starry heavens* and *descended* to earth from "higher" abodes to make their contact with humans. If not *literally* the "starry abodes," then we are speaking of beings that have achieved a "higher" vibrational existential-state and are able to access our world via the *"astral"*—which is directly named for the "stars."

 The ancient "Sumerian" cuneiform glyph—"AN"—is a "star" or eight-pointed *asterisk*—named for the *"istari"* or *"sky gods"* who come from (or reside in) the *"starry heavens."* As such, the sign indicates Anunnaki "gods" or "heaven," translated as "ILU" or "ILI" in later Babylonian-Akkadian languages, and represented by a simpler *fourway* "cross" sign. This determinative sign precedes *Anunnaki* names on tablet renderings, used to distinguish their "divine" nature. The same is even seem in orthodox religious lore with *divine, angelic* and otherwise "saintly" names surrounded with "crosses" when written down—particularly in anthologies of Christian rites called *missals*. We can see evidence throughout pre-Christian times, such as in Egypt and Mesopotamia, where the *cross* is indicative of "divinity," the *stars* and the *crossings of the gods*.

For our current purposes, this *Kabbalah*-oriented ceremonial primer has introduced two preliminary GD rites that frequently appear in modern applications of "ceremonial magic" and the "high magickal arts." They may be used in isolation for meditation, self-blessing and empowerment, but they also may be used in conjunction with other Rituals of the Stars for experiments in *Enochian magic* and *kabbalistic* "grimoires."

The "LBRP"—"Lesser Banishing Ritual of the Pentagram"—is found in opening and closing procedures of all operations of the GD *System* of magic. As either a preliminary banishing or a finalizing one, the rite is conducted to "clear," "banish" or "neutralize" existing energies of any space used to conduct magic—any space treated as "sacred" or consecrated as a temporary imitation of the ancient 'temple-shrines' of the *gods*. In modern "ritual magic" the LBRP is used to "cast a circle" or "consecrate" a space with the intention of doing magic—cleansing the air of any preexisting or negative energies at the beginning, as well as any resonant (or residual) energy remaining at the end of the working. While it is true that any area may become "charged" or else "enchanted" with repeated magical use, all "active energies" must be directed accordingly during a ritual—not allowed to linger. This is resolved in most standard practices.

 The form of the *pentagram* "traced" by the magician in the air for the LBRP operation is always "banishing"—which is a description of the "way" or "direction" that energy is traced for the star-pattern; essentially meaning where the starting point is and in what direction the lines trace the shape.

There are differing opinions—or traditions—in modern practice concerning the "colors" of energy to envision when tracing *pentagrams* for the LBRP. Some of the older (original) methods describe a white or silvery band of light, yet some other contemporary traditions—mainly those inspired by *Donald Michael Kraig*—have advocated use of the *blue ray*, possibly due to its protective qualities in some evocation rites.

The *pentagram* can be traced with a "magical implement"—such as a wand or dagger-blade—or it may be traced simply with the practitioners right (or projective) index finger. The challenge here is, of course, maintaining the visualization and energetic awareness of the *pentagrams* as the operator moves around the circle—and throughout the ritual work. When the center of a *pentagram* is pointed to, the operator should "feel" and "see" the *pentagram* as "activated," perhaps burning brighter than before—perhaps radiating a heat-like emission. The energy stream is followed, envisioning a continuous line from the center point of one *pentagram* to the start of the next as you move about the boundary of the ceremonial circle—consecrated sacred space—in a *deosil* or "counter-clockwise" (banishing) direction. At the end of the rite, the operator is surrounded by a band of four blazing interlocked *pentagrams*.

The Lesser Banishing Ritual of the Pentagram

• The LBRP begins in the eastern quarter where the operator performs the *Middle Pillar Rite* and *Kabbalistic Cross Rite*. Then, while still in the east, the operator should trace the banishing pentagram, point to the center and intone: **YHVH** (*yod-heh-vahv-heh*)

• Then, in the south, the banishing pentagram is traced, the center is pointed to and the invocation is: **ADNI** (*ah-doh-nye*)

• In the western quarter: **EHIH** (*eh-heh-yeh*)

• And in the north: **AGLA** (*ah-glah*)

• Carry the *ray of light* back to the east, connecting to the first *pentagram*, then stand with outstretched hands to speak:

> *Before me, Raphael. Behind me, Gabriel.*
> *At my right hand, Michael. At my left hand, Auriel.*
> *Before me flames the pentagram.*
> *Above and below me shines the six-rayed star.*

While it is difficult to trace definitive origins for this specific version of the rite, it was immediately clear to early "Mardukite Chamberlains" that the most antiquated 4,000-5,000 year old Mesopotamian inspiration could be nothing else than the *"Incantation of Eridu"*—also called the *"Incantation of Enki"* or *"Incantation of Marduk."* A few of the lines:—

> *I am the priest in ERIDU.*
> *I am the magician of BABYLON.*
> *My spell is the spell of ENKI.*
> *My incantation is the incantation of MARDUK.*
> *SHAMMASH (Samas) is before me.*
> *NANNA (Sin) is behind me.*
> *NERGAL is at my right hand.*
> *NINURTA is at my left hand.*
> *ANU, above me, the King of Heaven.*
> *ENKI, below me, the King of the Deep.*

The "Watchtowers" are a very ancient concept inseparable from modern practice of ceremonial magic—and even some other magical traditions, such as *Wicca*, which chose to incorporate it from early GD "grimoires" of ceremonial magic. Semantics are derived from ancient Mesopotamian "divisions" of command, stewarding and guardianship of specific *zones* and *domains*, as alluded to throughout mystical cuneiform tablet records concerning the *Anunnaki*. In fact, even the descriptive title "Watchers" is handed down from the Mesopotamian "*Igigi*"—"*those who see*" or even possibly "*overseers*"—but as related to the physical world, Watchtowers exist at the "*four corners*" of this cosmic dimension, guarded by figures meant to seal "*in*"—or "*out*"—appropriate degrees of energy specific to *Malkuth*, the lower material domain (in the *Hebrew Kabbalistic* model) that we are wired to experience in "typical"human form. This is one reason why many *kabbalistic* depictions of the lowest (10th) *sephiroth* —*Malkuth*—of the material realm is often depicted with a cross or "X" dividing the "circle" or "sphere" into *four quarters*, and subsequently attributed to the *four elements*.

Watchtowers are popularized in ceremonial magic from another GD rite within the same cycle as the LBRP—and as much as the LBRP is considered a "minor" method of "casting a circle" for *high magic* purposes, the "*Watchtower Ceremony*"—or "*Watchtower Formula*" as it is sometimes called—was employed for all the more "advanced" GD operations and experiments, such as *Enochian magic*. There are some underground "societies" that make use of the rite for "initiation" and "installation" ceremonies.

The "*Watchtower Formula*" follows a cumulative succession of "rituals" —those previously given—building upon the same *kabbalistic* formula. Divine Names used for this version are derived from the elemental or *Watchtower Tablets* of the *Enochian* system—which are meant to be present for the rite. Elemental, Watchtower or cross-quarter gate tablets appear frequently in such rites—the fact they *are* originally "tablets" lends us a possible hint to their ancient source. All of the other verbiage recited during the rite are direct passages from a treatise known among *esoteric* and "*Hermetic*" circles as the "*Chaldean Oracles of Zoroaster,*" given as Tablet-O within the "Mardukite Core" (such "*Necronomicon: The Anunnaki Bible*"). The rite employs traditional "ceremonial magic" rules—meaning access to "elemental tools," those based on significant artifacts from ancient temples: a *wand*, a *blade*, a *vessel* (for water; usually a cauldron or goblet-chalice) and a *pentacle* or *stone* (often crafted from a meteorite, moldevite or some other kind of heavenly material).

The Watchtower Ceremony

The temple is arranged with a double circle. *Enochian tablets*—or elemental "Watchtower tablets"—are placed between the two circles at their appropriate directions. A banner, flag or other representation can be made and used in place of "tablets" proper. If employed for *Enochian* magic, then the "*Tablet of Union*" and "*Sigillum de Aemeth*" should also be present on the "altar."

- Perform the "Middle Pillar Rite"
- Perform the "Kabbalistic Cross Rite"
- Perform the "LBRP"

• Go and stand in the south, raise your sword, saying:

Behold, all the phantoms have vanished and I see before me that sacred and formless fire that flames and consumes the hidden depths of the Universe and I hear the voice of the fire.

• Feel and see the sword radiate with fire, and say:

Oh-ee-peh Teh-ah-ah Peh-doh-key [OIP TEAA PDOKE]. In the names and letters of the Great Southern Quadrangle, I invoke thee spirits of the Watchtower of the South.

• Go to the west and take up the sacred chalice; sprinkle some of the water, saying:

Now therefore I, a priest of fire, summon the lustral waters of the sea and hear the wrath of the waves upon the shore, the voice of the water now and evermore.

• Feel the water element rising up within you, then say:

Em-pehheh Ar-ess-el Gah-ee-oh-leh [MPH ARSL GAIOL]. In the names and letters of the Great Western Quadrangle, I invoke thee spirits of the Watchtower of the West.

• Go to the east and raise your dagger (or wand); strike the air three times saying:

> *My mind extends through the realm of air. In the form-less air comes the vision and the voice, flashing, bound-ing, revolving, it whirls forth crying aloud.*

• Feel and see the winds of the air element, swirling about you as you say:

> *Oh-roh Ee-bah Ah-oh-zod-pee [ORO IBAH AOZPI]. In the names and letters of the Great Eastern Quadrangle, I invoke thee spirits of the Watchtower of the East.*

• Go to the north and take up the pentacle; shake it in the air three times and say:

> *I stoop down into a world of darkness, wherein lies un-known depths and Hades shrouded in gloom, delighting in senseless images; a black ever-rolling abyss, a voice both mute and void.*

• Feel Earth beneath your feet; become very aware of the ground as you intone:

> *Moh-are Dee-ah-leh Heh-keh-teh-gah [MOR DIAL HCTGA]. In the names and letters of the Great Northern Quadrangle, I invoke thee spirits of the Watchtower of the North.*

• Finally, go to the east and proclaim:

> *Holy art thou, Lord of the Universe. Holy art thou, whom Nature has not formed. Holy art thou, the Infinite and Mighty One, Lord of Light and of Darkness.*

"Mardukite Chamberlains" spent a significant amount of time exploring the *"Chaldean Oracles of Zoroaster"* for the Mardukite Core, form 2008 through 2010. The full work—of uncertain *ancient near eastern* origin —relays a primer of *"Hermetic Philosophy"* over the course of five tab-lets, or scrolls (papyri) in other versions.

The First Tablet describes "God" and the establishment of "soul-programs" residing at the "divine center" of all things and beings:—

> *"The true and indestructible God is known as 'Silence'*
> *By the Divine Powers [Anunnaki] of the Universe,*
> *And is known to the souls of humans*
> *through the power of the mind alone.*
> *There are no speakable names for this force,*
> *though 'he' has been known as IAO [YWH]*
> *Signifying that 'he' is above*
> *the Seven Pillars of Material Existence. . ."*

The Second Tablet illustrates the "Mind of God" as it expanded with the universe and its "intelligibles." Three *supernal rays* shine forth and solidify into *Seven*, but we are not to be "confused" by this fragmentation, for in wholeness, the tablet also relays: *"The Seven are Three and the Three are the One"*. . . All-as-One.

The *"Watchtower Ceremony"* opens with mention of the "formless fire," a concept that appears on the "First Tablet" of *Mardukite Tablet O-Series*. The "Father" whirls forth and his "intellectual fire" is what spreads intelligence throughout the universe. The "voice of fire" is the "voice of *Silence*"—the "voice of God." From the fire elemental *zone* in the south, the operator moves to the west to confront the water element—which is the next element described on the First Tablet. The "intellectual fire" spread and from the depths of the universe sprang up "intelligent fountains" that spread the "intelligence of God" into all life.

Perhaps the most obvious parallel between *The Watchtower Ceremony* and the *Mardukite Tablet-O Series* comes at the end of the working and similarly from the last (fifth) tablet, which opens with words even fitting to describe the Druid's mistletoe, among other things:—

> *"Do not fix your mind on the vast systems of Earth;*
> *For the plant of truth grows not upon the ground."*

Of course, there are many modern *magicians* and *sorcerers* that clearly overlooked this message and frequently did *just* that. And continuing:—

> *"Stoop not down unto this Darkly-Splendid World;*
> *Wherein lies a continuously faithless depth*
> *And 'Hades' shrouded in cloudy gloom,*

> *Delighting in senseless images,*
> *In a tortuous, winding, ever-rolling Abyss;*
> *Containing the lightless body – formless and void."*

Later on the tablet it relays:—

> *"So therefore, the Priest who governs the works of Fire,*
> *Must sprinkle about Waters of the loud-resounding Sea.*
> *Should you see a 'terrestrial demon' approach, scream at it!"*

Prior to the passage selected for the ritual, the tablet warns:—

> *"If you invoke the lower often, the Darkness will consume you.*
> *You will no longer see the Intelligent Light,*
> *And you will no longer be visible to the Light-Bearers,*
> *Who suspend themselves from vaulted skies of Heaven.*
> *Then will Three lightning bolts strike,*
> *And all things will be engulfed in chaotic thunders."*

The portion influencing the ritual passage continues:—

> *"Then comes the Fire,*
> *Flashing and extending through the rushes of the Air,*
> *Or a Fire most formless,*
> *Which carries the Vision and the Voice,*
> *Or a flashing light, abounding revolving,*
> *whirling forth and crying aloud."*

> *"There is an Incorruptible Flame*
> *above the Celestial Lights,*
> *Always sparkling, the Spring of Life,*
> *the Formation of All Beings,*
> *The original a-priori archetype of All things*
> *This flame produces all things,*
> *And no existence may perish except what it consumes.*
> *This flame cannot be contained to any single space*
> *It encompasses all of the Starry Heavens you can see."*

The entire *Mardukite Tablet-O* series closes with the lines:—

> *"Whosoever understands the meaning of these things;*
> *Shall not experience death."*

— 8 —
ENOCHIAN MAGIC OF DR. JOHN DEE*

Fascinated with astrology, *Dr. John Dee* (1527–1608) publicly predicted the time that *Queen Mary* would die and it came to pass. He was accused of using black magic to kill her and eventually imprisoned for it. When her sister, *Queen Elizabeth I* ascended the throne proper, she released *Dee* and made him her personal royal court astrologer. In spite of his position, financial stress forced *Dee* to continue his alchemical pursuits for the philosopher's stone. This interest led him to the company of a young rogue-seer named *Edward Kelley*—sometimes spelled *Kelly*. As little as we know truly of *Dee*'s life, we know even less about his partner *Kelley*, except that they spent many years together allegedly conversing with angelic spirits, which led to the birth of the <u>*Enochian System*</u>.

John Dee excelled at "ceremonial magic," so he performed the rites as a practicing magician, while *Kelley* skryed into a crystal ball to decipher messages and letters of the *Enochian Alphabet*. A very complex ritual system was created—or channeled, depending on your opinion of its origins—including construction of the "*Sigillum Dei Aemeth*"—

---

* Excerpt from "*Arcanum: The Great Magical Arcanum*" by Joshua Free.

The "*Enochian Tablet of Union*"—

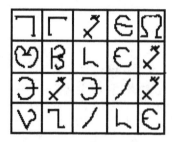

And the four "*Enochian Watchtower Tablets*"—

Enochian Air Tablet

Enochian Water Tablet

Enochian Earth Tablet

Enochian Fire Tablet

And the "*Enochian Language*" as a whole—

	Ceremonial	Cursive			Ceremonial	Cursive
B (pe)				**P (mals)**		
C,K (veh)				**Q (ger)**		
G (ged)				**N (drun)**		
D (gal)				**X (pal)**		
F (orth)				**O (med)**		
A (un)				**R (don)**		
E (graph)				**Z (ceph)**		
M (tal)				**W,U,V (Vau)**		
I,J,Y (gan)				**S (fam)**		
H (nahath)				**T (gisa)**		
L (ur)						

The Enochian Alphabet

...all of which are used to summon the power of angelic spirits, communicate inter-dimensionally, or else conjure them to physical appearance. We see traces of *Gnostic* beliefs in the system, rites heavy with *kabbalistic* influences and other *Divine Names*.

The relationship between *Dee* and *Kelley* started to turn when *Kelley* informed him that a spirit named *Madimi* instructed them to share their wives. While it is said that *Dee* eventually gave into *Kelley*, no one knows what really transpired except that the unique magickal partnership ended abruptly. This background and *Kelley*'s reputation for mystical hoaxes has led many scholars to question the validity of the *Enochian System*. The credibility of the system is probably derived more from *John Dee*'s contributions than *Kelley*'s.

> It is possible that over the centuries, much of the *Enochian System* has actually been "willed" into existence via the thought-forms of powerful entities created by their practitioners and energetic relationships with later magicians using the system.

As a derivative of *Kabbalistic* and other *Hermetic* systems, *Enochian Tradition* represents a further evolution of post-Babylonian *Anunnaki* systems. In fact, in the past several decades, both the "*Enochian System*" and the "*Babili System*" have been referred to by multiple authors as the "*Necronomicon*"—a semantic that the modern *Mardukite* movement also decided to carry for those who prefer it. What we do have in the *Enochian* methodology is not simply some arbitrary "Judeo-Christian" context for studying angelic phenomenon—it would seem to possess far greater *esoteric* or "Gnostic" applications—such as we might identify with those methods closely assimilating remnants of post-Babylonian occult systems, such as *Hermetics, Chaldean magic, Persian magi, &tc.*

The *Enochian System* is named for its patron from *Judeo-Christian* lore: Enoch. As a "biblical" figure in "orthodox" versions of *Judeo-Christian* writings, Enoch makes a very slight appearance in the *Old Testament*. He is more famously connected to other writings from the same period —*The Books of Enoch*. But esoterically, as a visionary messenger of his own race, his "persona" is closely linked to higher Mercurial energies that *would have been* interested in him—*Hermes, Thoth, Ningishzidda, Enki, Nabu,* &tc. But the ancient accounts are clear of one thing: he had direct encounters with "*Divine*" beings, otherwise called "*angels*."

— 9 —
THE ENOCHIAN SYSTEM OF MAGIC*

The *"angelic spirits"* that Enoch encountered brought him up "above" the earth to show and teach him many things otherwise forbidden or unknown to his people—the "human" race. As a result, Enoch is equated with the "messenger-class" of visionaries—or prophets—that served as "ambassadors" between humanity and the "Other," much like ancient priests—ambassadors between beings of the earth and the heavens. Much of this lore does not make its way into "approved" versions of scripture found in the *Holy Bible* or used for "orthodox" religion, but it does appear in other sources such as the *Dead Sea Scrolls* and *Books of Enoch*. It is from such sources that many esoteric students actually encounter derivative *Anunnaki* and *Igigi* lore, but in the semantic guise of "*Elohim*" and "*angels*" viewed within the Judeo-Christian worldview.

As an effective "ceremonial" application, *Enochian Magic* requires a set of the aforementioned *Enochian Tablets*—the four *Watchtowers* and the *Tablet of Union*—a set of *magical weapons* or "elemental tools" previously "consecrated" to the high magical arts, and finally, the *Sigillum Dei Aemeth* appears, inscribed on a disc of wax or wood, which may replace the traditional ritual *pentacle* on the altar. Furthermore, operators must have a thorough understanding of the *Enochian Keys* (or *Calls*) used for invocations, in addition to memorizing hierarchical "roll calls" of angelic spirit names from within the system—*angels*, *astral kings* and other *guardians* evoked for these rites.

There are two forms of *Enochian Magic* studied—and used—in the contemporary systems and traditions of the "*New Age..* The first is what we are already in the process of describing, which concerns evocation and spiritual interaction with *angelic* entities. A more advanced application of the system also exists, wholly dependent on an operator's ability to interact with the *Astral Plane* using "spirit vision." In the *Enochian* paradigm, the semantics describing separations of dimensional veils are called *aethyrs*. Contrasting the *Babili* "Gate-system" and the "sephiroth" of the *Hebrew Kabbalah*, the *Enochian* system fragments spiritual dimensions into "aethyr zones." During ceremonial magic the operator calls for these *angelic spirits* from the realms they presumably reside in.

---

*   Excerpt from "*Arcanum: The Great Magical Arcanum*" by Joshua Free.

Given the advanced nature of the operations, and the skills required to effectively access other dimensions using *"spirit vision,"* the "aethyrs" and *"starwalking"* methods are those least-employed in contemporary magical arts. This does not change its significance for our current purpose—to understand the last remaining example with a long-standing history of use that is still derived from the same *Anunnaki* and *Judaic* system origins. Certainly the semantics, styling and practical use of the magic has shifted greatly over the course of thousands of years.

"Divine Names"—or *words of power*—employed in the *Enochian System* are all derived from *"Enochian Tablets"*—the four *Watchtower* tablets and the *Tablet of Union*, derived from the other four. There are four main *"Watchtower Tablets"*—one for each of the cardinal directions or "quadrangles" (quarters) of the universe—but each of these tablets is also made up of four sections, divided by a "cross." A "cross-section" is also composed on each of the four smaller portions. In short, this means there are four watchtower tablets, each with a cross that separates four smaller sections—for a total of sixteen—that each contain a smaller cross. Philosophically, each of the four elemental tablets are subdivided into a microcosm of four elemental aspects.

The key to interpreting and correctly using the tablets involves understanding the quadrants. Whether used to consolidate a "Great Tablet" or differentiate the smaller sections of the "four" into "sixteen," the same formula key is used to divide sections into "elemental" quadrants:

AIR = upper left   WATER = upper right
EARTH = lower left   FIRE = lower right

Since each of the tablets are divided into "elemental quadrants," this provides for sixteen different elemental combinations—such as "earth of air" and so forth. The names of the "cross-angels"—as they are called in the *Enochian system*—are derived from the smaller cross found within each quadrant. The names of the "senior-angels" are found in the larger cross divides the four quadrants. Names and *sigils* of the *"aethyrs"* and their "governor" spirits are also taken from interpretations of the tablets and tracing out "sigil-lines" that coincide with the pattern of letters as they appear on the tablets.

We have described energetic "tracing" of *signs* previously in the form of "pentagrams" for the *Lesser Banishing Ritual of the Pentagram*, but in the practice of *Enochian magic,* the "hexagram" is the preferred sign.

337

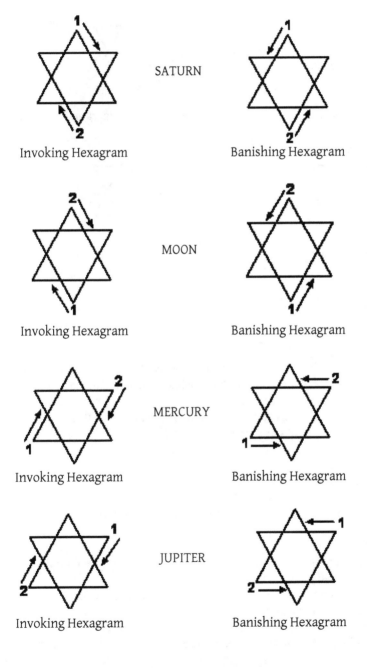

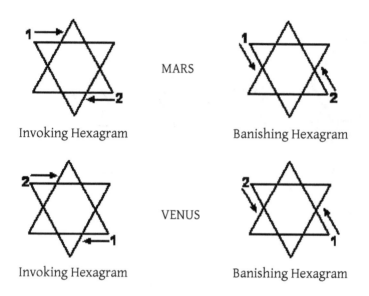

MARS

Invoking Hexagram   Banishing Hexagram

VENUS

Invoking Hexagram   Banishing Hexagram

The fundamentals for *Enochian Magic* are as follows:—

Prerequisite Knowledge
1. The name of the senior or angel to be evoked.
2. The direction/Watchtower to face, using elemental correspondences.
3. The Enochian Keys to be recited.
4. The hierarchy or order of succession to be called. Use this order:
   a) Divine Name of the element,
   b) King,
   c) Seniors,
   d) Cross-Angel: six lettered,
   e) Cross-Angel: five lettered.
5. The planetary-hexagram to be traced and the color to envision it.

Hints & Tips
1. Except for Kings, the hierarchy needs only to be followed until you reach the desired name.
2. A hexagram is traced only when you are evoking a Senior. All six must be used to contact a King.
3. Use an "invoking pentagram" if evoking Cross-Angels.
4. If evoking a Cross-Angel, you need only speak the names of the

Seniors, though some operators prefer to trace all corresponding hexa-grams.

5. Hexagrams are ruled by planetary forces, while the pentagrams are ruled by the elements.

Order of Operations
1. Enter the body of light and perform the Watchtower Ceremony.
2. Go to the appropriate direction/Watchtower and trace the hexa-gram(s) or pentagram envisioning it a color correspondent to the planet or element.
3. Intone the descending Enochian hierarchy from the designated ele-ment. When calling the Kings, you must intone each name of the Senior while synchronously tracing the appropriate hexagrams.
4. Repeat the name of the entity many times. Envision the name filling you and projecting from you. The spirit will appear in the traced star or some desired skrying speculum.
5. Perform the Lesser Banishing Ritual of the Pentagram (LBRP) when finishing the rite.

The Divine Names/Watchtowers

Air: Oro Ibah Aozpi (oh-roh ee-bah ah-oh-zod-pee)
Water: Mph Arsl Gaiol (em-peh-heh ar-ess-el gah-ee-oh-leh)
Earth: Mor Dial Hktga (moh-ar dee-al-el heh-keh-teh-gah)
Fire: Oip Teaa Pdoke (oh-ee-peh teh-ah-ah peh-doh-key)

Enochian/Elemental Kings

Air: Bataivah (bah-tah-ee-vah-heh)
Water: Raagiosl (rah-ah-gee-ohs-el)
Earth: Ikzhikal (ee-keh-zod-he-kah-el)
Fire: Edlprnaa (ee-del-por-nah-ah)

Enochian/Planetary Seniors

[Order listed: Mars, Jupiter, Moon, Venus, Mercury and Sun.]
Air: Habioro, Aaozaif, Htmorda, Ahaozpi, Avtotar, Hipotga
Water: Srahpm, Saiinou, Laoaxrp, Slgaiol, Soniznt, Ligdisa
Earth: Laidrom, Akzinor, Lzinopo, Alhktga, Ahmllvk, Likiansa
Fire: Aaetpio, Adaeoet, Alnkdood, Aapdoke, Anadoin, Arinnap

The Enochian Keys for Kings and Seniors

Air: 1, 2 and 3.
Water: 1, 2 and 4.
Earth: 1, 2 and 5.
Fire: 1, 2 and 6.

Enochian/Elemental Subordinate Cross-Angels

[Listed below in two names with the corresponding *Enochian Keys* to be used in parenthesis. These entities represent qualities reminiscent to the alchemical breakdown of each of the elements into sixteen combinations, even equated by some practitioners to the figures of *geomancy*.]

Air of Air: Idoigo, Aroza (3)
Water of Air: Lkalza, Palam (3 & 7)
Earth of Air: Aaioao, Oiiit (3 & 8)
Fire of Air: Aovrrs, Aloai (3 & 9)
Air of Water: Obgota, Abako (4 & 10)
Water of Water: Nelapr, Omebb (4)
Earth of Water: Maladi, Olaad (4 & 11)
Fire of Water: Iaaasd, Atapi (4 & 12)
Air of Earth: Angpol, Vnnax (5 & 13)
Water of Earth: Anaeem, Sonda (5 & 14)
Earth of Earth: Abalpt, Arbiz (5)
Fire of Earth: Ompnir, Ilpiz (5 & 15)
Air of Fire: Noalmr, Oloag (6 & 16)
Water of Fire: Vadali, Obava (6 & 17)
Earth of Fire: Volxdo, Sioda (6 & 18)
Fire of Fire: Rzionr, Nrzfn (6)

— 10 —
KEYS OF ENOCH: CALLS TO THE ANGELS*

Enochian Keys or *Calls* are used as incantation-prayers or invocations to the hierarchies of *angels* [*Igigi*] and the *archangels* [*Anunnaki*] in cere-monial applications of *Enochian magic*. They were divined by John Dee and Edward Kelley during their channeled inception of the system from an '*angel*' calling itself: *Ave*.

As with lore connected to other applications of what some might call the "*Necronomicon*," many esoteric students believe that the *Enochian Keys* potential to unleash forces that are otherwise sealed from the time-space of human existence—the most condensed physical perception of reality. That being the case, the *Enochian System* seems like a prime candidate of the available "New Age" applications of *Kabbalah* for doing just that: inviting or summoning "alien" forces into our world! But, this is not something likely to happen by "accident," since any success with this system is dependent on the operator's "true" understanding and compre-hension of related mysteries *Self-Honestly*. Here, we are not interested in simply inciting some "phenomenon," but as with the *Babili* system, we are interested in developing a "true and faithful" relationship with the "spiritual forces" we encounter and communicate with.

There is no reason to believe that the *Enochian System* is any closer, purer or better than the original *Anunnaki Babili* system—but for com-parative purposes, the *Enochian* secured high notoriety during the 20th century magical revival—likely due to its accessibility from the *Golden Dawn* and *Aurum Solis* literature. What follows are the "*Enochian Keys*" used for these methods, translated for the English language.

"The First Enochian Key"

I reign over you says the God of Justice, in power exalted above the firmaments of Wrath. In whose hands the Sun is as a sword and the Moon as a through-thrusting fire: Who measures your garments in the midst of my ventures and trussed you together as the palms of my hands: Whose seats I garnished with the Fire of Gathering: Who beauti-

---

* Excerpt from "*Arcanum: The Great Magical Arcanum*" by Joshua Free.

fied your garments with admiration: To whom I made a law to govern
the Holy Ones: Who delivered you with a rod and with the Ark of
Knowledge. Moreover you lifted up your voices and swore obedience
and faith to Him that lives and triumphs: Whose beginning is not nor
can ever be: Which shines as a flame in the midst of your palaces and
reigns among you as a balance of righteousness and truth. Move, therefore and show yourselves: open the mysteries of your creation. Be
friendly unto me. For I am the servant of the same, your God, the true
worshiper of the Highest.

"The Second Enochian Key"

Can the Wings of Wind understand your voices of wonder, O you the
Second of the First, whom the burning flames have formed within the
depths of my jaws: Whom I have prepared as cups for a wedding or the
flowers in their beauty for the chamber of righteousness. Stronger are
your feet than the barren stone and mightier are your voices than the
manifold winds. For you are becoming a building that is not, except in
the mind of the All-Powerful. Arise, says the First. Move, therefore unto
thy servants. Show yourselves in power and make me a strong seer of
things, for I am descended from Him that lives forever.

"The Third Enochian Key"

Behold, says your God. I am a circle on whose hands stand Twelve
Kingdoms. Six are the seats of the living breath, the rest are sharp
sickles or the horns of death, wherein the creatures of Earth are and are
not, except by my own hands that also sleep and shall rise. In the First, I
made you stewards and placed you on Twelve Seats of Government,
giving unto every one of you the power over Four, Five and Six, the true
ages of time: to the intent that the highest vessels and the corners of
your government you shall work my power: pouring down the Fires of
Life and increase continually upon the Earth. Thus you have become the
skirts of justice and truth. In the names of the same, your God, lift up, I
say to you. Behold, his mercies flourish and his name becomes mighty
against us, as unto the initiates of the Secret Wisdom of your creation.

"The Fourth Enochian Key"

I have set my feet in the South and have looked about me saying: Are not the thunders of increase numbered 33, which reign in the Second Angle? Under whom I have placed 9.639 whom none have numbered but One: In whom the Second beginning of things are and wax strong, which successively are the numbers of Time, and their powers are the First. Arise you Sons of Pleasure and visit the Earth: For I am the Lord your God which is and lives forever. In the name of the Creator, move and show yourselves as pleasant deliverers so that you may praise Him among the Sons of Men.

"The Fifth Enochian Key"

The mighty sounds have entered the Third Angle and become as olives on the olive mount, looking with gladness upon the Earth and dwelling in the brightness of the heaves as continual comforters. Unto whom I have fastened 19 pillars of gladness and gave them vessels to water the Earth with all of her creatures: And they are the brothers of the First and Second, and the beginning of the own seats which are garnished with 69,636 continually burning lamps, whose numbers are as the First, the End, and the midway content of time. Therefore come and obey your creation. Visit us in peace and comfort. Include us the receivers of your mysteries. For why? Our Lord and Master is of the All-One.

"The Sixth Enochian Key"

The spirits of the Fourth Angle are nine, mighty in the firmaments of water: the First has planted a torment to the wicked and a garland to the righteous: Giving unto them fiery darts to wash the Earth, and 7,699 continual workmen whose courses visit with comfort to the Earth, and are in government and continuance as the Second and the Third. Wherefore, come and follow my voice. I have talked of you and I move you in power and presence: Whose works shall be a song of honor and the praise of your *God* in your creation.

"The Seventh Enochian Key"

The East is a house of virgins singing praises among the flames of the First glory, wherein the Lord has opened his mouth and they become 28 living dwellings in whom the strength of man rejoices and are appareled with ornaments of brightness, such a work that fascinates all creatures: Whose kingdoms and continuance are as the Third and Fourth, strong towers and places of comfort, the seat of mercy and continuance. O you servants of mercy, move, appear, and sing praises unto the Creator of All. And be might among us. For to this covenant is given power and our strength waxes strong in our comforter.

"The Eighth Enochian Key"

The midday, the First, is as the Third Heaven made of 26 crystalline pillars, in whom the elders are becoming strong, which I have prepared for my own righteousness, says the Lord: Whose long continuance shall be as buckles to the Stooping Dragon and like unto the harvest of a widow. How many are there which remain in the glory of the Earth, which are, and shall not see death until this house falls and the Dragon sinks? Come away for the thousands have spoken! Come away for the Crown of the Temple and the robe of Him that is, was and shall be crowned King and divided. Come! Appear unto the terror of the Earth and unto our comfort and to those who are prepared.

"The Ninth Enochian Key"

A mighty guard of Fire with two-edged swords flaming, which have eight Vials of Wrath for Two times and a half, whose wings are wormwood and of the marrow of salt, have settled their feet in the West and are measured by their 9,996 ministers. These gather up the moss of the Earth as the rich man does guard his treasure. Cursed are they whose iniquities they are. In their eyes are millstones greater than the Earth and from their mouth runs seas of blood. Their heads are covered with diamonds and upon their hands are marble sleeves. Happy is he on whom they frown not. For why? The God of Righteousness rejoices in them. Come away and not your Vials, for the time is such that requires comfort.

"The Tenth Enochian Key"

The thunders of judgment and wrath are numbered and are harbored in the North in the likeness of an Oak whose branches are 22 nests of lam-

entation and weeping laid up for the Earth, which burns night and day:
And vomit out the heads of scorpions and active sulfur mingled with
poison. These are the thunders that 5678 times (in the 24th part of your
moment) roar with a hundred might earthquakes and a thousand times as
many surges, which rest not, neither know any echoing time herein. One
rock brings forth a thousand, as occurs in the hearts of men with their
thoughts. Woe! Woe! Woe! Woe! Woe! Woe! Woe! Woe! Woe! Hear, I
say, Woe! Be merciful to the Earth for her iniquity is, was and shall be
great. Come away! But not your mighty sounds.

"The Eleventh Enochian Key"

The mighty seat groaned aloud and there were five thunders, which flew
into the East and the Eagle spoke and cried in a loud voice: Come away!
And they gathered themselves together and became the House of Death,
of whom it is measured, and it is 31. Come away! For I have prepared
for you a place. Move therefore and show yourselves. Open the mysteries of your creation. Be friendly unto me, for I am a servant of the same,
your God, who is the true worshiper of the Highest.

"The Thirteenth Enochian Key"

O you swords of the South, which have 42 eyes to stir up the wrath of
Sin: making men drunken and empty. Behold, the promise of God and
His power, which is called amongst you a bitter string. Move and show
yourselves. Open the mysteries of your creation. Be friendly unto me,
for I am a servant of the same, your God, who is the true worshiper of
the Highest.

"The Fourteenth Enochian Key"

O you Sons of Fury, the legal heirs of the just, which sits upon 24 seats,
vexing all creatures of the Earth with age, which have under them 1,636.
Behold the Voice of God, the promise of Him, which is called amongst
you Fury or extreme justice. Move, therefore and show yourselves.
Open the mysteries of your creation. Be friendly unto me, for I am a servant of the same, your God, who is the true worshiper of the Highest.

"The Fifteenth Enochian Key"

O thou, the Governor of the First Flame under whose wings are 6,739, which weave the Earth with dryness: Which knows the secret of the Great Name: righteousness, and the Seal of Honor. Move, therefore and show yourselves. Open the mysteries of your creation. Be friendly unto me, for I am a servant of the same, your God, who is the true worshiper of the Highest.

"The Sixteenth Enochian Key"

O thou, Governor of the Second Flame, the House of Justice, who has your beginning in glory and shall comfort the just, who walks the Earth with 8,763 feet, which understands and separates the creatures. Great you are to the God of Conquest. Move, therefore and show yourselves. Open the mysteries of your creation. Be friendly unto me, for I am a servant of the same, your God, who is the true worshipper of the Highest.

"The Seventeenth Enochian Key"

O thou, Governor of the Third Flame who wings are the thorns to stir up vexation. And who has 7,336 living lamps going before thee: Whose God is wrath in anger, bind up thy loins and take notice! Move, therefore and show yourselves. Open the mysteries of your creation. Be friendly unto me, for I am a servant of the same, your God, who is the true worshipper of the Highest.

"The Eighteenth Enochian Key"

O thou, the might light and burning flame of comfort, which opens the Glory of God unto the center of the Earth. I whom the 6,332 secrets of Truth have their abiding, which is called in your kingdom of Joy and not to be measured. Be thou a window of comfort unto me. Move, therefore and show yourselves. Open the mysteries of your creation. Be friendly unto me, for I am a servant of the same, your God, who is the true worshipper of the Highest.

— 11 —
"AETHYRS" OF THE ENOCHIAN SYSTEM[*]

The *"Aethyrs"* are the fragmented spiritual dimensions from which angelic spirits of the *Enochian System* are called. This lore is at the heart of one of the most advanced operations of *high magick* in the New Age, *"Rising on the Planes,"* executed in its entirety from a "Body of Light" using ceremonial magick. It is a lengthy endeavor to work through all thirty of the *aethyrs* successfully—requiring a strong feat of concentration "spirit vision" ("astral skrying") while simultaneously conducting ritual gestures and incantations, although this can just as successfully be conducted on the astral plane.

In the original formulation of the system, John Dee, the ritual magician, required the aid of a seer or co-magician (Edward Kelley) to record the information accessed from the *aethyrs*, but otherwise, modern *aethyr* work is a solitary endeavor.

"Rising on the Planes" requires astral passage through (or attainment of) the first eighteen *Enochian Keys* before ceremonially executing the first of thirty cycles of *Call to the Aethyrs*. This "call" is the same for all *aethyrs* except that the title of each plane is replaced. Appropriate *sigils* of "angelic guardians/governors" of each *aethyr* should be carried as seals and "traced" (envisioned) while calling appropriate "Divine Name" for each spirit. *Aethyrs* are also aligned to a fundamental element, which determines the ritual direction to face (air-east, fire-south, water-west, earth-north) and the "elemental/magickal weapon" used to trace *sigils*.

Each *aethyr* must be accessed consecutively, though confusion occurs here since half of the traditions work from the thirtieth to the first and the other half follow the opposite regimen. According to modern magical lore, once relationships are established between the practitioner and the "guardian spirits" of the first eighteen *Enochian Keys*, then operation of the *Call to the Aethyrs* will be sufficient to access these planes via astral "spirit vision." Names and sigils of aethyrs—that follow here—are derived directly from the *Enochian Tablets*. The *"Call of the Aethyrs"* is referred to as the 19th-through-48th *Enochian Keys*, depending on the name of the aethyr inserted.

---

[*] Excerpt from *"Arcanum: The Great Magical Arcanum"* by Joshua Free.

1 LIL   a)   b)   c)

2 ARN   a)   b)   c)

3 ZOM   a)   b)   c)

4 PAZ   a)   b)   c)

5 LIT   a)   b)   c)

6 MAZ   a)   b)   c)

7 DEO   a)   b)   c)

8 ZID   a)   b)   c)

9 ZIP   a)   b)   c)

10 ZAX   a)   b)   c)

11 IKH   a)   b)   c)

12 LOE   a)   b)   c)

13 ZIM   a)   b)   c)

14 VTA   a)   b)   c)

15 OXO   a)   b)   c)

1. LIL (lee-lah) [water] Occodon, Pascomb, Valgars
2. ARN (ah-rah-noo) [water] Doagnis, Pacasna, Dialiva
3. ZOM (zoad-oh-me) [water] Samapha, Virooli, Andispi
4. PAZ (pah-zoad) [water] Thotanf, Axziarg, Pothnir
5. LIT (lee-tay) [water] Lazdixi, Nocamal, Tiarpax
6. MAZ (mah-zoad) [fire] Saxtomp, Vavaamp, Zirzird
7. DEO (day-oh) [fire] Obmacas, Genadol, Aspiaon
8. ZID (zoad-ee-dah) [fire] Zamfres, Todnaon, Pristac

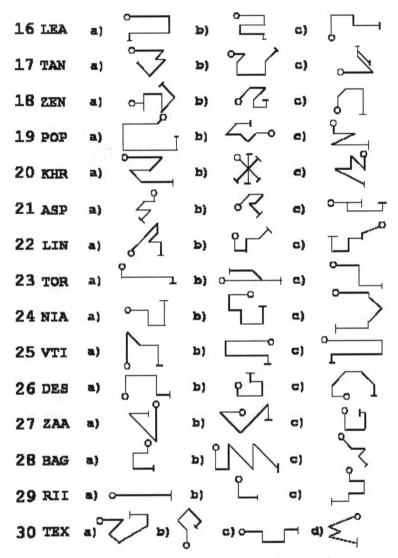

16 LEA   a)   b)   c)

17 TAN   a)   b)   c)

18 ZEN   a)   b)   c)

19 POP   a)   b)   c)

20 KHR   a)   b)   c)

21 ASP   a)   b)   c)

22 LIN   a)   b)   c)

23 TOR   a)   b)   c)

24 NIA   a)   b)   c)

25 VTI   a)   b)   c)

26 DES   a)   b)   c)

27 ZAA   a)   b)   c)

28 BAG   a)   b)   c)

29 RII   a)   b)   c)

30 TEX   a)   b)   c)   d)

9. ZIP (zoad-ee-pay) [fire] Oddiorg, Cralpir, Doanzin
10. ZAX (zoad-ahtz) [union] Lexarph, Comanan, Tabitom
11. ICH (ee-kah-hey) [water] Molpand, Vanarda, Ponodol
12. LOE (loh-aye) [fire] Tapamal, Gedoons, Ambrial
13. ZIM (zoad-ee-me) [fire] Gecaond, Laparin, Docepax
14. VTA (vah-tah) [air] Tedoond, Vivipos, Ooanamb
15. OXO (ohx-oh) [air] Tehando, Nociabi, Tastoxo
16. LEA (lah-ay-ah) [air] Cocarpt, Lanaconi, Sochial

17. TAN (tah-noo) [air] Sigmorf, Aydropt, Tocarzi
18. ZEN (zoad-en) [air] Nabaomi, Zafasai, Yalpamb
19. POP (poh-pay) [air] Torzoxi, Abaiond, Omagrap
20. KHR (kay-hay-ray) [air] Zildron, Parziba, Totocan
21. ASP (ah-ess-pay) [air] Chirspa, Toantom, Vixpalg
22. LIN (lee-noo) [air] Oxidaia, Paraoan, Calzirg
23. TOR (toh-ray) [earth] Ronoamb, Onizimp, Zaxanin
24. NIA (nee-ah) [earth] Orcamir, Chialps, Soageel
25. VTI (vah-tee) [earth] Mirzind, Obvaors, Ranglam
26. DES (day-ess) [earth] Pophand, Nigrana, Bazchim
27. ZAA (zoad-ah-ah) [earth] Saziama, Mathula, Korpamb
28. BAG (bah-gee) [earth] Labnixp, Focisni, Oxlopar
29. RII (ree-ee) [earth] Vastrim, Odraxti, Gomziam
30. TEX (tehtz) [water] Taoagla, Gemnimb, Advorpt, Dozinal

Rising of the Planes (Enochian Aethyr Rite)

1. Perform the Watchtower Ceremony.
2. Face the appropriate direction based on the elemental correspondence of the aethyr.
3. Enter the body of light.
4. Recite the *"Call-Key of the Aethyr"* inserting the appropriate name of the aethyr.
5. Evoke the Angelic Guardians (governors) of the aethyr while tracing their sigils in the air visualizing them in an appropriate color (element based).
6. Leave the body using skrying or astral projection, allowing the astral body (or mental projection) to rise freely on that plane/aethyr.
7. Retrace the sigils in reverse to dismiss the spirits and perform the Lesser Banishing Ritual of the Pentagram (LBRP) to complete the rite, negating any residual energies of the nemeton.

The *"Enochian Key to the Aethyrs"* is given here in two forms—in both *English* and *Enochian* languages. The English version provided is especially recommended for beginners—especially to this form of "magick." Practitioners should never intone incomprehensible words or formulas until the symbolism can be determined and understood. The same applies to *"Divine Names."* After operators are more proficient with the *Enochian System* (and language),they may use the Enochian version.

"*Enochian Key of the Aethyrs*"
(English version)

The heavens that dwell in the (*N.* aethyr) are mighty in the parts of the Earth and execute the judgment of the Highest. Unto you it is said: Behold the face of your God, the beginning of comfort, whose eyes are the brightest in the heavens, which provided you for the government of Earth and her unspeakable variety, furnishing you with a powerful understanding to dispose all things according to the providence of him that sits at the Holy Throne and rose up in the beginning saying: The Earth, let her be governed by her parts and let there be division in her that the glory of her may be always drunken and vexed in itself. Her course, let it circulate with the heavens and as a handmaiden let her serve them. One season, let it confound another, and let there be no creature upon or with her one and the same. All her members let them differ in their qualities and let there be no one creature equal to another. The reasonable creature of Earth, and men, let them vex and weed out one another and their dwelling places. Let them forget their names. The work of man and his pompousness; let them be defaced. His buildings; let them become caves for the beasts of the field. Confound her under-standing with darkness. For why? I repent that I have made man. One moment, let her be known, in another moment, a stranger. Because she is the bed of a harlot and the dwelling place of him that is Fallen. O ye heavens arise! The lower heavens beneath you; let them serve you! Govern those that govern. Cast down such as fall. Bring forth those who increase and destroy the rotten. Let no place remain in one number. Add and diminish until the stars are numbered. Arise! Move! And appear before the covenant of his mouth, which he has sworn to us in his justice. Open the mysteries of your creation and make us partakers of the undefiled knowledge.

"*Enochian Key of the Aethyrs*"
(Enochian version)

Madriaax d s praf (*N.* aethyr) chis micaolz saanir od fisis bal zizras Iaida. Nonca gohulim: micma adoian mad, Iaod bliorb, soba ooaona chis Lucifitias Piripsol, ds abraassa nonif net aaib caosgi od tilb adphant damploz, tooatnoncfg Miadz Oma Irasd tol glo marb Yarry Id oigo od torxup Iaodaf gohol: Ca osga tabaord saanir od Christeos yrpoil tiobl busdir tilb noaln paid orsba od dodrmni zylna. Elzap tilb parm gi piripsax, od ta qurist booapis L hibm ovcho symp od Christeos ag toltorn mirc q tiobl L el. Tol paomd dilzmo as pian od Christeos ag L toltorn parach asymp. Cordziz, dodpal od didalz L smnad: of fargt bams omaoas. Conishra od avavox, tonug Orsca tbl noasmi tabges levithmong. Un chi omp tibl ors. Bagle? Modoah ol cordziz. L capimao izomaxip, od cacocasb gosaa. Baglem pi tianta a babalond, od foorgt teloc vovim. Madriax torzu! Oadviax orocho aboapri! Tabaori priaz artabas. Adrpan cors ta dobix. Lolcam priazi ar coazior, of Quasb Qting. Ripir paoxt sala cor. Vml od prdzar carcg aoiveae cormpt. Torzu. Zacar. Od zamran aspt sibsi butmona, ds surza tiaballa Odo cicle qaa, od ozozma plapli Iadnamad.

— 12 —
THE TRADITIONAL KABBALAH*
:: AN APPENDIX ::

 1. Kether: "The Crown"
Divine Name: Eheieh ("I am")
Color: White
Essence: Frankincense
Archangel: Metatron
Angelic Order: Chaioth ha Qadesh ("Holy Creatures")
Virtue: Completion of the Great Work
Anunnaki: Enlil
Archetype: A venerable bearded king
Archdemon: Satan (or Moloch)
Qlippoth: Thamiel ("The Contenders")
Heavenly Sphere: Rashith ha Gilgalim ("Primum Mobile")
Alchemical: Mercury
Resonance: 'B' – note
Pathwork: Return to the Source
Part of the Body: The Head

 2. Chokmah: "Wisdom"
Divine Name: Jah ("The Lord")
Color: Gray
Essence: Eucalyptus & Musk
Archangel: Raziel (or Ratziel)
Angelic Order: Auphanim (or Ophanim)
Virtue: Devotion
Anunnaki: Enki
Archetype: A bearded male
Archdemon: Beelzebub
Qlippoth: Ghogiel ("The Hinderers")
Heavenly Sphere: Malzoth ("Wheel of the Zodiac")
 Alchemical: Salt
Resonance: 'A#' – note
Pathwork: Vision of God
Part of the Body: Brain

---

*   Excerpt from "*Arcanum: The Great Magical Arcanum*" by Joshua Free.

3. Binah: "Understanding"
Divine Name: YHVH (Jahovah) Elohim ("Lord God" or "Anakim")
Color: Black
Essence: Chamomile & Myrrh
Archangel: Tzaphkiel
Angelic Order: Aralim ("The Thrones")
Virtue: Silence
Anunnaki: Adar/Ninib-Ninurta
Archetype: A female matron
Archdemon: Lucifuge
Qlippoth: Ghogel ("The Concealers")
Vice: Avarice
Heavenly Sphere: Shabbathai ("Saturn")
Alchemical: Sulphur
Resonance: 'A' – note
Pathwork: Vision of Sorrow
Part of the Body: The Heart

4. Chesed: "Mercy"
Divine Name: El ("The Mighty One")
Color: Blue
Essence: Cedar & Nutmeg
Archangel: Tzadkiel
Angelic Order: Chasmalim ("The Shinning Ones")
Virtue: Obedience
Anunnaki: Marduk
Archetype: A crowned king
Archdemon: Astaroth
Qlippoth: Agshekeloh ("The Destroyers")
Vice: Pride & Hypocrisy
Heavenly Sphere: Tzadek ("Jupiter")
Alchemical: Silver
Pathwork: Vision of Love
Part of the Body: Right Arm

5. Geburah: "Strength & Severity"
Divine Name: Elohim Gabor ("God of Battle" or "Lords of War")
Color: Red
Essence: Cypress & Pine
Archangel: Khamael (or Camael)
Angelic Order: Seraphim
Virtue: Courage & Vitality

Anunnaki: Nergal
Archetype: A warrior and chariot
Archdemon: Asmodeus
Qlippoth: Golohab ("The Flaming Ones")
Vice: Cruelty
Heavenly Sphere: Madim ("Mars")
Alchemical: Gold
Resonance: 'F#' – note
Pathwork: Vision of Power
Part of the Body: Left Arm

6. Tiphareth: "Beauty"

Divine Name: YHVH (Jahovah) Eloah va-Daath ("God Manifest")
Color: Yellow
Essence: Jasmine & Rose
Archangel: Raphael
Angelic Order: Malachim ("The Multitudes")
Virtue: Devotion to the Great Work
Anunnaki: Utu (Shammash)
Archetype: A boy king
Archdemon: Belphegor
Qlippoth: Tagiriron ("The Disputers")
Vice: False pride
Heavenly Sphere: Shemesh ("Sun")
Alchemical: Iron
Resonance: 'F' – note
Pathwork: Vision of Harmony
Part of the Body: The Chest

7. Netzach: "Victory"

Divine Name: YHVH (Jahovah) Sabaoth ("Lord of Hosts")
Color: Green
Essence: Patchouli & Rose
Archangel: Haniel
Angelic Order: Elohim ("The Gods" or "Anakim")
Virtue: Selflessness
Anunnaki: Inanna/Ishtar
Archetype: A naked beautiful woman
Archdemon: Baal
Qlippoth: Nogah ("Ravengers" or "Raven Cult")
Vice: Lust & Impurity
Heavenly Sphere: Nogah ("Venus")

Alchemical: Copper
Resonance: 'E' – note
Pathwork: Vision of Beauty
Part of the Body: Right Leg

8. Hod: "Glory"

Divine Name: Elohim Sabaoth ("Lord God of Hosts" or "Lord of Gods")
Color: Orange
Essence: Rosemary & Wisteria
Archangel: Michael
Angelic Order: Beni Elohim ("Sons of God" or "Nephilim")
Virtue: Truth
Anunnaki: Nabu (Nebo), Hermes/Thoth
Archetype: A hermaphrodite
Archdemon: Adrammelech
Qlippoth: Samael ("The False Accusers")
Vice: Dishonesty
Heavenly Sphere: Kokab ("Mercury")
Alchemical: Tin
Resonance: 'D' – note
Pathwork: Vision of Splendor
Part of the Body: Left Leg

9. Yesod: "Foundation"

Divine Name: Shaddai El Chye ("The Almighty One")
Color: Violet
Essence: Lavender & Myrtle
Archangel: Gabriel
Angelic Order: Cherubim ("The Strong")
Virtue: Independence
Anunnaki: Nanna
Archetype: A handsome naked man
Archdemon: Lilith ("The Seducer")
Qlippoth: Galamliel ("The Perverse One")
Vice: False Idleness & Stagnation
Heavenly Sphere: Levanah ("Moon")
Alchemical: Lead
Resonance: 'C' – note
Pathwork: Vision of Unification
Part of the Body: Genitals

10. Malkuth: "The Kingdom"

Divine Name: Adonai ha Aretz ("Lord of the Earth")
Color: Black, citrine, russet & olive
Essence: Carnation & Sandalwood
Archangel: Sandalphon (or Metatron Manifest)
Angelic Order: Ashim or Issim ("Souls of Flame")
Virtue: Discernment
Anunnaki: Kia (Earth Planet?)
Archetype: A young crowned lady
Archdemon: Nahema ("Child Strangler")
Qlippoth: Nahemoth ("The Child Stranglers")
Vice: Dependency
Heavenly Sphere: Elemental Kingdoms
Alchemical: Philosopher's Stone ("Mercurial Philosophum")
Resonance: 'A' – note
Pathwork: Vision of Elementals & work with "Holy Guardian Angel"
Part of the Body: Feet and/or whole body system

—APPENDIX B—
THE ANUNNAKI TAROT
(LIBER T : EXCERPTS)

THE
ANUNNAKI
TAROT

Consulting the Babylonian
Oracle of Cosmic Wisdom

JOSHUA FREE & KYRA KAOS

— 0 —
: INTRODUCTION :
THE BABYLONIAN ORACLE OF COSMIC WISDOM
by Joshua Free

Of nearly 25 years actively involved with the modern "New Age" or "metaphysical" revival, I have now spent over ten of them as Director of the "Mardukite Research Organization." All during this time I collected notes for a guidebook, hoping I would one day be partnered with a graphic artist that could both appreciate efforts to bring my *Anunnaki Tarot* to light and be able to enhance ancient specimens of Mesopotamian art that fit my specification—rather than apply modern art to ancient archetypes.

Ancient archetypes of civilization actually originate in Mesopotamia—so, rather than take an arbitrary theme and impose tarot symbolism onto it, my esoteric knowledge base of Anunnaki traditions allowed me to quite easily bridge these two aspects in a way both historically authentic and mystically valid as a practical tool of modern "Mardukite neo-Babylonian spirituality."

This is not the first time that Mesopotamia makes an appearance in tarot —however, it is the first time that the post-Sumerian or "Mardukite" Babylonian paradigm/worldview is represented properly. Where some have presented what they call Babylonian, in reality we are given combinations of the Babylonian and pre-Mardukite or Enlilite systems interchangeably and often placing emphasis on deities and myths that aren't central to Mardukite Babylonian religion.

I selected the title *Anunnaki Tarot* for this oracle to differentiate from other artistic manifestations of a Babylonian tarot that previously emphasized Sumerian motifs or the "Epic of Gilgamesh" but not Mardukite Babylon as reflected in a tablet catalogue the Mardukite Research Organization prepared as "*Necronomicon: The Anunnaki Bible*" or "*The Complete Anunnaki Bible.*" The specifically Mardukite tablets display a mystical tradition of Babylon under the patron Anunnaki deity Marduk, whose son Nabu established the tradition with a proliferation of cuneiform tablets supporting the systematization of Anunnaki tradition.

— A —
: THE BABYLONIAN ORACLE :
ANUNNAKI ARCHETYPES OF THE MAJOR ARCANA
by Joshua Free

0. Adamu . . . The Fool
1. Marduk . . . The Magician
2. Teshmet . . . The High Priestess
3. Sarpanit . . . The Empress
4. Anu . . . The King of Heaven
5. Nabu . . . The High Priest
6. Divine Union . . . Lovers
7. Winged Disc . . . The Chariot
8. Elder Sign . . . Stength
9. E.A.–Enki . . . The Hermit
10. Tablet of Destiny . . . Wheel of Fortune
11. Enlil . . . Justice
12. Marduk's Exile . . . The Hanged Man
13. The Cosmic Tree . . . Death
14. The Path . . . Temperance
15. Tiamat . . . The Devil
16. Marduk's Temple . . . The Tower
17. Inanna–Ishtar . . . The Star
18. Nanna–Sin . . . The Moon
19. Shammash (Šamaš) . . . The Sun
20. Anunnaki Assembly . . . Judgment
21. An-Ki . . . The Universe

— B —
: THE BABYLONIAN ORACLE :
CONSULTING THE WISDOM OF ANUNNAKI TAROT
by Joshua Free

There are no absolute standards or rules for working with an oracle—all traditional symbolism and practices are the result of observations and experimentation spanning hundreds, if not thousands, of years. This being said: there is a general trend or consensus among classic teachings of mystics and magicians that lends us hints and clues toward developing a more personal approach as one grows with experience in using this type of "cartomancy" (or card symbol divination).

A preliminary familiarity with the actual cards (and imagery) offers greater success of using their oracular value. The same is true concerning their mythic and historic backgrounds within the specifically Babylonian "Mardukite" worldview (paradigm) —all of which is concisely described on the previous pages of this book, of which may also be supplemented with other material.

As a personal tool—or sacred tool—oracles are always treated with respect and often are kept away from "casual" view or the arbitrary handling from others. Many who use tarot cards and other such devices today will often keep their "pack" or deck wrapped in a dark material, often black, as a physical and energetic shelter. This also maintains an aura that they are not everyday common place items—that they are sacred. They should, however, carry your own personal individual "charge." This is accomplished naturally by your handling of them and use in meditations.

When used as an oracular device, the tarot cards are shuffled and "cut" based on the intuition of the practitioner. They may also be "fanned." When they are read for others, some will allow that person to perform this step; others are more particular, either allowing no one else to handle their tools at all—or else, only allowing another person to touch them when a card is to be selected from the fanned pack, or when the deck is to be cut.

Diviners and seers using oracular devices will develop their own unique methods of practice. Personal standards become "ritualized" over time with repeated use and familiarity—forming a *tradition*. They are so numerous in fact, that entire books are dedicated to little else. Various theories also exist correlating cartomancy phases to left-right brain activity where it is suggested to use this-or-that hand for cutting or laying out cards, &tc. Likewise, some diviners utilize reversed meanings in their interpretation, returning to the deck any fallen cards during shuffles in the same manner they fell.

In addition to games and fortune-telling, tarot cards are also mnemonic devices for key archetypes and esoteric lessons, much like the *Nordic Runes* or *Druidic Ogham*. Use of a preselected "significator" card in the readings materializes this. It is placed beneath of, or substitutes, the card that best represents the basis of the question/need or general state of the *querent* or "Seeker"; e.g. *lovers* for love, *chariot* for travel, &tc.

The arts of divination and oracular use is something that can only be described in a "how-to" book such as this, which mainly emphasizes the unique Anunnaki elements into an already well-established method. A preexisting background in esoteric arts of concentration and meditation, or previous use of divinatory systems, is not required, but may be beneficial. For those coming upon this lore "early" on their path: the methodology presented within this book and card set is more than adequate to base an ongoing developmental pursuit.

It is important to note—contrary to how many others may present similar oracles—that this current "system" is a *tool* for personal exploration and spiritual growth or evolution. It draws from the most ancient archetypal symbolism and iconography on the planet to display a complete "method" of gaining *insights* from ritual, meditation or divination that is consistent with roots of its ancient symbolism and the modern "New Age" methods of practice. It is *only* a tool or catalyst— the *real* power being: you.

The basic premise behind *cartomancy* is simple: There is a series of variable cards or symbols, each carrying a specific theme or array of key meanings; there is a series of variable determinations or positions a possible card or symbol may occupy; and finally, someone—observer or interpreter—must make a correlation between placement of symbols and the situational query.

Whereas the symbolism of the archetypes or cards has been given previously, the following section describes manners that the cards may be laid out—called a *layout* or *spread*. These "spreads" are specifically designed to compliment Anunnaki themes of Babylonian tradition, but they are only suggestions. Any similar type of layout can be substituted for personal preference.

There is one final main point of discussion before turning you loose on the oracle—a matter of the degree or level of cultural or ceremonial (ritual) intricacy incorporated into the practice of divination. This, again, is subject to personal preference, but will be important for some of our readers here.

The act of consulting an oracle is a spiritual exercise in meditation that is treated as formal or casual as the seer requires. Some people have treated "tarot" cards as little more than a game—whereas others have used its symbolism as a tool for personal exploration, growth and development—or as an aid to outlining and planning personal endeavors. It is important that any oracle remain a personal clarifying tool, not as a replacement or substitute for using good judgment; a perfecting catalyst, not a crutch to carry the weight.

In ancient times, powers of the oracle are exercised by a "seer"—a specialized priest or priestess of the temple. A sacred space would already exist within the temple for this operation, but a modern practitioner can easily designate space, appropriating an altar and carpet within a defined circle. Boundaries of the circle may be marked by a line of consecrated "Flour of Nabu"—also called the "Flour of Nisaba" on some older tablets. Sacred space may be decorated to personal taste, if none of it is distracting.

An altar cloth or "spread cloth" may be on the altar—a piece of cloth material used only to lay out the cards on. Some people use this to wrap up their cards between "readings."

A prayer or invocation may facilitate initial energetic movement or exchange, else "communication." This projects or speaks intentions of the seer, followed by the act of "meditation," which is a reception of information—the part where a seer must be able to hear, listen or receive the answers sought; contemplating and understanding what is given.

MARDUKITE
10TH ANNIVERSARY

Would you like to know more???

ENTER THE REALM OF THE

**MARDUKITE
CHAMBERLAINS**

**mardukite.com
necrogate.com**

Necronomicon: The Anunnaki Bible : 10th Anniversary
Collector's Edition—LIBER-N,L,G,9+W-M+S
(Hardcover)

*The Complete Anunnaki Bible: A Source Book of Esoteric
Archaeology* : 10th Anniversary—LIBER-N,L,G,9+W-M+S
(Paperback)

Necronomicon: The Anunnaki Bible : 10th Anniversary
Pocket Edition—LIBER-N,L,G,9+W-M+S
(Abridged Paperback)

*Gates of the Necronomicon: The Secret Anunnaki Tradition of
Babylon* : 10th Anniversary Collector's Edition—
LIBER-50,51/52,R+555
(Hardcover)

The Sumerian Legacy: A Guide to Esoteric Archaeology—
LIBER-50+51/52
(Paperback)

*Necronomicon Revelations—Crossing to the Abyss: Nine Gates of the
Kingdom of Shadows & Simon's Necronomicon*—LIBER-R+555
(Paperback – Release: May 30, 2019)

*Necronomicon: The Anunnaki Grimoire: A Manual of Practical
Babylonian Magick* : 10th Anniversary Collector's Edition—
LIBER-E,W/Z,M+K
(Hardcover)

*Practical Babylonian Magic : Invoking the Power of the Sumerian
Anunnaki*—LIBER-E,W/Z,M+K
(Paperback – Release: June 21, 2019)

*The Complete Book of Marduk by Nabu : A Pocket Anunnaki
Devotional Companion to Babylonian Prayers & Rituals* :
10th Anniversary Collector's Edition—LIBER-W+Z
(Hardcover)

*The Maqlu Ritual Book : A Pocket Companion to Babylonian
Exorcisms, Banishing Rites & Protective Spells* :
10th Anniversary Collector's Edition—LIBER-M
(Hardcover)

*The Anunnaki Tarot : Consulting the Babylonian Oracle of
Cosmic Wisdom (Guide Book)*—LIBER-T
(Paperback – Release: June 21, 2019)

NABU—JOSHUA FREE ("Merlyn Stone")
Chief Scribe & Librarian of New Babylon

CPSIA information can be obtained
at www.ICGtesting.com
Printed in the USA
LVHW061554170723
752574LV00056B/51/J